THE BATTLE OF GLENDALE

THE BATTLE OF GLENDALE

*The Day the South Nearly
Won the Civil War*

Jim Stempel

McFarland & Company, Inc., Publishers

Jefferson, North Carolina, and London

LIBRARY OF CONGRESS CATALOGUING-IN-PUBLICATION DATA

Stempel, Jim, 1948–
    The battle of Glendale : the day the South nearly won the Civil
War / Jim Stempel.
        p.   cm.
    Includes bibliographical references and index.

    ISBN 978-0-7864-6300-8
    softcover : 50# alkaline paper ∞

    1. White Oak Swamp, Battle of, Va., 1862.   I. Title.
E473.68.S74   2011
975.5'291—dc22   2011007638

BRITISH LIBRARY CATALOGUING DATA ARE AVAILABLE

Front cover: Painting by Don Troiani, www.historicalimagebank.com

Manufactured in the United States of America

McFarland & Company, Inc., Publishers
  Box 611, Jefferson, North Carolina 28640
  www.mcfarlandpub.com

Table of Contents

Preface   1

Prologue   5

1. The Great Skedaddle   13
2. A View from the *Gazelle*   29
3. Kearny le Magnifique   37
4. Morning   49
5. Orders at Daybreak   58
6. Delay on the Charles City Road   64
7. The Rear Guard of All God's Creation   70
8. Dithering at White Oak Swamp   77
9. The Long Wait   84
10. A Perfect Model of a Christian Hero   92
11. A Battle of Axes   99
12. For the Nonce Below Their Wanted Tension   105
13. Riot on the River Road   113
14. Misfortune's Plaything   120
15. A Thing Understood as It Really Is   127
16. The Gallant Jenkins   133
17. Go Build a Bridge   139
18. A Reckless Impetuosity I Never Saw Equaled   145
19. Nightfall   153
20. I Had Gained Command of the Quaker Road   158
21. One Blood-Chilling Cry of Pain   165

Table of Contents

22. I'll See You All in Hell 173

23. Cowardice or Treason 179

24. The Lost Day of the Lost Cause 186

Epilogue 195

Chapter Notes 203

Bibliography 211

Index 213

"When one thinks of the great chances in General Lee's grasp that one summer afternoon, it is enough to make one cry to go over the story how they were all lost."
— *Confederate general Edward P. Alexander*

I am concentrated into one;
He is divided into ten.
I am Ten to his One;
Many against his Few.
Attack few with many,
And my opponent Will be weak.
— *Sun-tzu,* The Art of War

Preface

It has become commonly accepted, indeed almost an axiom of modern American history, that the South could not have won the American Civil War. Cited in support of this proposition are the gross disproportions in population, finance, and manufacturing capacity between the two regions. Added to this list are the miles of Northern railroad and telegraph lines, the naval and merchant fleets that simply dwarfed their Southern counterparts, and so on. These factors have been amply catalogued, were all true, and were undoubtedly significant in terms of the conflict's ultimate resolution.

But probabilities do not win wars. Wars, rather, are won and lost on the field of battle, won at times even when the probabilities appear grimly improbable. If this were not true, we would not today recall names such as Marathon, New Orleans, or Bastogne. The Soviet Union would have overwhelmed tiny Finland in the Winter War of 1940, the United States might still be a part of Great Britain, and Goliath might have crushed young David even before he had uncoiled his sling.

The argument made in this book, then, is that there were times — slim indeed, and few at best, but times nevertheless — when the South did, in fact, have the opportunity to win the Civil War. By this I do not mean a mere theoretical possibility, a remote statistical formulation cobbled together by modern scholarship, something far more akin to clever fiction than history. Rather I mean a *real* chance, an actual day and a precise time when in fact the stars aligned, so to speak, to afford — even if ever so fleetingly — an undeniable opportunity for Southern independence.

This book is about what is in my opinion the best of those limited opportunities, a day in June 1862 when the "gods of war" offered up to the South a moment of unparalleled opportunity. Indeed, it was a tactical arrangement so favorable for Southern arms that, not only *could* Confederate forces have won the war that day, but that by any reasonable accounting they *should* have won, and indeed, they came within a hair of doing so. But they

1

did not, and recalling that day many years later, Confederate officer turned historian Edward P. Alexander would lament, "When one thinks of the great chances in General Lee's grasp that one summer afternoon, it is enough to make one cry to go over the story how they were all lost."[1]

The action that day centered on, but was not exclusive to, a small Virginia crossroads of no particular significance called Riddell's Shop by some, Charles City crossroads by others, Glendale by most. Historically this has been classified more or less a minor rearguard action during the more famous Seven Days battles, when Union general George McClellan disengaged from Lee's army about Richmond and retreated to the safety of the Federal gunboats on the James River, Lee in hot pursuit. Events then swept rapidly forward to the significant action the following day at Malvern Hill, and few stopped to think or paused to grasp just what the Confederacy had failed to accomplish at Glendale. Since then, and much like an unappreciated orphan, this engagement has wandered the Civil War landscape under various names — Nelson's Farm, Riddell's Shop, Charles City Crossroads, Frayser's Farm, but generally Glendale.

What were those "great chances" Alexander referred to, and how did they all unravel that June afternoon? That is the substance of this book.

In the end what we will discover is that it is a most human tale, one of confusion, ineptitude, and exhaustion, all mingled with the finer elements of heroism, brilliance, and valor. Most remarkably, from the Southern perspective it is a story that turns on any number of almost stunning command failures, perhaps the most significant of all being that of Thomas "Stonewall" Jackson.

Just weeks removed from his brilliant Valley Campaign that enthralled the South and horrified the North, Thomas J. Jackson was in early June of 1862 already one of the most tested, aggressive, and energetic officers in service of the Confederacy. Yet on this particular June afternoon, when all that was needed to fashion a decisive Southern victory was a modest push by his force against the Federal rear guard in order to hold it in place, Stonewall Jackson — possibly exhausted beyond response — simply pulled his cap down over his eyes, seemingly incapable of movement. "It is said that Jackson fell asleep and either was not or could not be aroused by his staff officers. Night came."[2]

Because of Jackson's seeming exhaustion, the Valley Army would engage in little more than what Alexander later styled an "absurd farce of war,"[3] and the Federal rear guard — and along with it the most promising opportunity for independence the South would ever see — slipped away into the shadows of late afternoon. "It was the bitterest disappointment Lee had ever sustained, and one that he could not conceal."[4]

On such slim, indeed almost inexplicable, oddities, do the spokes of history at times turn.

J.S. • Libertytown, Maryland • Spring 2011

Prologue

The day was warm, the sky blue, and a light breeze played through the ship's rigging that morning off Newport News, Virginia. Two Federal wooden warships, the *Congress* and the *Cumberland*, lay at anchor, bobbing on a light chop, the day's wash still slapping on a balmy breeze.

It was about 12:30 P.M. when the thing was spotted, far off to the south in the Elizabeth River, a smokestack and a massive black roof inching along in the water. It was March 8, 1862, a Saturday, and suddenly heads began to turn. "I wish you would take the glass and have a look over there, sir," remarked the quartermaster of the watch. "I believe *that thing* is a-comin' down at last."[1]

The drums began to beat general quarters, the laundry was pulled from the rigging, and sailors quickly prepared for battle. Yet it would take almost an hour for the huge, lumbering mass to get close enough to make out the metal plates that formed its casement and the tubes of the guns that lined her hull. There was no question now. It was the *Merrimack* (rechristened *Virginia* by the Confederate Navy, but she would be called almost exclusively *Merrimack* by friend and foe alike), and in the next twenty-four hours she would change the face of naval warfare, and as a chance byproduct, the course of General George B. McClellan's planned spring offensive on the Virginia peninsula.

The *Merrimack* closed steadily, almost cavalierly, to within two hundred yards of the Federal warships. "The *Congress* then fired a full broadside point-blank. Nine hundred pounds of hurtling metal smashed fully home. In horror the gunners saw the balls ricochet into the air like pebbles off a roof."[2]

The *Merrimack* was unscathed and unfazed by the broadside she'd received. No damage had been done. She came about and fired a four gun broadside of her own, tearing the *Congress* to shreds. Inside the stricken *Congress* smoke poured, blood ran like water, and men lay in pieces. The dawn of the ironclad had arrived.

Leaving the stricken *Congress* behind, the *Merrimack* turned and headed straight for the *Cumberland*, firing a shot with its forward gun that exploded among the marines below, then ramming her dead on the bow. Then the *Merrimack* backed away full astern, turned and found a position off the *Cumberland's* bow where it could rake the dying vessel with impunity. "Every one of the *Merrimack's* shots cut a swath of gore."[3]

By day's end, both Federal warships, once the pride of the Northern fleet, were a shambles. Moreover, the flagship *Minnesota* had been run aground and, come morning, would in all probability be blown to pieces once the formidable Rebel ram returned from its mooring in Norfolk. Against the Confederate ironclad, the wooden ships of the blockading fleet had proven powerless.

The *Merrimack*, like all her sister ironclads produced by the Confederacy during the course of the Civil War, had been built as part of a strategic plan conceived by Stephen Mallory, Confederate secretary of the navy. Mallory reasoned correctly that the South, with its limited manufacturing and ship-building facilities, could not hope to match the formidable Federal Navy on a boat-per-boat basis. Rather his vision was to employ a number of fleet commerce raiders that would prey on and disrupt Northern shipping world-wide, while also producing a few ironclad warships capable of taking on the Federal blockade. Ironclad batteries had already been developed in Europe to a certain degree, and it was Mallory's conviction that, if designed and built correctly, a single ironclad might destroy every wooden war vessel it encountered. Thus the *Merrimack* was originally conceived, not just as an important new weapon, but literally a breakthrough weapon that might alter, or even end, the war.

The *Merrimack* had originally been a frigate under construction by the Federal Navy at the Norfolk Navy Yard at the beginning of the war. When the yard had to be abandoned by the Federals at the outset of hostilities, the *Merrimack* was scuttled, and the yard put to the torch. The remains of the ship were in turn discovered by the fledgling Confederate Navy — which boasted not a single vessel when Mallory took the job as secretary — raised, and reconfigured into the ironclad design. Despite numerous design flaws — which would soon become apparent — the *Merrimack* still represented a new and formidable weapon. Indeed, for one afternoon — but for one afternoon only — Stephen Mallory achieved a portion of his strategic vision, a seemingly invulnerable vessel, capable of destroying every Federal wooden craft it encountered, and this shocking breakthrough was hardly lost on the Federal government's war planners in Washington.

The morning following the *Merrimack's* debut off Newport News, Sunday, March 9, was a day unlike any other in American history. News of the fleet's debacle in Hampton Roads had reached the White House via telegraph, and a special Cabinet meeting had been called to discuss the disaster. The group was utterly dumbfounded. Based on the reports they had received, it appeared the Confederates had indeed developed an invincible weapon, a craft that might soon render the entire Federal Fleet and its blockade of the Southern coast obsolete.

President Lincoln was reportedly so excited he could hardly speak. Secretary of War Edwin Stanton was beside himself. The *Merrimack*, he railed, would sink every vessel in the navy, capture Fort Monroe, cut off Burnside in the Carolina sounds, retake Port Royal, and lay New York and Boston under "contribution." McClellan's grand Peninsula campaign would have to be canceled to protect the government from this "formidable monster."[4] What, after all, was to stop it? In attendance was the Young Napoleon himself, General George McClellan, who according to one witness sat "dumbfounded and silent." It was, according to Navy secretary Gideon Welles, the "worst moment of the war."[5]

Unknown to virtually everyone present, however — but suspected by Navy secretary Welles — the Union's own ironclad, the *Monitor*, had just the evening before pulled into the waters off Newport News, and in the glowing light of the burning hulk of the *Congress*, taken up a blocking position in defense of the stranded *Minnesota*. That Sunday afternoon the *Merrimack* returned to finish off the helpless frigate, only to encounter the tiny *Monitor*, a cheese box on a raft, as it has been called ever since, and the two vessels would slug it out for hours to a virtual draw, as crowds jammed the shores of the Chesapeake Bay to watch.

The *Merrimack* finally withdrew, damaged but not done in, and the *Monitor* took up a position near Fortress Monroe, the Federal bastion on the bay. At the time little was known of the *Merrimack*'s true capabilities or intentions, thus caution was the word, lest the beast be permitted to roam free once again.

Unlike the *Merrimack*, which had been conceived and designed from the top down, the *Monitor* had evolved from the genius of one man — John Ericsson. "John Ericsson was a true genius of the nineteenth-century industrial revolution. Prickly, difficult, and extremely egotistical, the fifty-eight-year-old Swedish engineer was convinced there was absolutely nothing beyond his capacity to invent or improve upon."[6]

Ericsson's design was so novel, so radical in its conception, that when brought before the navy's ironclad board, they hardly knew what to think of it. "The ship measured 172 feet long, by a boxy 41 wide, with just over a 10-

foot draft. The hull was composed of two elements: an overhanging, armored raft deck, nearly awash, and a lower, timber hull holding the machinery, magazines, and berthing spaces."[7] On the deck sat a pilot house and a revolving turret that would house two 11 inch Dahlgren naval rifles. That was it.

No one in the navy had ever seen anything like it, and the response was cool. But the president had seen and liked it, and Secretary of the Navy Gideon Wells thought the design had merit, thus Ericsson's plan was ultimately accepted. A contract was written, calling for the delivery of the ironclad within 100 working days. Working frantically in his East River boat house in Brooklyn, New York, Ericsson had the *Monitor* completed by late January 1862, slightly over schedule, but acceptable nevertheless. During the next month her crew was gathered and trained, and in early March, with reports of the *Merrimack*'s imminent completion, the *Monitor* shoved off for Virginia waters.

Thus was naval history made that day in Hampton Roads near Newport News, naval blueprints altered forever, and it would be the gritty little *Monitor* with its swiveling gun turret that would set the standard for naval designs of the future. Indeed, every dreadnaught and battleship of the twentieth century had direct bloodlines back to the *Monitor*.

Since November of the preceding year, and sporadically over the better part of five months, George McClellan, commander of the Federal Army of the Potomac, had been ever so slowly planning his Peninsula campaign, a design to take the Confederate capital at Richmond from the flank via a water route through the Chesapeake Bay. As an unintended consequence of the *Merrimac*'s debut and continued lurking presence about Hampton Roads, those plans had now to be either shelved entirely or altered.

General George McClellan had arrived in Washington in the fall of 1861 after having conducted a short, limited, but reasonably successful campaign in western Virginia. After the First Battle of Bull Run, a time when Federal successes were few and failures abundant, his arrival had been naturally well received, and soon McClellan was rewarded, not only with command of the Army of the Potomac, but also with promotion as general-in-chief of all Federal forces. An organizer and motivator of high skill, McClellan quickly put the battered remnants of the Bull Run army back into camp and back onto track. The army soon grew in both size and morale, was paraded, inspected, and drilled endlessly in its Washington camps, but did not venture out against the Confederates, though they were certainly near at hand.

Meanwhile, just across the Potomac River from Washington, scarcely 25 miles away, the Rebel army under General Joseph Johnston remained on station, fresh from its victory at Bull Run, and presumably spoiling for a fight. McClellan — as would be his overriding characteristic throughout his periods of command — vastly overestimated the size and capabilities of this force, and as a consequence refrained from direct confrontation. As a result, little in the way of actual combat was even attempted by the Federal commander, and what little *was* attempted devolved into failure and fiasco. Over the dragging weeks and months McClellan began to lose favor with the press, Congress, and, finally, President Abraham Lincoln. The massive army McClellan had gathered was costing the republic huge sums daily, yet the Young Napoleon seemingly had no idea just how to employ it, or how best to deal with the Confederate legions he conceived just the other side of the river. The war to save the Union was going nowhere.

McClellan's Peninsula Campaign was thus conceived as a means of solving two menacing problems, menacing, if not in reality, at least in George McClellan's mind. The first was how to strike a potentially lethal blow at the Confederacy without having to actually confront an entrenched and superior foe — superior, at least, by McClellan's calculations — Johnston's army at Manassas. Secondly, how could the Young Napoleon silence his growing ranks of detractors?

By loading his entire army onto a vast fleet and shipping it down the Chesapeake Bay to a point only a few days' march from Richmond where it might debark and move by land on the Rebel capital, McClellan reasoned he could cleverly bypass Johnston's legions while seizing the offensive, thus simultaneously silencing his critics. It was two birds with one stone.

Moreover, the plan would put his army on Johnston's flank and rear, thus compromising the Confederate's Manassas position, while making sensible use of the Union's vast seaborne superiority. If all went as planned, McClellan would move without risk and win the war almost without fighting. His plan, he thought, was grand, sensible, and achievable.

As the campaign was initially conceived, the Army of the Potomac would march to Annapolis, Maryland, where it would board a fleet for transfer to Urbana, Virginia, a small village on the south bank of the Rappahannock River. From there McClellan calculated a two or three day march on to Richmond, which the Young Napoleon intended to overwhelm before Johnston's army, or any other Rebel army, for that matter, could respond. Once situated between Johnston's Confederate force in Northern Virginia and the smaller Rebel army on the peninsula near Yorktown, McClellan might then turn and slay them in detail, crushing each as he pleased, in time frames suitable to his liking. While this plan had certain obvious holes and omissions, it also had considerable merit — if accomplished with speed. (The fact that

McClellan himself might, in such a position, be crushed by two converging Rebel forces apparently did not resonate in his thinking.)

Still, nothing much at all came of the peninsula strategy until late winter 1862. By then McClellan found himself under so much pressure from the government and press to do *something* that he was in serious danger of removal if he did not. The plan to move on Urbana was initially approved by the president — contingent upon McClellan leaving behind enough force to safeguard Washington — but then the *Merrimack* steamed out of Norfolk straight into history and ruined everything for the Federal commander. Even with the Union's *Monitor* patrolling the waters off Fortress Monroe, there was no guarantee "the monster" would not break loose again, bypass both the fort and *Monitor*, and ravage McClellan's helpless fleet as it landed on the banks of the Rappahannock. Suddenly the Urbana landing site had disaster written all over it. What to do?

Before McClellan had time to even catch his breath and reconsider his options, even more bad news arrived at his doorstep. On Sunday morning, March 9, as McClellan, President Lincoln and the cabinet were debating the shocking repercussions of the *Merrimack*'s attack off Hampton Roads, two contrabands slipped into Union lines outside of Manassas with interesting news — the Confederate army was abandoning its position and retreating south toward Fredericksburg![8] These reports were received by a New Jersey brigade commanded by a fierce, one armed brigadier general of high reputation, Phil Kearny, and Kearny's response was immediate.

"Kearny acted swiftly. Instead of awaiting definite orders he advised his Division Commander, General William B. Franklin, of what he had learned and then sent the entire New Jersey Brigade forward in a widely spread formation."[9] This was followed up the next day when Kearny's brigade moved through Fairfax Court House, Centreville, then into the vacated Confederate entrenchments at Manassas. What they found dotting the abandoned Confederate works were mounted logs painted black to appear as cannon from a distance. The "formidable" Confederate position McClellan had been loathe to assault had turned out to be little more than a clever fraud. George McClellan looked the fool, and the newspapers had a field day at his expense, naming the painted fakes "Quaker guns."

Kearny wanted to press the Rebels as they retreated south toward the Rappahannock River, but McClellan would have none of it. Kearny, a fierce soldier who would play a major role during the fighting at Glendale, was disgusted by McClellan's lack of initiative, and feared the worst for it: "The ... truth is that instead of letting me and others push on after the panic-stricken foe and forcing him to fight a big battle and probably ending the war — for the enemy's panicky flight promises us sure success — McClellan has brought us all back. The result will be that the Rebels ... thinking us afraid of a real stand-up fight ... will take daring action against us ... while we strike timidly at them."[10]

Thus it came to pass that George McClellan, desperate to get out of Washington and accomplish *something*, shifted his landing site from Urbana, where a landing force might be attacked, destroyed, or stranded, to Fortress Monroe, itself at the tip of the Virginia peninsula. Here the landings could take place under the frowning naval guns of the fort, and the patrolling eye of the *Monitor*. There, the Young Napoleon reasoned, his army could disembark in safety, then ultimately move straight up the peninsula on Richmond. The march from that point would of necessity involve confronting the Rebel force on the peninsula, and a trek of more distance than a landing at Urbana would involve, but the trade-offs were, to McClellan's mind at least, well worth the alterations. Some things would be given up, but others would be gained. As McClellan proclaimed in early February, "We can take Fort Monroe as a base, & operate with complete security, altho' with less celerity & brilliancy of results up the Peninsula."[11]

By then Joseph Johnston's Confederate army had already slipped back to a new line behind the Rappahannock River, not due to McClellan's activity, but simply due a new strategic conception dictated by Richmond. But it did not matter. Receiving assurances from the navy that his plan — despite the dreaded *Merrimack*— was still feasible, in late March 1862, the movement was put into motion. George McClellan departed Washington for Virginia's peninsula proclaiming, "I shall soon leave on the wing for Richmond — which you may be sure I will take."[12]

In reality, the shift from Urbana to Fortress Monroe, in order to avoid the lurking presence of the *Merrimack*, was a modest tactical alteration, but from small acorns do mighty oaks at times grow. The *Merrimack's* maiden sortie into Hampton Roads, like a small stone tossed into a still pond, created a sequence of ripples, the effects of which would prove far ranging.

Not only would ports of debarkation be altered, but timetables eventually changed. Armies on both sides would react and move, and senior officers would be wounded, forcing staffing changes at the highest levels. New men with different strategic visions would emerge, events would be twisted into new forms, and history subsequently altered.

In that sense the clash between the *Merrimack* and the *Congress* that bright Saturday afternoon might be considered simply the first scene of a much larger drama, a drama that would begin on the blue waters of the Chesapeake Bay off Newport News, only then to end some three months later in the Virginia countryside at Glendale south and east of Richmond on a single afternoon when the most promising opportunity for Southern independence would be fumbled away, and the day lost.

Then again, the drama, of course, would not really begin or end at either.

CHAPTER 1

The Great Skedaddle

In late June 1862 the Army of the Potomac, the Union's principle fighting force, found itself struggling south on the narrow roads that led through the Chickahominy Swamp east of Richmond, Virginia. The weather was warm, drinking water poor, and malaria a constant problem.

The roads on the Virginia peninsula had proved an endless difficulty for months. When the weather turned dry the roads became a powdery dust that coated the marching troops, filling their shoes, pockets, and nostrils. When it rained the roads turned into an ungovernable soup that swallowed men, cannons, wagons, and animals alike.[1] One young officer from Boston recalled, "It has rained like the devil last night all day and tonight and you may guess what the mud is in a clayey soil where it was a real annoyance before — Marching will have to be slow for the roads have constantly to be made or mended for artillery (of wh. there is a great deal) The men and officers are wet enough you may believe but there is real pluck shown now as these are real hardships to contend with."[2]

That pluck was now being severely tested. The trek south had been harried, long, and tedious. The going had been both slow and fearful. Yet only days before this same Army of the Potomac had been positioned at the very gates of Richmond, poised for a dash into the city that might have ended the rebellion. Indeed, so close had the Federal force come to the Confederate capital, that its advanced pickets had been able to set their watches by the toll of the church bells in the defiant city.[3] Now the Union Army was stumbling south on the narrow, red dirt Virginia roads, retreating toward the James River for reasons most troops found inexplicable. Defeat seemed to have been snatched from the jaws of victory. How had this come to pass?

Three months prior in late March, Union commander George B. McClellan — styled the Young Napoleon by many Northern newspapers — had loaded his army onto a vast, commandeered fleet of varied description and shipped them down the Chesapeake Bay to Fort Monroe at the tip of the Virginia peninsula. His aim had been a sensible one, to bypass the Confederate army deployed in a blocking position along the Rappahannock River near Fredericksburg, Virginia, and thus land in an area where he might march on Richmond by the flank, essentially unopposed.

To McClellan's credit, the waterborne advance had been executed with remarkable precision. Over a period of only three weeks the Army of the Potomac, numbering some 121,500 men and vast stores of equipment, had been transferred to the Virginia peninsula, and by early April the army was in a posture to begin offensive operations.[4] It had been a logistical operation that bordered on the miraculous.

The stage had been set for a rapid advance and a stunning Federal victory, but this was not to be the case. The reason for this was a caution on the part of George McClellan that seemingly bordered on paranoia, the sense that he was constantly the victim of unscrupulous Washington politicians and intriguers, that he was being forced against his best military judgment to strike a foe twice his own strength, etc., etc. McClellan constantly envisioned the enemy in vast numbers and, it seemed, behind every tree.

This paranoia was both fed and sustained by a Federal intelligence system run by the detective Allan Pinkerton, principle of the Pinkerton National Detective Service, an operation that consistently produced for McClellan grossly inflated estimates of Confederate strength. Often these estimates were based on spurious information, or at times, no factual evidence whatsoever.[5]

Yet according to Edward Porter Alexander, then in Confederate service outside of Richmond, the South also had a system in place that was hardly scientific but was nevertheless far more accurate and trustworthy than was McClellan's for judging enemy strength. This system relied fundamentally on Northern newspaper accounts, which were then simply cross checked. Throughout the war this method proved remarkably accurate for the projection of Union Army strength and allowed Confederate military leaders to plan accordingly.[6]

Edward Porter Alexander had both an interesting and involved Civil War experience. Born to a wealthy plantation family in Washington, Georgia, he was graduated third in his class from West Point in 1857. Prior to the outbreak of hostilities, Alexander served on the faculty at West Point, took part in the western expedition to quell the Mormon War, and helped develop a flag signal system, later utilized by both sides during the conflict. He was considered an expert engineer and artillerist, at the time the most scientific of battlefield applications. During the course of the war he rose to the rank of brigadier general, and was considered by Robert E. Lee to be one of his few indispensable lieutenants.[7]

After the war Porter Alexander excelled in business, governmental assignments, and academics. In the early years of the twentieth century he produced the first critical examination of the Civil War written by a veteran, and a work still considered by many a classic.[8] Writing in a humble, charming style, Alexander's recollections are fascinating, and we will turn to his observations from time to time in order to get a first hand look at events as they evolved during the Seven Days, and, more specifically, the fighting he witnessed at Glendale. And it was Alexander who was at a loss to explain why McClellan could not have employed the same simple intelligence techniques as did the Confederates to clarify enemy numbers:

> Why the enemy, by similar obvious methods, did not, also, always know our strength, remains a mystery. But McClellan had a bureau under Pinkerton to estimate for him, from reports of spies, prisoners, and deserters, and implicitly believed, by preference, the most absurd and impossible of all their reports. As an illustration may be taken his report of October, 1861, in which he estimates the Confederate army on the Potomac as "not less than 150,000 strong, well-drilled and equipped, ably commanded and strongly intrenched."
>
> In fact, the Confederate army at the time was only about 40,000 strong. It was poorly drilled, and wretchedly equipped, and it had practically no intrenchments whatever.[9]

It is impossible to understand the remarkable opportunity presented the Army of Northern Virginia at Glendale in June 1862 without understanding George McClellan's consistent acceptance of these gross overestimates of Confederate strength, and the distorted military options they in turn seemed to justify in his mind. "George McClellan's conviction that he was forever outnumbered was the one constant of his military character."[10] Irrational estimates bred irrational fears, which in turn seemed to demand irrational action.

McClellan would therefore advance his army that spring from Fortress Monroe across the Virginia peninsula with a caution and speed stubbornly and steadfastly resistant to military reality. Fantasizing, for instance, a vast Rebel army defending Yorktown — when in fact the Confederates were initially outnumbered 121,000 to 13,000[11] — he laid siege to a position he could have stormed in an afternoon, wasting a month in the process. "Another opportunity as good as that offered McDowell at Bull Run was here [at Yorktown] offered McClellan, who could have rushed the position anywhere. He contented himself, however, with some cannonading and sharp-shooting."[12] After almost a month's siege, McClellan finally took Yorktown after Confederate forces, sensing the initiation of a massive artillery bombardment, simply abandoned the position and began falling back to another line of defense.

George McClellan's military conservatism, his "glacial deliberation,"[13] his "slows" as Abraham Lincoln once styled McClellan's infuriating lack of initiative, have been well documented by numerous historians. At Glendale, however, it would require far more than a bad case of the "slows" on the part of George McClellan for the Army of the Potomac to be placed in a posture where it might be destroyed in a single afternoon. For this it would require an act bordering on dereliction of duty, and a moral failure of the first magnitude.

In response to McClellan's landing on the Virginia peninsula, the Confederate army, commanded that spring by General Joe Johnston, abandoned its blocking position along the Rappahannock River and ultimately joined

Edward Porter Alexander — On Lee's staff at Glendale, Alexander also handled reconnaissance duties during the Seven Days battles. Later promoted to brigadier general, Alexander would be considered the Confederacy's most accomplished artillerist by war's end (NARA).

the forlorn Rebel garrison at Yorktown. That position was then abandoned in the face of overwhelming Federal numbers, and Johnston fell back to a defensive line in front of Richmond with the Chickahominy River across his front. Johnston's force in defense of Richmond was significantly smaller than that of McClellan's. "He had seven divisions, 27 brigades, numbering about 60,000 infantry and artillery."[14] Johnston's plan was to defend the capital as best he could, and hopefully strike a blow at McClellan if and when the opportunity arose, a blow that would either send the Federal army reeling, or at least even the odds between the two combatants.

Through Williamsburg — where a brief rearguard action was fought on May 5 — and up the peninsula McClellan's army trudged throughout May, finally arriving before Richmond at Mechanicsville around May 24. There the Army of the Potomac began falling into position and throwing up earthworks as it went. Porter Alexander describes the position: "His [McClellan's] right flank, on the north bank of the Chickahominy, rested upon Beaver Dam Creek, a strong position which Johnston's engineers had selected for our own left flank, before we left Yorktown, when Johnston contemplated fighting on that bank. Thence, the Federal line extended southeast along the Chickahominy some three miles to New Bridge. Then, crossing this stream, it bent south and ran to White Oak Swamp, where the left rested, giving about four miles on the south side in a line convex toward Richmond, and scarcely six miles away at its nearest point."[15]

Thus was the stage set for a major contest just east of the Confederate capital, a contest in which McClellan hoped to reduce the Rebel defenders through siege tactics, then sweep them aside in one massive assault. Behind his meager earthworks, Johnston waited, biding his time until an opportunity to strike presented itself. The only question was would Johnston or McClellan strike first?

In Richmond near panic ensued as the Federal army approached, yet McClellan was not the only fear. Moving south from Fredericksburg and headed straight toward Richmond was another massive Federal corps under Irvin McDowell, a corps numbering some 30,000 troops. For Southern survival, this prospect was frightening. If McDowell were allowed to continue south unchecked, it was feared he would connect with McClellan's right flank, and create a monster envelopment of the Confederate capital, an envelopment of some 130,000 to 140,000 troops that Johnston could not possibly hope to oppose.

A curtain of darkness seemed to befall Richmond. Fearful citizens jammed the rail stations, filled the roads and boats leading out of town. Congress adjourned, the gold reserves were prepared for shipment, and the government's papers packed for transfer.[16] Doom seemed at hand, yet that looming doom was narrowly avoided. How?

Serving as an assistant to Confederate president Jefferson Davis, General Robert E. Lee had on May 16 sent to Thomas "Stonewall" Jackson far off in the Shenandoah Valley this secret instruction: "Whatever movement you make against Banks do it speedily, and if successful drive him back toward the Potomac, threatening that line."[17] This was, in effect, an order for Jackson to create a diversion in the Shenandoah, a threat that might march its way all the way down the Shenandoah Valley toward the Maryland line, thus potentially threatening even Washington. If successful, it was hoped Jackson might galvanize Northern fears and force a redeployment of McDowell's now threatening corps. This was surely a gambit, but under the circumstances, a gambit well worth trying. The rest, as they say, is history. Stonewall Jackson marched, fought, marched some more and fought much more, immortalizing himself and his small army in the now classic Valley Campaign of 1862.

Joe Johnston, still hunkered down outside of Richmond, was poised to strike McClellan before that army could be reinforced, when suddenly important intelligence was received. "McDowell had suddenly stopped his advance, and his troops seemed to be falling back on Manassas. What had happed was that Jackson had again broken loose in the Valley and defeated Banks at Strasburg on May 23, and at Winchester on May 25, and was moving on the Potomac...."[18]

Wyman White, then serving with the 2nd United States Sharpshooters attached to McDowell's corps near Fredericksburg, recalls the moment:

> The regiment with the rest of the brigade were ordered and crossed the Rappahannock River, climbed St. Mary's Heights, and marched on to Fairview Plantation, eight miles south of the river.... Then we returned across the river to Falmouth and kept up the march on the road toward Catlett's Station arriving at that place on May 31st. The column in this move was the whole of the First Army Corps under General McDowell and a division of troops in command of General Shields. This Division had but just come into Falmouth over the same road from the Shenandoah Valley, where they thought they had disposed of Stonewall Jackson.[19]

Jackson's advance down the Shenandoah (the Shenandoah is geologically more elevated in the southern portion of the Valley than it is in the north, thus the seemingly odd reference of moving north as "down" the valley) had raised eyebrows and fears all across the North. In response to these fears, McDowell had been promptly recalled, fulfilling Lee's fondest hopes, and Johnston was now left to contend with McClellan alone. Richmond heaved a collective sigh of relief.

McClellan, meanwhile, interpreted McDowell's recall as yet further evidence of the intent on the part of Washington politicians and intriguers to destroy him, further shaking his already questionable grasp of military reality. "It was one more sickening proof of the 'hypocrisy, knavery & folly' of those in Washington, he raged. 'Heaven save a country governed by such counsels!'"[20] This further stoked the fires of George McClellan's irrational misgivings, his paranoid fantasies, and further complicated his already odd decision making. Indeed, so delusional had McClellan become that he now believed — or at least reported to believe — that he was facing an immense Confederate force opposing him, perhaps twice his own number.

On May 31 Joe Johnston launched his much anticipated attack on McClellan's army south of the Chickahominy River. The tactical objective of this attack was to overwhelm part of McClellan's force south of the Chickahominy River before it could be reinforced by the rest of McClellan's army deployed north of the river. The rough objective was a country intersection about ten miles due east of Richmond known as Seven Pines. Unfortunately, orders were not clearly provided, or at least clearly understood, and the assault would go horribly bungled. By day's end little, if anything, had been accomplished. "In exchange for the temporary occupation of a square mile or so of woodland, two abandoned lines, ten guns, some 6000 small arms, a handful of prisoners, and miscellaneous loot, Confederate losses had been excessive."[21]

While little had been gained by either side at Seven Pines (called Fair Oaks by the North), the combat had been fierce, the casualty counts high, and the fighting generally reflective of what would become the norm for Civil War engagements. In 1862 neither side was yet prepared for the carnage that was to come, for while over the preceding decade battlefield weaponry had changed, infantry tactics had not.

The vast majority of Civil War officers had received what little battlefield experience they had gained during the Mexican War. At that time the standard infantry issue weapon was a smoothbore musket of limited range and accuracy. Thus to achieve maximum firepower, large concentrations of men had to be marched close to an enemy position in order to deliver a large volley, or concentration, of fire. Since the smoothbore musket had a maximum range of perhaps only 400 yards, and a killing range of even less, the tactic made sense and the carnage proved limited.

By the beginning of the Civil War, however, the standard infantry issue weapon was no longer the smoothbore musket of Mexican War vintage, but the 1861 Springfield rifle. This weapon fired a fifty-eight caliber, soft lead minié-ball with a range of nearly 1,000 yards. Suddenly the old massed infantry tactics had been rendered obsolete, but for the first few years of Civil War combat, no one seemed to take notice. The old Mexican War tactic of marching large concentrations of troops across open fields of fire prevailed on both sides of the conflict. The result on the battlefield was virtually mass murder, and at Seven Pines — only the second significant engagement fought in the East at the time — the carnage proved predictably horrific.

Colonel John Gordon, who over the years would rise to fame as one of the Confederacy's more stellar officers, describes the horror on the field at Seven Pines: "My field officers and adjutant were all dead. Every horse ridden into the fight, my own among them, was dead. Fully one half of my line officers and half my men were dead or wounded.... In water from knee-to-hip-deep, the men were fighting and falling, while a detail propped up the wounded against stumps or trees to prevent their drowning."[22] For those units heavily engaged, the toll had been enormous. Again, John Gordon: "The losses were appalling. All the field officers except myself had been killed. Of forty-four officers of the line, but thirteen were left for duty. Nearly two thirds of the entire command was killed or wounded."[23]

Those fighting on the Federal side fared little better. Oliver Wendell Holmes, Jr., provides a glimpse of the carnage he observed the following day as he crossed the field of battle: "Today is pleasant and hot — It is singular with what indifference one gets to look on the dead bodies in gray clothes wh. lie all around — (or rather did — We are burying them today as fast as we can —) As you go through the woods you stumble constantly, and, if after dark, as last night on picket, perhaps tread on the swollen bodies already fly blown and decaying, of men shot in the head back or bowels — Many of the wounded are terrible to look at — especially those fr. fragments of shell."[24]

One unexpected result of the slaughter at Seven Pines, however — and one that would play large as the war progressed — had been the serious wounding of General Joseph Johnston himself. Porter Alexander, riding with Johnston's staff at the moment, describes the scene: "Gen. Johnston & the staff stood out in the field watching until a little before sundown when the general received a musket ball in his shoulder & in a moment or two afterward a fragment of shell broke some of his ribs & brought him to the ground. A litter was brought up, & he was put on it & started back to hd.qrs. Darkness soon stopped the firing, after which I followed & overtook the litter bearers."[25]

Confederate command immediately devolved upon General Gustavus Smith, Johnston's second, but Smith physically collapsed under the newfound responsibility — suffering what today would in all probability be diagnosed as a nervous breakdown — and could not stand up to the task.[26] Confederate president Jefferson Davis responded immediately by appointing Robert E. Lee commander, and the campaign around Richmond from that moment forward took on a different character, and one that would hardly serve as an agreeable tonic for George McClellan's already troubled psyche. Lee's qualities as a military leader were at the time unknown and untested, but they would not remain unknown or untested for long.

Robert E. Lee was the offspring of a renowned Virginia family, and a career soldier of high reputation. His father had been the famous Revolutionary War hero "Light Horse Harry" Lee, and Robert had graduated West Point in the class of 1828, second in standing only to cadet Charles Mason.[27] Lee had led an exemplary career, serving with distinction in the war with Mexico, and he had been offered, but refused, the command of Federal forces

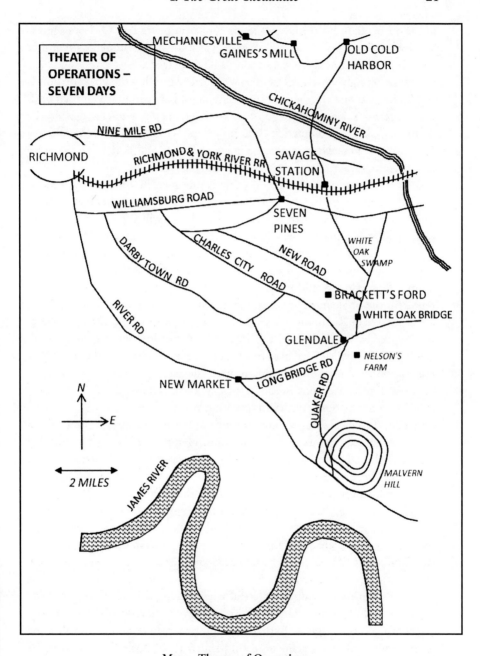

THEATER OF OPERATIONS – SEVEN DAYS

MECHANICSVILLE

GAINES'S MILL

OLD COLD HARBOR

CHICKAHOMINY RIVER

NINE MILE RD

RICHMOND

RICHMOND & YORK RIVER RR

SAVAGE STATION

WILLIAMSBURG ROAD

SEVEN PINES

WHITE OAK SWAMP

DARBY TOWN RD

CHARLES CITY ROAD

NEW ROAD

BRACKETT'S FORD

RIVER RD

WHITE OAK BRIDGE

GLENDALE

NELSON'S FARM

NEW MARKET

LONG BRIDGE RD

QUAKER RD

N
E

2 MILES

JAMES RIVER

MALVERN HILL

Map — Theater of Operations

at the outbreak of hostilities by the Lincoln administration. Of Lee's aggressive inclinations and military skill little was known as he took command in early June 1862, but these were soon to be displayed.

Interestingly, Porter Alexander, while off examining the lines surrounding Richmond one afternoon, came upon an old acquaintance familiar with Lee. Alexander, fearful that the new Confederate commander might not be up to the task, asked pointedly: "Our only hope is to bounce him [McClellan] & whip him somewhere before he is ready for us, and that needs audacity in our commander. Has Gen. Lee that audacity?"

The response: "Alexander, if there is one man in either army, Federal or Confederate, who is, head & shoulders, far above every other one in either army in audacity that man is Gen. Lee, and you will very soon have lived to see it. Lee is audacity personified."[28]

That remark, now many years and much study later, would seem to appear almost prescient. Indeed, audacity, the willingness to take the offensive despite long odds, would mark Lee's Civil War career, and it would surely represent the single most important factor in the turning back of McClellan's army outside of Richmond. It seems Lee's going over to the offensive alone, the "aggressive" as he would call it, and not the situation on the ground, unhinged George McClellan's already fragile state of mind to the point that making poor, almost inexplicable military decisions seemed suddenly prudent. And those decisions would in turn lay the groundwork for the remarkable Confederate opportunity in late June at Glendale.

Lee's first decision was not to renew offensive operations after taking over the reins of command at Seven Pines. He preferred instead to marshal his strength and bide his time until the right opportunity presented itself. There was little question, however, that he ever considered waiting, as had Johnston, to absorb the enemy's blow, rather than going over to the offensive to deliver a strike. "He reasoned that if he permitted McClellan to remain in front of Richmond, the superior Federal artillery soon would blast its way into the city. A defensive behind temporary fortification was necessary until the Confederate Army could be disposed and, if possible, reinforced. Then it would assume the offensive."[29]

Lee's plan would not be a tactical scheme designed to hamper, confuse, or harass his Federal adversary, a Fabian strategy conceived to delay or impede the coming Union assault. Rather it would be a plan designed to rollup the entire Federal line, to send it reeling south in confusion, perhaps to its destruction in the thickly tangled woods, rivers, and streams east of Richmond. It would be a plan conceived to rid Richmond of the monstrous Federal invasion, hopefully soon, and hopefully forever.

And when he struck it would be with overwhelming force. As Alexander points out, Lee intended to marshal every available body of troops to the task: "The principal feature of Lee's proposed plan had long been the bringing down of Jackson from the Valley to attack the enemy's right wing. Even before Jackson had extricated himself from the pursuit of his enemies, on June 8, Lee had written him to set on foot the arrangements to mislead the enemy as to his intentions."[30]

False rumors were circulated to confound McClellan. The cavalry under J.E.B. Stuart was sent on a reconnaissance in force around the Federal right in order to firmly locate the enemy's flank and supply line. An entire division was sent off from Richmond to Jackson in the Shenandoah Valley in a ruse to persuade the Federal commander that Lee's army was first amply manned, and secondly that something was soon to be afoot in the Valley. Both worked. On June 18, clearly taken in by the Confederate games, McClellan wrote President Lincoln, "If ten or fifteen thousand men have left Richmond to reinforce Jackson, it illustrates their strength and confidence."[31]

McClellan hesitated to attack, assuring Washington of action while finding reason after reason to delay. "On June 2, which was his best opportunity, he was only waiting for the water to fall in the Chickahominy. On June 7 he was waiting for McCall's division ... which arrived on the 12th and 13th. On June 16 he was waiting for two days to let ground harden."[32]

Phil Kearny, the fiery, one armed brigadier who had stormed after Johnston's army back at Manassas in March, had not been fooled by George McClellan's procrastination. Indeed, with remarkable foresight he appraised McClellan's performance and predicted the probable outcome: "Here we are at deadlock again. Manassas over again — both parties entrenched up to the eyes; both waiting for something to occur. It only required McClellan to put forth ... his military might and Richmond would have been ours. But no; delay upon delay.... I am puzzled to divine the next act of the drama. It will be either another inexplicable evacuation, or the suffocation of this army by the seizure of our communications when least expected."[33]

Secret arrangements were made by Lee to bring Jackson's entire command down from the Valley via Ashland and to be in position to strike the opening blow of a substantial Confederate assault on the extreme Federal right — precisely as Phil Kearny had predicted, to cut off the Federal army from its line of supply and communication along the York River Railroad.

The offensive was to begin on the morning of June 26, all other commands to move on the sound of Jackson's guns.[34] But Jackson, mysteriously, did not arrive as expected. Then without proper orders the division under

A.P. Hill attacked the Federal position at Beaver Dam Creek late in the afternoon, and was in turn severely repulsed.

Why had Hill attacked? Where was Jackson? Lee's great plan had misfired seemingly as badly as had Joe Johnston's at Seven Pines.

Or had it? "Yet however grim the failures of the day, General Lee had succeeded in one vitally important respect: he had captured the initiative. Equally important, he had indelibly impressed that fact on the mind of his opponent. Just five hours after the fighting at Mechanicsville ended, General McClellan determined he must retreat from Richmond."[35]

Only hours after a decided Federal *victory*, George McClellan, the Young Napoleon, had decided to abandon the effort to seize Richmond, and retreat instead to the safety of the James River. There the Union gunboats with their massive naval guns could cover his redeployment, while he might establish a waterborne supply line to his army, or evacuate if necessary.

This decision to retreat cannot be justified in terms of the military facts; indeed, it cannot be justified logically. It can be justified only through what must have been the twisted state of McClellan's mind at the moment. He had created so many phantoms with which to do battle that those phantoms had now seemingly risen to consume him. One day later McClellan would appear virtually enfeebled by the turn of events. "His demoralization, which had begun two days before with the report that Stonewall Jackson was approaching, was now complete."[36]

No doubt factoring into George McClellan's decision to retreat before Richmond were important naval actions that had transpired on the waters near Hampton Roads, then later on the James River below Richmond. In early May, with McClellan's forces in command of most of the lower Virginia peninsula, the Confederate hierarchy in Richmond had concluded that Norfolk, isolated on the eastern side of the Chesapeake as it was, could not be adequately reinforced or supplied, and was therefore indefensible. The only sensible course of action, distasteful though it be, was to abandon the city and redeploy its garrison to better use.

On May 9 the crew of the *Merrimack* suddenly realized to their dismay — no one had thought to inform them of the decision — that Norfolk had in fact been evacuated of all Confederate troops, and the city abandoned. Suddenly, the *Merrimack* was on her own. What's more, for the Confederacy this created a strategic dilemma, for the *Merrimack* had been the only defense against the Federal fleet sailing directly up the James River and reducing the Rebel capital to rubble.

The captain of the *Merrimack* ordered almost every piece of equipment that was not absolutely necessary for the ship's operation tossed overboard in an attempt to raise her draft and make a run up the James River for Richmond, but even that would not do. The *Merrimack*'s draft remained far too low to even attempt the run, and there seemed no option but to scuttle the boat. On May 11 the crew departed and the *Merrimack* was run aground and set ablaze. When the magazine finally blew there was virtually nothing left of her. The crew hiked a distance, caught a train, and headed off for Richmond. The mighty *Merrimack* was gone, and the James lay open and undefended.

It did not take the Federal Navy long to discover the fate of their monster adversary, nor to grasp its meaning. On May 15 a five-ship Federal flotilla headed up the James, bound for Richmond. What they found, however, was that seven miles south of the city, on a

Robert E. Lee — Commander of the Army of Northern Virginia and today regarded as one of the finest military leaders in American history (Library of Congress).

bend in the James, the Confederates had hastily constructed a naval battery on high ground called Drewry's Bluff that dominated the river.

Waiting there for them was the *Merrimack*'s crew, manning several large naval guns, and as the Federal flotilla rounded the bend they received a fusillade of metal for their efforts. The guns on Drewry's Bluff sat so high the Federal ships could not elevate their own sufficiently to adequately respond, and the small flotilla was battered to no avail and finally had to retire. While the Federal attempt to run up to Richmond had ended in dismal failure, the news that the James was wide open and now in Union hands clear up to Drewry's Bluff no doubt was music to George McClellan's ears. Here, now, was a safe haven, should he need one.

George Brinton McClellan, like Robert E. Lee, was a West Point graduate who had fought with distinction in the war with Mexico. After that war, he served as an official observer for the United States to the Crimean War. He was considered a rising star in the military but resigned from the army in 1857 to take up a position with the railroad. With the outbreak of the Civil War, McClellan returned to military service, and was promptly given command of the Department of the Ohio.

There McClellan directed operations that brought him both success and immediate national acclaim. Soon after the disastrous Federal defeat at Bull Run in the summer of 1861, McClellan was given command of the forces defending Washington, and within months promoted to general in chief of United States forces. His rise had been meteoric. Born of a wealthy family from Philadelphia, in pedigree McClellan and his adversary, Robert E. Lee, would seem remarkably similar. In performance, however, they were soon to prove remarkably dissimilar.

The Federals would fight again the following day at Gaines's Mill, only to lose disastrously when McClellan refused to send ample reinforcements to his embattled 5th Corps, still north of the Chickahominy. But by then it did not matter. Orders had already been issued, the tents struck. The lead elements of the Army of the Potomac had already departed for the James River, hopefully to elude en route the massive Confederate army that existed only in George McClellan's tortured mind.

Now we must return to the beginning of the tale, to the tired, dusty Federal troops struggling south on the red dirt roads bordering the Chickahominy swamp. These Union soldiers were marching on the few narrow roads that led south across the peninsula, tired and in most cases fearful, exhausted, and confused. Named by the Federal troopers who stumbled south, what forever more would be known as the Great Skedaddle had begun.

Oliver Wendell Holmes, Jr., then a young lieutenant with the 20th Massachusetts Volunteers, recalled the constant fighting, turmoil, and exhaustion of the retreat: "We have had hard work for several days — marched all night — lain on our arms every morn'g & fought every afternoon — eaten nothing — suffered the most intense anxiety and everything else possible — I'm safe though so far — But you can't conceive the wear & tear — Lowell is probably dead bowels cut."[37]

While the peninsula had a number of roads running east and west from Richmond out toward Hampton Roads, running north and south were very few. As a consequence, much of the army's retreat took place on a single road, causing great confusion and delay. Through a single channel the entire army had to pour. Their supply depots had been burned, their wounded compatriots left behind. But that was by no means the worst of it.

"Unknown to us," Porter Alexander explained, "another circumstance was rarely in our favor. The Federal army was temporarily without a head. On the 29th, and July 1, McClellan, on each day, left his army without placing any one in command during his absence, while he did engineer's duty, examining the localities toward which he was marching. Had the Confederates accomplished their reasonable expectations, the criticism of McClellan would have been severe."[38]

Severe is to say the least. The Young Napoleon had ridden far ahead, abandoning his retreating army in the guise of an engineering errand, presumably to find a suitable location for his new base of operations on the river. This all done without the appointment of a second in command; thus were the individual corps commanders of the Army of the Potomac left to fend for themselves. On June 30, as his exhausted troops prepared to do battle for their lives at Glendale, George McClellan was already at Haxall's Landing on the James, "without telegraphic communications and too distant to command the army."[39] That afternoon he would be the welcome guest aboard a naval gunboat headed up river.

George McClellan — Called the Young Napoleon by writers of the era, McClellan showed enormous capability as an organizer of men, but almost none as a fighting general (Library of Congress).

But McClellan's men would not fare quite so nicely. Once again, Oliver Wendell Holmes, Jr., explains what the confusion and terror of the retreat was like for the ordinary foot soldier.

> June 29 we started from the trenches on our retreat — at Fair Oaks passed Rocket Guns & great quantities of stores wh. had to be destroyed — Went a little further & formed in line. Co" I & B (the R. & Left. Co") went out as skirmishers & my Co. as support. Our own side fired shell & cannister into us (hurt no one luckily) and the 5th N.H. Regt. Behaving badly I had to fall back on the Regt. Afternoon marched to Savage's Stat" where lots more stores were destroyed and a hospital stood where all the wounded had to be left to the enemy. Here the enemy shelled us — Several men hurt none of our Co. Major was touched but not hurt. Later there was tall musketry (we sharing but little) and a South Car Brigade was chewed up.[40]

In the face of an aggressive enemy George McClellan, the commanding general of the Army of the Potomac, had fled the field. Worse still, he had left his army to fend for itself on unfamiliar territory, to fight in detail, and quite possibly be destroyed in detail. McClellan had provided his Confederate adversary an opportunity almost beyond calculation, and an opportunity only time has brought into clear focus.

It is impossible to understand the circumstances offered Southern arms that day in late June at Glendale without understanding these facts. Never before, and never after, would Robert E. Lee's Army of Northern Virginia — or any other Confederate army, for that matter — be provided a similar opportunity: a moving adversary, bereft of command, strung out over miles of unfamiliar, narrow roads, incapable of unit cooperation and therefore mutual defense. On June 30, 1862, the Army of the Potomac had been abandoned by its own leader, placed in the unenviable position of not merely being harassed, roughly handled, or defeated by the closing Confederate foe, but potentially annihilated.

CHAPTER 2

A View from the *Gazelle*

On the morning of June 28, while there was joyous celebration in and about Richmond due to the apparent Federal retreat, at General Lee's headquarters the mood remained restrained. For the Confederate high command it still remained unclear what, exactly, had transpired. A bloody battle had been fought and won at Gaines's Mill, that seemed clear, but Federal intentions and movements remained a puzzle.

Officers with field glasses studied the changing scene just to their east and noted something of interest. "Soon the bright panorama beyond the river-valley began to be obscured. An ever-lengthening cloud began to rise. It was not the smoke of a silent battle; it was dust, and it could only have been raised by laboring horses and marching men. Now there came distant flashes, echoing heavy explosions. Magazines were being fired! McClellan was on the move — but why and whither?"[1]

The question was no longer whether or not McClellan's army had been put into motion — that, indeed, had been made manifestly clear. The question, rather, was just where the Federal army was headed, and what McClellan intended to do once he got there. It was difficult for Lee to believe, understanding the sheer size of the Union force arrayed before him, that McClellan did not intend to stay and fight. The firing of supplies smacked more of panic than of a planned redeployment. But what did the Federals have to panic about?

As the Confederate high command envisioned it that June morning, if McClellan's army was, in fact, in motion, he had essentially two options. "It was a question whether they would go to the James River near City Point, where their fleet & supplies could meet them; or whether they would seek to recross the Chick. lower down & go back to the York."[2] Was McClellan retreating or simply redeploying, maneuvering, perhaps, to strike Richmond along a more advantageous axis, or slipping away to safety? On the morning after the battle at Gaines's Mill, all this remained a matter of specula-

29

tion, but speculation of the most intense variety. The facts had to be uncovered.

Getting a good look at just what was transpiring proved difficult. For the better part of a month the Federal army had constructed a network of formidable earthworks facing Richmond to shield their advance, and now those earthworks served to screen all movement behind them. A corporal's guard could hold off a division from behind those mounds, so a reconnaissance, even one in substantial force, seemed a poor option — it would simply be shot to pieces.

Just what was happening beyond those manmade hills remained for Lee on the 28th maddeningly unclear. The dust clouds behind the great earthworks appeared to be slowly inching east, but that did not clarify the situation either, for the few roads in that area demanded an easterly movement, at least initially, whether McClellan was headed south toward the James, or east toward the York River.

It was necessary to pierce the cloud of mystery, to get a good look behind those fortifications. Lee had to know what was happening. But how?

If McClellan were in fact headed east toward the York River, it was reasoned, he would at some point have to cross the Chickahominy River further downstream. It was decided, therefore, to have those bridges and fords watched closely.

Additionally, on the far left of the Confederate position a reconnaissance in force was sent out beyond the Federal earthworks to probe east toward White House, the massive supply depot the Federal Army had constructed on the Pamunkey River.[3] Was the depot still functioning? Were the bridges and fords along the lower Chickahominy under Federal guard? Was there Union cavalry on the prowl, infantry dug in on the ridges commanding the river, artillery unlimbered to command the bridges? Until he had a clear indication of Federal intent, Lee could not risk a move. Not enough yet was known, and the wrong move could easily prove fatal.

On the far right of the Confederate line yet another technique was put into play to try and clarify both the Federal movement and its probable destination. "Some weeks before this campaign began, Doctor Edward Cheves of Savannah conceived the idea of making a balloon for military observation."[4] Cheves had purchased most of the silk in Charleston, then varnished it using a "witches brew" of old rubber car springs dissolved in oil to make the silk airtight. Christened the *Gazelle*, the balloon worked remarkably well, and was moved to Richmond in late June. Lacking pure hydrogen, it had to be daily pumped full of gas from the Richmond Gas Works, and as such the balloon was of but limited range. The *Gazelle* could reach an altitude of

1,000 feet on a tether line, but it leaked gas at such a rate that the craft had to be regularly refilled. While the balloon was thus limited in both air time and range from the gas works, while in the air it proved an effective craft.[5]

Selected to command this innovation was Porter Alexander, soon to gain distinction for his handling of Longstreet's artillery that final day at Gettysburg. But Alexander had also handled intelligence matters previously for General Beauregard after Manassas and was a trained signalman and observer. He was a natural choice for the job.

"Well, on the receipt of this balloon, Gen. Lee ordered me to take charge of it, & go up in it, to observe, specially, any transfers or crossing of the Chickahominy — from one side to the other — during the approaching battles on the north side, & also any indications of any disposition of the enemy to assume the aggressive on the south side. And I was ordered to provide signals to be displayed to indicate whatever I might see."[6]

Fearful of heights after a fall over a cliff while a cadet at West Point, Alexander was petrified he would become so overwhelmed that he might literally jump out of the balloon once aloft, but he actually found the experience captivating: "The Balloon had not risen 50 feet before I felt as safe & as much at home as if I had lived in one for years.... If balloons were plenty I could imagine one's acquiring the 'balloon habit,' & going up every day just to gaze down."[7]

Alexander's first ascension took place on the Williamsburg Road during the battle of Gaines's Mill. There he spotted smoke from the battle, and observed Federal reinforcements crossing the river. He signaled this information back to the ground using "four big, black-cambric balls, stretched over telegraph wire hoops, & I devised a little signal code of one or more of these balls, hung out below the balloon, & copies were given to all the principal officers all along our lines."[8] But from the area directly in front of Richmond, the view was limited, and the Yankee columns seemed to have disappeared behind a sea of woodland. Alexander had to come up with a better idea if he was to get a good look at the Federal retreat.

So to increase the balloon's optical reach, Alexander came up with the clever notion of attaching the tether to a small tug named the *Teaser*, which then towed him along the James down river toward Malvern Hill. This technique worked well, and for days Porter Alexander soared high above the water, spyglass in hand, the one and only aeronaut in Lee's army. "During the next several days I made several ascensions both day & by night, when the locations of camp fires would betray troops who could not be seen by day, the object being to locate the routes over which the enemy was retreating."[9]

Sadly, in early July the *Teaser* would run aground; a Federal gunboat approached with guns ablaze, and both the *Gazelle* and the *Teaser* had to be abandoned. Porter Alexander escaped unharmed, but thus ended Alexander's days as an aeronaut. But his ingenious efforts in the air during the Seven Days campaign may well have been one of the most sophisticated aerial reconnaissances prior to World War I and the introduction of the biplane.

Through all these efforts, in the air and on the ground, using aeronauts, cavalry, engineers, and infantry, interesting reports slowly began to accumulate. Then late in the afternoon of the 28th Robert E. Lee finally received the firm sort of intelligence he had been waiting for — Stuart's cavalry had reached the lower Chickahominy bridges and found them fired and the supply depot at White House in smoky ruins.[10] This seemed conclusive. McClellan would not have burned bridges he intended to cross, nor put the torch to a vast supply depot needed to sustain his army. It did not appear that the Federal army was headed for the York River. The cloud of mystery had begun to disperse, and a more meaningful picture crystallize in its place: McClellan appeared to be headed south toward the James River.

Then on the morning of the 29th Lee received even more conclusive evidence. Two engineers from Longstreet's command had performed a reconnaissance across the Chickahominy River: "The great, frowning works around Golding's Farm were empty! This was the key position south of the Chickahominy. McClellan had abandoned his attempt to take Richmond. Lee's spirits rose."[11]

Just why the Federal army had turned away from its objective remained an unknown for Robert E. Lee, a mystery, truth be told, but it was a mystery that no longer mattered. Facts were all that mattered, and the facts — for the moment, at least — appeared clear. McClellan had put his monstrous army on the move south toward the James. A force that could not have been attacked without enormous loss behind those giant earthworks by the Confederates, now appeared entirely vulnerable on the narrow, dusty roads leading south toward the river.

For Robert E. Lee and his lieutenants, this remarkable news must have seemed almost too good to be true. Indeed, the entire aim of Lee's offensive had been to force the Federal army away from Richmond, and then into the open where it might be attacked and destroyed. Now McClellan seemed to have graciously provided for both.[12] The only question confronting Robert E. Lee on the morning of June 29 was when, where, and how to get at the Federal army. "If McClellan was establishing a base on the James, the whole of the Army of Northern Virginia should be concentrated south of the Chickahominy and hurled against the enemy while he was in the confusion of change."[13]

Playing nicely into Lee's planning was the fact that south of the Chick-ahominy River the road system greatly favored the Confederates in any pursuit of a foe moving south. Three roads led more or less east from Richmond, while there was fundamentally only one route south, and this a collection of roads, all of which would have to be controlled by the Federals in retreat. If Lee himself had drawn the map, he could not have drawn it to much greater advantage.

From north to south, the map revealed the east bound routes as the Charles City Road, the Darbytown Road, and farther south, running along the north bank of the James, the River Road. Lee, familiar with the area, immediately grasped the strategic significance of the road grid, and planned his pursuit accordingly. Each route could be used to concentrate the Confederate Army on or near a single point.

Confederate infantry was at the time organized loosely in four commands under generals Jackson, Longstreet, Huger, and Magruder. Alexander explains Lee's plan for pursuit on the morning of the 29th: "Magruder, immediately behind the enemy on the Williamsburg road, was ordered to pursue down that road. Huger, on the Charles City road, was ordered down that road. From the battle-field of the 27th [Gaines's Mill], A.P. Hill and Longstreet were ordered to cross the Chickahominy at New Bridge, and passing in rear of Magruder and Huger to move by the Darbytown, the next road to the right.... Jackson, with the largest force, was directed to pursue by the shortest and most direct route."[14]

Put simply, Lee intended to send three columns moving from west to east on the three roads previously mentioned, while Jackson pursued the Federal rear from north to south. While this plan required proper coordination, each Confederate column would be moving on its own separate road, supported by the other columns on their left and right. It was a reasonably sound plan. Somewhere in the woods east of Richmond Lee knew one or all of those pursuing columns would strike the lumbering Federal retreat with their immense train of wagons, horses, and artillery, hopefully reducing it then to smaller pieces that could be devoured in detail.

Critical to this design was Stonewall Jackson. Jackson was intended to handle the largest of Lee's converging columns, marching on the shortest route toward the Federal rear. Generally this would have seemed a simple task for the Stonewall of Shenandoah Valley fame, but for two days that famous Stonewall had yet to put in an appearance.

At Mechanicsville on the 26th Lee's entire plan had hinged on Jackson's opening the general assault at the first light of day. Not only did Jackson not open on time, but his Valley Army never showed up, instead going into

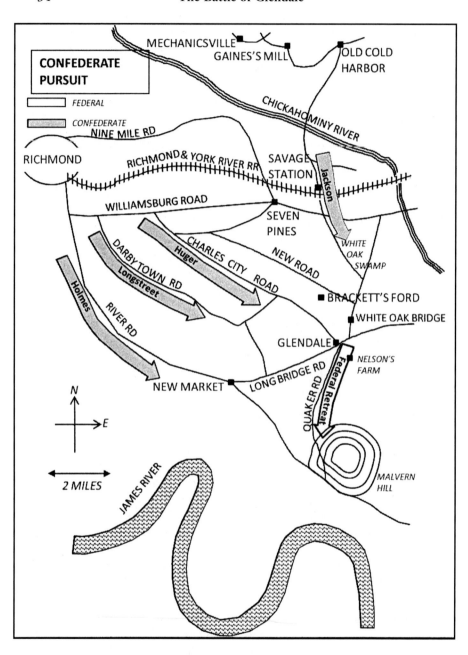

Map — Confederate Pursuit

bivouac in the late afternoon with the sound of guns ringing in the distance.[15] A.P. Hill, moving impatiently and without orders, had sent his division forward against a strong Federal position at Beaver Dam Creek, and his division was severely repulsed for his effort. Those were the guns that Jackson's men had heard as they went into bivouac, and thus was Lee's debut turned from one of high promise to fiasco. The following day at Gaines's Mill Jackson would finally arrive, but then late, and ineffectively. While Gaines's Mill would ultimately prove a Confederate victory, it would be won at a terrible cost, and not because of Jackson sluggish efforts, but despite them.

Not mincing any words, Porter Alexander offers a harsh critique of Jackson's performance: "He nowhere, even distantly, approached his record as a soldier won in his every other battle, either before or afterward. As one reads of his weak and dilatory performance day after day, and recalls what he had always been before, and always was afterward, one feels that during these Seven Days he was really not Jackson. He was a different individual. He was under a spell!"[16] What sort of spell might Jackson have been under?

Thomas "Stonewall" Jackson — Architect of the famous Shenandoah Valley Campaign of 1862, which is considered a classic by many military experts, but Jackson consistently failed during the Seven Days Campaign outside of Richmond (Library of Congress).

Since March Jackson had been maneuvering and fighting in Virginia's Shenandoah Valley. Throughout April, May, and early June, Jackson had marched, countermarched, and fought innumerable battles against three separate Federal armies sent to corner and crush him. His success had changed the face of the war. "With a force that never had exceeded 17,000 men of all arms, he had cleared the enemy from the greater part of the Shenandoah. What was far more important, he had used this small force so effectively that he had forced President Lincoln to change the entire plan for the capture of Richmond."[17]

Later Jackson would engage in a long and tiring trip to meet with Lee in order to coordinate the plan of attack at Mechanicsville set for June 26, return to the Valley, then turn and march his army from the Valley to the outskirts of Richmond. Jackson, a man seemingly driven by willpower alone, may well have, by the time he had reached the vicinity of Ashland, simply pushed himself beyond the power of will.

Henry Kyd Douglas, on staff with Jackson at the time, relates that the general often slept only when time would permit: "For awhile I was wont to wonder if the General ever slept; but I soon found out that he slept a great deal, often at odd times. If he had just five minutes to spare for that recreation, he could sleep four and half minutes of it and be wide awake when the five minutes were up."[18] But that sort of physical regimen has limits, and by the opening of the Seven Days battles, Stonewall Jackson may well have surpassed his. Put differently, Jackson's stunning victory in the Valley that temporarily saved Richmond, may have set the table for eventual failure during the Seven Days, and a failure that would have far reaching repercussions, not only for Lee's ambitions, but for the course of American history.

But on the morning of June 29 for Confederates all hopes were high. If McClellan's position had not been firmly fixed, his direction had, and that alone due to the road grid revealed his rough position. If Southern forces could move rapidly they could intercept him, cut him off from the James, and destroy the Federal army in detail. At that moment victory, indeed, independence seemed within grasp.

Orders were issued for the long columns to move. Jackson was to press south on the Nine Mile Road toward White Oak Swamp. Longstreet was to march east on the Darbytown Road, as was Huger on the Charles City Road.

And if the casual observer of the day were to trace the wandering course of those roads across the face of a map with nothing more than the tip of a finger, he would discover that eventually all three come roughly together not far at all from a small blacksmith's shop owned by a man named Riddell, a country crossroads called Glendale.

CHAPTER 3

Kearny le Magnifique

Confederate expectations were no doubt high on the morning of June 29, and rightfully so. By all reports, the situation on the ground favored them immensely. Yet aside from the broad principle of pursue and destroy, the fact of the matter was, on the morning of June 29, the Confederate plan of battle remained sketchy. Yes, the assignments had been made for the direction of march, and yes those orders were sensible, but where, when, and how those marching Confederate columns might actually encounter the Federal army remained a vague prediction.

The general plan of action was simply divide and conquer, but where, exactly, the enemy might be encountered and the columns subsequently severed, remained unclear. Dividing the geography below the Chickahominy River was a long, low confusion of trees, brambles, and water with few crossing points known as White Oak Swamp. It was Lee's basic aim to cut off a significant portion of the Federal force north of the swamp, capturing or destroying that portion, while Holmes, Huger, Longstreet, and Hill moved by the flank to confront the portion below the swamp, perhaps the following day.

Thus while hopes were high, what actually prevailed that morning was not certainty at all, but rather the fog of war, a confusion of possibilities, and in war where confusion lurks, the probability of mistakes, errors, and miscalculations increases exponentially. Add to this formula the human elements of fear, ignorance, illness, and exhaustion, and suddenly what appears theoretically a lopsided victory for one side or the other can often devolve into little more than a prescription for bewilderment and failure. So it would be for Confederate aspirations on June 29.

The first to fall prey to this malady would be Confederate general "Prince" John Magruder. Ordered by Lee to move at once down the Williamsburg Road and strike the Federal flank or rear — in fact, whatever force he found before him — Magruder stumbled and fumbled through a day of excitement and turmoil. "Whatever the exact nature of the information that reached him, Magruder became convinced that the enemy was preparing to attack him in numbers far exceeding his own."[1] Somehow Magruder had managed to persuade himself that an enemy in obvious flight had turned about, and for some inexplicable reason, had gone over to the offensive.

Indeed, it required a remarkable set of calculations on Magruder's part to arrive at such a conclusion. In essence he would have to believe that McClellan had abandoned a defensive position of massive earthworks — which were almost unassailable from the Confederate perspective — in order to lure the Rebel army into battle on the narrow roads and woods east of Richmond, a tactic obviously fraught with dire possibilities for the Federal high command

John Bankhead Magruder — Commanded a division under Robert E. Lee during the Seven Days but fatigue and illness would compromise his performance (Library of Congress).

This would have been a strategy perhaps worthy of Napoleon, as he had done, in fact, at Austerlitz where he bamboozled and destroyed the coalition forces that opposed him through maneuvering off the high ground. But by making such a comparison Magruder would of necessity have to have confused George McClellan, the "Young Napoleon," with the real article, and Magruder had already seen enough of McClellan's cautious, lumbering tactics on Virginia's peninsula to know the difference between the two. Indeed, at Yorktown it had been Magruder who had bamboozled McClellan by cleverly marching his limited forces every which way in order to give McClellan the appearance of vast numbers, a theatrical ruse the Young Napoleon had swallowed hook, line, and sinker. Nevertheless, Magruder concluded to ignore Lee's order to advance and decided instead to hunker down until reinforced sufficiently to lead an attack down the Williamsburg Road.[2]

Finally, by late afternoon, and long after any true opportunity to cut the enemy off had been squandered, Magruder pushed forward a limited force east along the tracks of the York River Railroad, as if testing the waters with his toe. "Out of six Brigades present, he used only two and a half."[3] A violent clash occurred, thereafter known as the battle of Savage Station, but by late in the day little, if any, of Lee's plan had been realized on Magruder's portion of the battlefield.

In fairness to Magruder, it seems, due to the excitement of battle, and caught in the throes of responsibility, he had been suffering from an acute stomach ailment, and had slept little in days.[4] The combination of illness and exhaustion had undoubtedly made him unbalanced, and incapable of sound decision making. Regardless, for his efforts he received this disappointed note from General Lee: "General, I regret much that you have made so little progress to-day in pursuit of the enemy. In order to reap the fruits of our victory the pursuit should be most vigorous. I must urge you then again to press his rear, rapidly and steadily. We must lose no more time or he will escape us entirely."[5]

For Confederate and Federal alike, this was a time of exhaustion and anxiety. Both armies were on the move night and day, often skirmishing when and where they stumbled upon one another. The wounded lay where they fell, as did often the dead. Confederate colonel John Gordon, who had emerged from the carnage at Seven Pines unscathed, had this unnerving tale to tell of the exhausting Confederate pursuit:

> The fighting between the armies of McClellan and Lee was so nearly continuous, and engagement succeeded engagement so rapidly, that at some points the killed were hurriedly and imperfectly buried. I myself had a most disagreeable reminder of this fact. The losses in Rode's brigade, which I was then commanding, had been so heavy that it was held with other troops as a reserved corps. Our experiences, however, on the particular day of which I now speak had been more trying, and after nightfall I was directed to move to a portion of the field where the fighting had been desperate the preceding day, and to halt for the night in a woodland. Overcome with excessive fatigue, as soon as the designated point was reached I delivered my horse to a courier and dropped down on the ground for a much-needed rest. In a few moments I was sound asleep. A slightly elevated mound of earth served for a pillow. Frequently during the night I attempted to brush away from my head what I thought in my slumber was a twig or limb of the underbrush in which I was lying. My horror can be imagined when I discovered, the next morning, that it was the hand of a dead soldier sticking out above the shallow grave which had been my pillow and in which he had been only partially covered.[6]

Of the four Confederate columns put in motion that morning, Magruder fumbled away the moment, while Longstreet, Hill, and Huger had moved off to the southwest in good order. This left only Jackson to press the Federal rear down the Nine Mile Road from the north. For the two days prior Jackson had failed in his responsibilities. How had Stonewall faired on the 29th?

Edward Porter Alexander offers this appraisal: "But General Jackson with his great force did not move, & and the only reason that he did not is that it was Sunday. It is usually stated that he was delayed by necessary repairs to the Grapevine Bridge which was his shortest line of advance, but I have the authority of Gen. Hampton for saying that the necessary repairs were very slight & were executed Sunday morning by a lieutenant & not over twenty men."[7]

Henry Kyd Douglas, riding with Jackson at the time, offers this partial insight into the general's travails: "General Jackson, having sent Ewell toward the White House, remained almost stationary with the rest of his corps during the 28th and 29th. He had much difficulty that night, however in repairing Grapevine Bridge. When this was done, causing a delay much to be regretted, he crossed the Chickahominy and united with General John B. Magruder."[8] Why Jackson remained stationary for two days might be asked, and if the work at Grapevine Bridge was so tedious, why was it to be regretted?

Jackson's odd behavior during the Seven Days battles has baffled historians ever since. "Was the strain of hard days and sleepless nights sapping his initiative? The driving power of the Valley Campaign — was it being lost?"[9] These are fair questions, and questions numerous critics have asked. Was Jackson's delay a matter of religion or the exhaustion previously mentioned? Whatever the reason, Jackson's odd behavior would not only continue, it would grow even stranger.

While Jackson's mental state at the time remains questionable to this day, one thing, however, *was* certain. Jackson's force had not moved far, as Douglas readily admits, and had certainly not trapped or held the fleeing Federals north of White Oak Swamp. By evening they were across, and had posted a rear guard on the ridge overlooking the bridge, and that rear guard would have to be dealt with the following morning. Lee was disappointed; precious little had been accomplished, and a great opportunity had been squandered. But all was not lost.

To the contrary, in fact, considering the positions of his troops, the direction of the roads, and the slowness of the marching Federal column, an even better opportunity awaited the following day. "Gen. Lee was concentrating everything for one grand attack the next day, with his whole force, upon the enemy at Charles City cross roads [Glendale]."[10]

Hill, Longstreet, and Huger were closing rapidly from the west, and would be in easy striking distance of the crossroads the following morning. Jackson, despite his dilatory performance of the past three days, was still in position to attack, break, or at least hold in place the Federal rear guard at White Oak Swamp. Holmes, moving west on the River Road, was in position to take and hold Malvern Hill, an eminence dominating the James south of Glendale, thus cutting off the Federal retreat. In the morning the Federal army, along with all of its supplies, wagons, and artillery, would be strung out between White Oak Swamp and the James River, a distance of about ten miles, and perilously thin at points.

Any child could see from the map that the entire Federal retreat had of a necessity to filter through one crossroads town, that narrow little junction near Riddell's Shop called Glendale. Thus if Lee could take Glendale or the road just to the south, he would split the Federal army in two, and once split in two it would be entirely vulnerable to envelopment and destruction.

The sheer imbalance in men, equipment, and financial resources that favored the Union would naturally weigh heavily in the Federals' favor during the course of any protracted war. Thus if the South was ever to win its independence, Lee knew, it would have to be done with a quick and altogether shattering victory, a success so stunning and complete that it would not only destroy the enemy's forces, but leave the Federal government powerless to pursue its goals. The history of warfare, however, was not replete with examples of such inverted opportunities, yet none ever studied had been tactically superior to the one that confronted Robert E. Lee at that moment.

Thus the taking of the crossroads was absolutely critical, and Robert E. Lee — true to his nature — had arranged a concentration of overwhelming force to accomplish the task. He had given orders for Magruder to swing his six brigades (12,000 men) to the west in support of Longstreet. On the Charles City Road Huger was already closing with 9,000 troops, and between Hill and Longstreet Lee counted another 23,000 effectives. In the morning he would bring to bear a full 44,000 troops[11] on the tiny village of Glendale, more than enough to overwhelm any Federal resistance they might encounter. Once the crossroads had been taken and the road leading south to Malvern Hill secured, one column might turn north, the other south, and crush between them any remaining Federal resistance.

For Robert E. Lee, with the coming dawn the opportunity of a lifetime awaited; if he could take and hold Glendale, the war appeared won.

For Robert E. Lee, the war may have appeared to have been speeding toward a promising conclusion that evening, but in war, as in games of chance, Lady Luck often plays a mischievous role. Seemingly with the wave of an unseen wand victory can be turned into defeat, or just as easily, vice versa. Like a dealer in a backroom card game, Lady Luck shuffles, then deals the cards to all those who have anted up in the game of war. The accomplished commander plays his cards well, hoping to overcome poor fortune with skill, while the unskilled commander stumbles in the task, hoping Lady Luck will somehow smile on his misfortune. But skillful or unskillful, in the right, or in the wrong, the cards are always dealt, and the hands must be played accordingly.

On the evening of June 29, 1862, the South had surely been dealt the strongest hand it would ever play during the course of the American Civil War, the equivalent, perhaps, of five shiny aces. Lady Luck had smiled, and if one had been leaning over Robert E. Lee's shoulder at the time and reading his cards, it would certainly have appeared that the game was up for the Federal cause.

But Lady Luck always deals both ways, sometimes, it seems, from the bottom of the deck, and while the Federals had no doubt played themselves into a calamitous situation, some interesting cards still fell their way. These cards were nothing, of course, like the lovely aces that had been dealt the Southern cause, but they were scrappy, tough, and game nevertheless. Maybe Lady Luck knew what she was doing, or perhaps these cards had been slipped from the bottom of the deck, but one way or another — and as shall be documented in due course — a number of fortunate cards were drawn by the Federal cause that day, a few of which were named Meade, Hooker, and Kearny.

For two days the massive Federal army had been stumbling its way south on the dry, dusty roads of Eastern Virginia. "During the day and into the night Federal columns were halted for hours in miles-long traffic jams. Men fell asleep where they stood or sat."[12] The field hospital at Savage Station had been abandoned, and a massive supply depot put to the torch. Rising black clouds of smoke filled the sky, and supplies seemingly by the city block had either been burned or destroyed by order of the Young Napoleon. Nothing could be left behind that might augment the Rebel cause, thus destruction had become the word of the day.

Along the roadside discarded equipment lay scattered from Gaines's Mill to White Oak Swamp, then on into Glendale along a winding course of almost fourteen miles. Yet because of the inept Confederate pursuit, the lumbering Federal columns had still somehow managed to slip across White Oak Swamp bloodied, confused, and demoralized, but hardly bowed.

At Savage Station three full Federal corps — Heintzelman's, Sumner's, and Franklin's[13] — had been deployed to serve as a rear guard, yet because the commanding general had left the field without appointing a second, no controlling hand was present to guide events. Their orders, contrary to Magruder's worst fears, had been simply to hold their ground until night enveloped the field, then fall back with the rest of the army.[14] The three corps commanders were thus left to try and cover the army's rear while retreating as best they could. Naturally, confusion ensued.

Heintzelman, reasoning his corps was no longer needed to help hold the rear, began moving south in the afternoon, virtually unbeknownst to the other commands, and crossed White Oak Swamp on his way toward the James.[15] Marching under Heintzelman were the divisions of Joe Hooker and Phil Kearny and, by the sheer luck of the draw, these two divisions would be placed in positions the following morning that would bear the brunt of Lee's attack on Glendale. Two more proficient fighters could not be found in the Army of the Potomac.

Joseph Hooker is today best remembered as the failed commander of the Army of the Potomac, the man outflanked and outfought by Robert E. Lee — and, of course, Stonewall Jackson — at the battle of Chancellorsville, Virginia, in the spring of 1863. Rumors of drinking, card playing, and womanizing further tarnished his reputation, but prior to Chancellorsville, few soldiers in the Army of the Potomac advanced further or faster on merit than did Joe Hooker. In slightly over a year Hooker rose through the grades of brigade, division, and corps command, then was ultimately promoted

Joseph Hooker — Joseph Hooker rose rapidly through the ranks of the Army of the Potomac, and was known as one of its finest fighting generals. Promoted to the command of the army in 1863, he would lose the battle at Chancellorsville when flanked by Stonewall Jackson (Library of Congress).

to the command of a grand division under Ambrose Burnside. It was a remarkable record, a meteoric ascendance, and all of it earned on the field of battle. While questions of Joe Hooker's bravado, morals, and braggadocio were fair enough, no one ever questioned his willingness or ability to fight.

Hooker had graduated with the West Point class of 1837, where he was known as much for his bad behavior as he was for an outstanding academic record. In the war with Mexico he earned three brevets for gallantry, and gained enormous experience handling troops. In 1853 Hooker resigned his commission while on post in California, and would not return to military duty until the outbreak of the Civil War. By then he had firmly established two contentious feuds with senior officers that would weigh heavily in his military career. One was with Henry Halleck, the other Winfield Scott. Joe Hooker seemed the sort that is either loved or hated, and there is little doubt that many hated Joe Hooker, generally, it seemed, for his enormous ego and unstoppable, intemperate talk.

Wrangling a commission from the White House in late summer 1861, Joe Hooker joined the Army of the Potomac as a brigadier, and his star at once began to rise. After the first battle at Bull Run — which was fought before he was commissioned — his commands saw action in virtually every engagement the Army of the Potomac participated in. At Second Bull Run he was in the center of things, while during Lee's Maryland campaign of 1862 Hooker was particularly conspicuous.

At South Mountain he led a flanking movement that forced D.H. Hill to ultimately abandon the mountain, and at Antietam he almost accomplished the unthinkable — driving Stonewall Jackson's division from a defensive position. Indeed, had Hooker not been seriously wounded in the effort, and had McClellan responded to Hooker's urgent pleas for reinforcements instead of dithering, the Army of Northern Virginia may have been swept from the field that September morning.

It was on the peninsula with McClellan that Joe Hooker had established his early reputation as a hard fighter. A division commander at the time under Samuel Heintzelman, Hooker's command fought admirably at Williamsburg, Seven Pines, and Oak Grove. At Williamsburg Hooker was the lead in the pursuit of a retreating foe. His job was to pitch in to the Confederate rear when and where found, and this Joe Hooker accomplished with abandon. His division fought well and hard but was in time overwhelmed by numbers and the utter lack of Federal support. For all intent and purposes, Hooker was fighting on his own, a single division against overwhelming odds, and as the afternoon wore on his lines began to sag, then break. Frantic messages went out for support, but McClellan had remained behind at Yorktown, out of touch with events, and there was little control over the Federal dispositions.

Hooker's call for support was finally answered, not by George McClellan, but rather the fiery, one armed general, Phil Kearny. Kearny, like Hooker, in command now of an infantry division, was miles behind the front when the day's action began at Williamsburg.

Today Phil Kearny is scarcely remembered for his role in the American Civil War, but at the time he may have arguably been the most competent field officer in *either* army, and he was certainly the most experienced. Hearing the sound of guns in the distance, and learning that Hooker was in trouble, Kearny responded with an immediate and furious dash to the front.

Nothing would stop him. When stalled wagons were encountered on the muddy road to Williamsburg blocking his path to the fighting, Kearny responded with venom. Furious, he roared at the teamsters standing helplessly nearby, "Tip those wagons out of my way! I've been ordered up to the fight! I'll permit no wagons to hamper me!"[16] When the teamsters balked, arguing that the wagons were stuck too deep in the mud to be moved, Kearny would have none of it. "Move them, I say!" he screamed. "Or I'll put the torch to them!"[17] Not surprisingly, the wagons were somehow moved, and Kearny's division slogged on through the muck and mud to the front.

Bounding onto the field of battle, Kearny found the front confused, Hooker's lines thinned or broken, men running every which way. Kearny rode up to a group of Union soldiers in apparent confusion under trees nearby. "What's this?" he demanded hotly. "Why aren't you in action?"[18]

The soldiers replied that the situation was so confused they could not tell friend from foe. They no longer knew where the Rebels were.

"You don't know!" Kearny bellowed. "Here, I'll show you!"

To the amazement of the huddled troops, Phil Kearny took off at the gallop directly into the center of the storm. Spurring his horse across the muddy field, the woods suddenly exploded with the white puffs of rifle shots, all directed at the galloping general. Then Kearny turned again, galloped back across the field, and returned to the huddled troops. He rose in his saddle and pointed. "There!" he screamed, pointing back toward the Confederate position. "There's the target! Now, go in and kick those rebels out!"[19]

Kearny led his division onto the field, and Hooker's demoralized troops drew new life. "It's Kearny! It's Kearny!" they cheered, waving their hats in the air. An officer in Hooker's division recalled the inspiring sight. "I saw Kearny come on the field ... and of course had heard what a fierce fighter he was ... but in all my days I never witnessed anything to equal what I saw him do.... He rode in front of the enemy's lines, exposing himself so the

Rebels would uncover their position."[20] As he led his troops onto the field at Williamsburg at the age of 47, Phil Kearny had already become an American legend.

For Philip Kearny there had never been any doubt what career he wanted to pursue in life — soldiering. Born to an extremely wealthy family in New York, he desperately wanted to attend the military academy at West Point, but his father forbade it, and he attended Columbia College instead, where he graduated with honors in 1834. While his college studies had been in law, he yearned for the cavalry, and when at the tender age of 21 he received a substantial inheritance from his grandfather's estate, he was prepared to move on. Kearny packed his bags, said goodbye to the practice of law, and headed off for the frontier. Shortly thereafter he secured a commission as an officer in the cavalry at Fort Leavenworth, Kansas.

In Kansas Kearny displayed such uncommon promise that he was specially selected by the secretary of war to attend the prestigious French Cavalry School at Saumur. There he served as aide-de-camp and studied tactics while attached to the famous *1st Chasseur d'Afrique*, consid-

Philip Kearny — Fearless and aggressive, at the war's inception Kearny was the most accomplished filed officer on either side of the conflict. Promoted rapidly, Kearny would be shot down fighting a rear guard action at Chantilly, Virginia, only days away, as rumored, from high command (NARA).

Phil Kearny (on horseback) leading his troops onto the field in relief of Joe Hooker's division at the Battle of Williamsburg as drawn by Alfred R. Waud (Library of Congress).

ered one of the most elite cavalry units in the world, and Kearny tasted battle for the first time during the French war in Algeria. Charging with a pistol in one hand, a sword in the other, and his horse's reins in his teeth — as was the distinctive style of the *Chasseurs*— Kearny so impressed the French with his flamboyance under fire that he was awarded the Legion d'honneur, and would be known forevermore as "Kearny le Magnifique."[21]

Kearny returned home, and later during the war with Mexico earned even greater distinction, leading a fierce cavalry charge at Churubusco, just outside the gates of Mexico City. Despite the bugle call to retreat, Kearny continued forward until his left arm was shattered by an artillery burst, a wound that later required the amputation of his arm at the shoulder. Kearny's service in Mexico brought the highest praise from General Winfield Scott, then commander in chief of U.S. forces, and one of the most respected military men in the world. When asked of Kearny's potential, Scott said simply, "If ever a man were a born soldier he is Phil Kearny. Soldiers will follow such a man to the very gates of hell."[22] By war's end, Kearny's reputation was unequaled.

Now 47 years old, Kearny was still a dashing, energetic, and fearless warrior, in that sense everything George McClellan would never be. On the peninsula Kearny had nursed a slow boiling disgust for the Young Napoleon, and his tactics of delay and avoidance. He was convinced that the Federal Army had the abundant manpower to take Richmond, and he was not fooled by McClellan's gross overestimates of enemy strength. "My men can hear the bells of St. Paul's," he told a friend. "If only the Young Napoleon gathered his nerve and loosed one tremendous blow ... I can promise that we would take Richmond at our ease."[23]

When Kearny got word that McClellan intended to retreat from the works before Richmond to the James River, he could not believe his ears. Demanding an interview, he and Joe Hooker stormed into McClellan's quarters, both insisting that Richmond could easily be taken with a mere division or two. Kearny knew that it was Magruder's Confederate troops on his front, and Kearny had not been fooled by Magruder's theatrical tricks of marching columns of troops about to give an impression of strength. "Rebel resistance is too spotty for large forces," Kearny told Heintzelman. "I know Magruder. He's a faker — an actor. Let me call his hand."[24]

But as previously told McClellan's mind had already been made up, his spirit broken. He refused permission for the assault, and Kearny flew into a rage. General Hiram Berry was a witness. "Phil unloosed a broadside. He pitched into McClellan with language so strong that all who heard it expected he would be placed under arrest until a general court-martial could be held. I was certain Kearny would be relieved of his command on the spot."[25]

Perhaps George McClellan had been intimidated, or perhaps he had coolly calculated that one day he would need a man of Kearny's fierce abilities, or perhaps he realized instinctively that arresting Kearny for his insistence on fighting, while insisting himself on retreat, would not play well with the administration in Washington, or the national press. But for whatever reason, Phil Kearny was not arrested for his outburst, but was returned instead to his command.

Thus as Samuel Heintzelman's corps moved south that afternoon from Savage Station, it was with Joe Hooker and Phil Kearny firmly in charge of their divisions. By late in the day they were across White Oak Swamp well on the march toward Glendale, and for Federal hopes of survival, they represented two important cards on the table.

CHAPTER 4

Morning

Both armies stirred early that morning, June 30, 1862. During the night thunderstorms had swept through the area, drenching tired men on the march, tired men on horseback, and tired men wherever they had collapsed to try and gather a few hours sleep. Stonewall Jackson, drenched in his tent by the pounding storm, early in the morning moved to a wagon, but managed very little rest that night.[1]

When the troops awoke they found the ground soaked, decent, dry firewood at a premium, and the prospect of imminent battle virtually assured. Dawn came clear and calm, a light mist from the cooling rains hanging along the low swamps and creeks, a blue sky slowly revealing itself as the sun rose. The promise of great heat was in the air.

While battle was almost assured that morning, either at White Oak Swamp where the Federal rear guard hovered awaiting attack at any moment, or more certainly at Glendale, where few of the Federal officers taking in the surrounding countryside failed to take notice of the network of roads that led from Richmond seemingly directly to their doorstep. But in the Civil War, as it had been since war had appeared in the human chronicle thousands of years prior, today as always it would not simply be the enemy that each side would have to master to their advantage, but the land itself, the geography of the battlefield and surrounding terrain that would have to be used to advantage, or neglected to disadvantage. The ground running from the Chickahominy River south to the James was abundant with opportunities for both.

Thus as the first rays of light spread from the rising sun from east to west that morning, they fell upon a landscape that loomed as either a potential ally or antagonist for either side. Just how all that would play out would be determined by the skill of the opposing combatants.

The ground over which the question of Southern independence would be struggled for — at least, on this day, and on this field — was by and large lowlands, the alluvial plain of Virginia, which millions of years prior had served as a wide, long shoreline for the Atlantic Ocean. Numerous old rivers snaked their way east through the region, generally running through ravines of considerable depth. While the rivers themselves were often narrow and not terribly deep — thus both easily fordable and bridgeable for a 19th century army on the move — because of the depth of the gorges through which they ran, the flat nature of the ground that surrounded them, and the numerous feeder tributaries that nourished them, in wet weather they could suddenly, become an impassable torrent surrounded by an impassable swamp of almost indeterminate scope. All of this environmental chaos was solely dependent upon the amount and duration of rainfall. A sudden thunderstorm, for instance, could trap man and beast alike in an instant in a nightmare of fast running creeks, marshes and bogs. Surrounding these rivers grew a dense jungle of trees, brambles, and matted vegetation that even on good days was difficult to penetrate. On bad days these marshes were dangerous, often impassable.

North of White Oak Swamp, the Chickahominy River ran through a low lying swamp bed of its own, the varying width dependent upon the range of rainfall. The river could at times run through numerous stream beds, again all dependent upon the amount and duration of any precipitation. In a prevailing dry spell the Chickahominy dwindled to what most would consider a middling creek, while in a season of heavy rains, the river could swell to a flooding morass.

Across this river both armies had to maneuver, often at fords or upon hastily constructed bridges of questionable stability and engineering. In the race to the James so far the Federal army had, with much good fortune, and excellent engineering, weathered the storm.

A few miles south of the Chickahominy, and snaking its way on a roughly southeasterly course, ran the Great White Oak Swamp. The swamp was about ten miles in length, dumping into the Chickahominy River below Bottoms Bridge, which in turn flowed into the James not far from Williamsburg. The north bank of the swamp consisted generally of a gradual, or sloping approach, while the south bank was higher, and consisted of a ridge of more dominating hills. The bottom lands along the creek were dark, swampy, and thick with trees, brambles, and brush.

There were three usable fords in the White Oak Swamp at the time of McClellan's retreat: the first, Jordan's, some two miles below Savage Station; the second, called Fisher's, yet another mile downstream; and a third, Brackett's, still two miles south of Fisher's.[2] In dry weather all could be crossed easily by marching infantry, but the spring of 1862 had been particularly wet, and the creek was therefore considered impassable unless bridged.

The Federal army by pluck, luck, and Confederate ineptitude, had managed to bridge the creek along these fords, and cross over to the southern bank by the morning of June 30. The bridges were then all destroyed to make crossing difficult for the approaching Southern forces in pursuit. Thus White Oak Swamp, which General Lee had intended to use to his advantage during the pursuit of the 29th, would now prove an obstacle during the pursuit on the 30th. For the Federal rear guard had now taken a position on the higher, dominating hills on the southern bank, and would have to be moved by force of arms. Here, then, it was the Federal army, either by luck, skill, or a combination of both, that had used the ground to its advantage, and the Confederates who had fumbled away a considerable opportunity.

From White Oak Swamp a small network of roads twisted south to Glendale, from which a single avenue, the Quaker Road, continued south toward the James, traversing a significant plateau called Malvern Hill along its course. Here there also ran a welter of local and farm roads, none of which were recorded or marked, and all of which might instantly confound the unsuspecting traveler. Importantly, it should be noted that the well organized McClellan had numerous maps of the terrain created before embarking on his campaign, while the Confederates — although on their own, native ground — had almost none.[3]

Malvern Hill, located just a mile or so north of the James River, dominated the surrounding landscape, most of which was open, cultivated farmland at the time. The northern slope of Malvern Hill rises slowly, and when approached from the north appears more a rising plateau than hill. The crest of the plateau was open at the time, offering good views, thus clear fields of fire, to any defender. Any approach by opposing infantry would be spotted from the crest, especially on the one road leading south, and easily opposed by artillery from the plateau's summit at a distance. Two creeks snaked along the edges of the hill from north to south emptying into the James River, but these were modest and could be forded at numerous points by motivated infantry.

There was little question that Malvern Hill, if thoroughly occupied by a large force employing significant artillery, in 1862 represented a formidable defensive position. If, on the morning of the 30th of June, Confederate forces, therefore, could move quickly to the summit, the Federal retreat toward the river might be cut off and thwarted. If, on the other hand, Union forces were allowed to cross over in force and occupy the plateau, with their advantage in men and artillery, the hill would represent an almost impregnable defensive platform, and an obstacle Confederate forces might consider leaving well enough alone — with one intriguing caveat.

The southern rim of Malvern Hill is much steeper than the north, and the James River flows deep, blue, and wide less than a mile behind the position, which represents a tactical situation not generally favorable to the defense. True, if used effectively by the Federal Navy, the James River might prove a distinct advantage, for its gunboats were numerous and both their firepower and range considerable. But if an aggressive attacker could breach the defensive lines on the summit of Malvern Hill — which was narrow and somewhat confined — the position might be carried with dire consequences. With their back to the river, any defender might easily be forced to stumble downhill in confusion then be quickly trapped and destroyed against the river. Thus it could be said that Malvern Hill offered extreme advantages and extreme disadvantages simultaneously, quite possibly a blessing or perhaps a curse, depending on how the game was played.

Contrast this mix with the Federal position assumed at Gettysburg roughly one year later — which Porter Alexander characterized as the most favorable ever taken by either army during the war — which also consisted of a low ridgeline with open and ample fields of fire. But the field at Gettysburg was much more elongated than Malvern Hill, thus offering a far greater disbursement of troops along the line. Moreover, the ground directly behind Cemetery Ridge was not dominated by a river, but rather additional ridgelines which in retreat would not have served as an impediment, but rather a potential advantage. Thus while Malvern Hill looked impressive for the defense, serious potential liabilities lurked nevertheless.

So how to date had each adversary managed to cope with the geography of war? As already noted, on the Confederate side both Magruder and Jackson, through delay, confusion, and probable exhaustion, had failed to seriously bring the Federal rear guard to bay and thus allowed the Yankee force to slip away south across White Oak Swamp. Not only did this fail to capture a portion of McClellan's army north of the swamp where it could be trapped and destroyed, but now — since the Yankees had destroyed their bridges behind them — the Confederate advance would have to face the Yankees dug in on the southern bank. Here the ground was high and dominating and thus presented a far more difficult task than it would have the day before. As far as Malvern Hill was concerned, on the morning of the 30th the precise location of McClellan's forces was still not known to the Confederate high command, thus it was hoped that Malvern Hill could still be seized and utilized.

From the Federal perspective, the retreat had gone well, if simply by means of good fortune and hard marching. Crossing White Oak Swamp represented a major accomplishment. What remained now was to consolidate if possible on Malvern Hill while communicating with the navy for artillery support from the James. How all this would play out, we shall now see.

———

Douglas Southall Freeman, recounting the history of Lee's Army of Northern Virginia, notes the almost contagious optimism that infused Lee's army as it enjoyed the first rays of light that June 30. "The Decisive day, June 30, broke 'cloudless and calm' upon thousands of confident soldiers who expected McClellan's army to be destroyed ere night fell again."[4]

While the Confederates approached the day with high hopes, the Federal Army just to the east still labored its way south toward the river James. Herds of cattle and a supply train numbering some 5,000 wagons were still struggling south on the dusty roads, somewhere between White Oak Swamp and Malvern Hill. Sweat, dust, and curses filled the air. There were arguments, fights, and constant blockages as the massive train slowly inched its way toward the river. God alone knew how many more hours, or perhaps days, it would take before all hands were safe.

Thus while Confederate thoughts that morning reverberated with notions of victory and independence, for the Yankees, dust deep in flight, concerns centered on simple survival. This was to be the sixth day of fighting and marching, the sixth of the now famous Seven Days, and the Federal Army — those portions of it, at least, that had managed their way passed Mr. Riddell's Shop — had quite literally stumbled into Glendale, exhausted and unnerved, overnight. Ignorance breeds fear, and few of the retreating Yankees — officers included — had any idea what was occurring behind them even a mile or two away. Every near or distant report of musketry brought fears of imminent peril; perhaps Stonewall Jackson's dreaded Valley army was about to charge from the woods or down some country lane to sweep them all away!

The perilous significance of the road network that wound its way into Glendale had been pointed out to General George McClellan, and thus arrangements had been made to guard the retreating columns below White Oak Swamp that day. These dispositions — which will soon be described in detail — seem to have been arranged by the general commanding, but as there was no guiding hand present to help in the placement of the various units as they came up overnight (McClellan, along with his staff, had ridden off for Haxall's Landing on the James), the positions were taken up somewhat haphazardly, and as a result less than even adequately. While conforming to what appears a sensible overall defensive scheme, the detail of proper unit coordination and placement were either ignored, or simply lost in the confusion of the march.

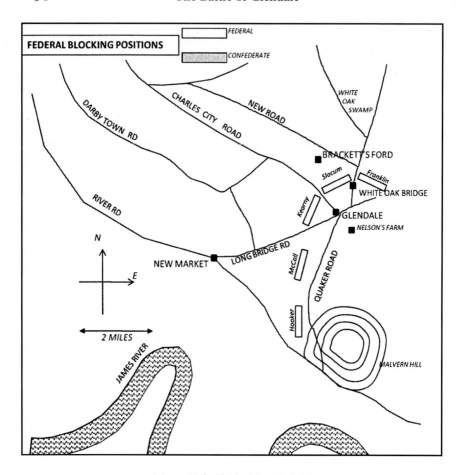

FEDERAL BLOCKING POSITIONS

FEDERAL

CONFEDERATE

WHITE OAK SWAMP

DARBY TOWN RD

CHARLES CITY ROAD

NEW ROAD

BRACKETT'S FORD

Slocum

Franklin

WHITE OAK BRIDGE

RIVER RD

Kearny

GLENDALE

NELSON'S FARM

N

NEW MARKET

LONG BRIDGE RD

McCall

QUAKER ROAD

E

Hooker

2 MILES

JAMES RIVER

MALVERN HILL

Map — Federal Blocking Positions

The result was a jumble of divisions, out of touch with one another, often with their flanks in the air — that is, not supported by another friendly unit, or anchored on a natural defensive barrier such as a hill or creek. Thus a hard rush at any number of spots along this defensive perimeter could have penetrated the position with ease and ultimately compromised the entire arrangement. Yet, under the circumstances, it was remarkable that even this much — inadequate as it was — had been accomplished.

As the sun rose that morning, and the troops scavenged for what food they could find for breakfast, the Federal defense began at White Oak Swamp in the north, then turned south and west to a point near where the Charles City Road entered Glendale. From there the line proceeded due south — and west of the Quaker Road, which it had to defend — to a point approximately one and a half miles below Riddell's Shop. The appearance of the arrangement was somewhat like that of a cavalryman's boot, the toe south, at the bottom, the top laces at White Oak Swamp, but with holes and gaps, some looming, all along the way. The line faced west, prepared for an assault all knew would of necessity have to come down the two roads previously mentioned. From the toe of the boot to the far right flank overlooking White Oak Swamp, the line stretched about four miles.

At White Oak Swamp the Yankees deployed a strong rear guard on the southern ridge overlooking the creek. There corps commander William Franklin had posted over three divisions of infantry and six batteries of artillery.[5] This was a force comparable to Stonewall Jackson's on the other side of the swamp, but unlike Jackson, who would have to attack this morning, on the defensive, and well posted. From the heights the Federal artillery, theoretically at least, commanded the approaches to the swamp. It should be noted, arranged as they were, both of Franklin's flanks were uncovered, and thus in the air and open to assault.

To the south and west, with a gap of almost a mile and a half between it and Franklin's rear guard at White Oak Swamp, was posted the division of Henry Slocum, also of Franklin's corps.[6] Here Slocum had gone into position with his left flank resting near the Charles City Road, while deployed in the woods facing northwest. Slocum's objective was to guard against any Confederate crossing that might take place along the swamp fords farther east toward Richmond, and which might then sweep down on the Federal right flank or rear from that direction. Here too, both of Slocum's flanks were uncovered.

From Slocum's position just above the Charles City Road, the Federal line — covering the approaches to Glendale from the west — ran due south for about two miles. Here Heintzelman's two divisions (Kearny's and Hooker's) fell into place, with McCall's — a single division from the 5th Corps — in between.

This arrangement created obvious problems for communication and coordination along that stretch of the line, but the most dramatic problem was the condition of McCall's division itself. This unit had seen heavy fighting at Mechanicsville, and very hard fighting at Gaines's Mill, where the 5th Corps had had to stand and slug it out alone with most of Lee's army. Used piecemeal by the corps commander at Gaines's Mill, when the Federal position finally collapsed late in the day, McCall's division paid a heavy price for the effort in comrades killed, wounded, missing, and captured. Now they were being placed into the very center of what was expected to become, at any moment, a very hot position, and asked to fight again.

Handling a brigade in that corps, but not terribly well known at the time, was General George Gordon Meade. Meade, like most of the upper echelon of officers in the Army of the Potomac, was a graduate of the U.S. Military Academy at West Point, in his case, the class of 1835. Meade, like Robert E. Lee, had been a career soldier, and had served in the war with Mexico. George Meade and Joe Hooker were virtually polar opposites. Unlike Hooker, Meade had come to be admired and respected by his fellow officers, and unlike Hooker he did not cut the image of a battlefield commander. Where Joe Hooker rode into battle on a white horse, sword swaying, dressed in a fine, fresh uniform, Meade appeared common to the point of drabness, and was unlikely to arouse much in the way of passion in his men.

Yet George Meade had always led from the front, fought with distinction and good sense, and would one day — like Hooker — rise to the command of the Army of the Potomac on the basis of merit alone. He had fought with distinction at Fredericksburg, leading the only brigade to break the Confederate line that day, and would do so again at Chancellorsville. Colorless where Hooker was flamboyant, not prone to lofty ambitions, while Hooker plotted and intrigued for advance, circumspect where Hooker was imprudent, George Meade would prove himself over time a first rate fighter and a careful tactician. He would lead the Army of the Potomac one day to its greatest victory at Gettysburg, and on the morning of June 30, 1862, his brigade had been placed directly across the Long Bridge Road, the route leading into Glendale from the Darbytown Road.

Thus it was that three of the most proficient fighters in the Army of the Potomac — two of which would one day rise to army command — had been placed, by either a kind

George Meade — A brigadier general at Glendale, Meade would rise to command of the Army of the Potomac and provide the North its greatest Civil War victory at Gettysburg (Library of Congress).

and all knowing Providence, or simply the luck of the draw, in positions of critical importance.

Just to the south of Glendale, at the toe of the boot, so to speak, Joe Hooker had deployed his division facing west, confident of attack that morning. A mile or so north of Hooker, Meade's brigade was now in a blocking position across the Long Bridge Road, the very route of Longstreet's march. And waiting defiantly, with his left flank near the Long Bridge Road, and his right on the Charles City Road — precisely where the bulk of Lee's morning offensive was scheduled to strike — was the man who had cursed George McClellan to his face for even contemplating retreat, whom Winfield Scott had insisted men would follow to the very gates of hell, perhaps the most respected, experienced fighter in either army — Phil Kearny.

All the cards were now on the table. Soon the game would begin.

CHAPTER 5

Orders at Daybreak

War, as generally presented in our history books, seems conceived as a somewhat cerebral affair, if not a dry exercise in pure logic, then at least something akin to it. Battles are frequently portrayed rather like a grand chess match, with large blocks of troops — brigades, battalions, divisions, etc.— being shifted here and there across the landscape by either knowing, or foolish, commanders like the pawns or rooks on a chessboard. Lower level officers receive their orders and respond accordingly, again, carefully calculating their decisions based on the facts as they understand them. Thus any errors that are committed in war are viewed from this perspective as errors of comprehension, or experience, or even a simple lack of intelligence. The commanders and officers are then judged accordingly, the number of dead, wounded, and missing tabulated, winners and losers assessed, the page turned.

This sort of presentation, however, robs war of some of its most visceral elements, elements that historians tend to exclude from their critical equations, but factors that are in the end the very essence of war. This historical perspective, then, is often quite unfair, not because it is wrong, but because it is limited. Absent from this formula are confusion, terror, exhaustion, illness, ignorance, and simple human dread. Neglected are the miles, days, and perhaps weeks on the march, the poor food and horrendous conditions, the cold and heat, the snow and rain, the rivers that must be crossed, and the mountains that must be climbed. Lost is the mind shattering reality of the battlefield, of friends blown to pieces, blood spilled like water; the fearful roar of guns; the screams, cries, and howls of the dying, indeed, the hundred or so soul numbing realities that men in war must endure.

These factors all combine to reduce human physical and mental capacity, to sap the spirit, and over time force poor, even incomprehensible decisions from even the finest minds. *That* is the true nature of war, and it can never, if fairness be a concern, be removed from the grim calculus of battlefield decisions.

Perhaps General Robert E. Lee had known this all along, or perhaps it was just then beginning to dawn upon him, but one way or another, it was apparent that on the morning of June 30 he had decided to take some action. If McClellan's army was still going to be trapped north of the James River and ultimately destroyed, General Lee realized that the fiasco of the 29th could not be repeated. The conception he'd had the day before of an aggressive pursuit had simply evaporated during the long hours of the preceding day as does a morning mist evaporate before the rays of a rising sun. Alexander rightly observes: "Looking back on the course of events, it is interesting to inquire wherein lay the weakness of this [Lee's] order, apparently so simple and obvious in its execution. Yet the pursuit, from this moment, was bootless and a failure."[1] Nothing of value had been accomplished. That could not happen again.

Thus Lee headed off early that morning to meet with several of his lieutenants, to explain face to face what today was to be expected, to clarify his orders, to set things straight. He rode first to Savage Station where he found Prince John Magruder still in a state of high anxiety, seemingly much too actively engaged. Magruder, suffering from the effects of illness and fatigue, seemed even to his own staff a sad reflection of his former self. The man who had bamboozled McClellan at Yorktown to the applause of the entire South, seemed now oddly mercurial and incapable.

Major Joseph Brent of Magruder's staff looked on in dismay. "As our troops were bivouacking upon each side of the railway, it took a considerable time to march them up and get ready for the route. General Magruder was on horseback, galloping here and there with great rapidity. He seemed to me to be under a nervous excitement that strangely affected him. He frequently interposed in minor matters, reversing previous arrangements and delaying the movement he was so anxious to hasten. I looked on with great sadness at what seemed to me a loss of equilibrium in a man I knew to be earnest and indefatigable in the discharge of duty."[2]

If this odd behavior was so obvious to Major Brent, surely Lee observed it as well while verbally providing Magruder his orders that morning at Savage Station. Whatever Lee's assessment of his lieutenant might have been remains unclear; the outcome, however, is not. Magruder was removed from the pursuit of the Federal rear guard and ordered instead to march into a general reserve behind Longstreet and Hill on the Darbytown Road.

Later, during a stop along the march, Major Brent — at the urging of his fellow officers — approached Magruder with his concerns. "Well, Major, you are right," Prince John replied. "I am feeling horribly. For two days I have been disturbed about my digestion, and the doctor has been giving me medicine, and I fear he has given me some morphine in his mixture and the smallest quantity of it acts upon me as an irritant. And besides that, I have lost so much sleep that it affects me strangely; but I fully appreciate your kindness in speaking to me, and I will endeavor to regain my self control."[3]

Exhausted, ill, and apparently mildly drugged, it was a wonder Magruder could function at all. He was clearly in no condition to lead men into battle that morning, and his explanation does much to help explain his actions and activity — or lack thereof — of the previous day. While he certainly deserves sympathy, it remains a fact that exhausted men are bound to make exhausted decisions, for which men in war pay with their lives, and campaigns go muddled. Lee's decision regarding Magruder was therefore sound, and an intelligent first step toward recovering the initiative he desperately sought that day.

Indeed, prior to Lee's visit, Magruder had still been despairing of a Federal attack on his front, despite the fact that the Yankees had withdrawn overnight. Magruder, as can now be understood, seems to have lost touch with reality, and was battling little more than his own irrationally induced fears. As Alexander explains, "During the night, the entire Federal force had crossed the White Oak Swamp and McClellan had accomplished one half his retreat safely."[4] Thus was Magruder sensibly removed from a central role in the day's unfolding drama. "Lee, early on the 30th, had withdrawn Magruder's six brigades, now about 12,000 strong, from Savage Station, and brought them down the Darbytown road within striking distance by 2 P.M., and had halted them at that hour near Timberlake's store."[5]

One event that had served to mildly allay Prince John's fears that morning had been the arrival of Stonewall Jackson at his headquarters around 3:30 A.M.[6] While this may have served as a tonic for Prince John, knowing that substantial help was now near at hand, for Stonewall it did not bode well.

Stonewall Jackson had been roused from sleep that night by the drenching rains of a substantial thunderstorm. He had moved to a wagon to try and sleep, but was apparently so wet and uncomfortable that by around 1:00 A.M. on the 30th he'd given up entirely any effort to rest.[7] Stonewall issued instructions for the Valley Army to move out at first light toward Grapevine Bridge over the Chickahominy, then called for his horse and rode off. It may be assumed, therefore, that Jackson had been able to gather at least a few hours sleep prior to the storm, but hardly enough to overcome the deep seated exhaustion that appeared to have had him in its grip for days.

Moreover, the order to move the Valley Army had been left in the hands of Major Robert Dabney, a devout Presbyterian minister with no prior military experience, whom Jackson had become particularly fond of. Dabney had served Jackson well, if briefly, as a staff officer in camp, but now Stonewall had gone so far as to have entrusted Dabney with the position of chief of staff, a position the good minister was wholly unprepared to handle.

Stonewall Jackson's profound religious sensibilities at times ranged far beyond the practical, and his command would suffer for his irrational resolutions. We can only assume that Jackson presumed God would smile upon and reward his choice of Dabney in this critical role and at this particularly critical time, no matter how impractical. This was not Dabney's fault. It was Jackson's. Kyd Douglas, then on Jackson's staff— and no critic of the general — explains the obvious: "The General's Chief of Staff, Major Dabney, an excellent officer in camp, was not equal to this occasion in the field. With no previous training, he had not been in the army more than three months and had no experience to fit him for the demands of his position. While he did his duty faithfully, he could not be of any service to the General in such an emergency; and as for training a staff to its duties, he knew nothing about it."[8]

It would seem, therefore, that two serious problems plagued the Valley Army at dawn on the 30th. The first was a commander, Stonewall Jackson, who in all probability was on the verge of exhaustion and perhaps physical breakdown, while his second in command, ordered to move the Valley Army promptly on its way that morning, was himself utterly incompetent to the task. These two negatives would hardly bode well for the crisp and vigorous pursuit General Lee was hopeful to accomplish that day, and would actually, although unintentionally, serve to sabotage it.

At any rate, after meeting with Prince John that morning, and providing him with direct verbal orders, General Lee met face to face with Stonewall Jackson on the road to Savage Station. Sadly, no record of this meeting exists, and neither officer ever offered a report as to what, precisely, was discussed. So we are left to speculate as to Lee's attitude toward his lieutenant, and the exact nature of the orders Jackson received. Fortunately, a young artillery officer was nearby who later recorded his observations. That officer was Robert Stiles,[9] and what he recalled is of considerable interest.

To begin with, Stiles noted that Jackson was brimming with nervous energy that morning, and that he began talking to Lee in a very animated fashion, drawing a design in the dirt with the toe of his boot. This design was in the fashion of a triangle or diamond (or so it appeared to Stiles from a distance), which Jackson traced in a slow, deliberate, or halting manner. As he traced this design Stonewall glanced up at Lee repeatedly, then anxiously down at his diagram, back and forth, and so on, until the design in the dirt was finally complete. When the final line Jackson had been tracing at last intersected the first he'd drawn, Stonewall lifted his foot, stomped down on the diagram emphatically, and exclaimed loud enough for Stiles to hear: "We've got him!"[10] Then according to Stiles, Stonewall "signaled for his horse, and when he came, vaulted awkwardly into the saddle, and was off."[11]

Jackson's diagram was in all probability little more than a very rough sketch of Lee's overall offensive scheme for the day, the lines etched by his boot representing the converging Confederate columns, perhaps intersecting the Yankees' line of retreat. Once McClellan had been cut off from the river, attacked in the rear (by Jackson himself) and broken at Glendale, then Stonewall grasped plainly that McClellan's army would be done.

Interestingly, despite all the nervous energy and animation, Stonewall would not ride far that morning, nor would he immediately attend to matters of the pursuit, despite his outward display of conviction. In fact, if taken together, both Magruder's and Jackson's behavior that morning seem oddly similar. Both seemed to have been motivated by the same nervous, jerky, impetuous sort of energy that is often an indication of impending collapse, and it is difficult to say just what General Lee may have seen in Jackson's demeanor that morning that he had not already observed in Magruder's. Whatever the case, Magruder was ordered off in support on the right, while Jackson was handed over the task of the direct pursuit of the Federal rear guard.

What, exactly, that pursuit entailed remains to this day unclear. Whether Lee wanted Jackson to attempt a breakthrough at White Oak Swamp, or simply a vigorous demonstration in order to hold the Federals in place while the full force of Confederate arms fell on Glendale, was never clarified by either. Surely, however, Lee expected more of Jackson than to curl up under a tree and fall asleep while the entire Valley Army sat on its arms, which is exactly what Stonewall would eventually do.

Over the years much debate has thus ensued as to the reason for Stonewall Jackson's poor showing during the battles of the Seven Days, most critically on the 30th of June at Glendale. Some have argued that religion was behind Jackson's serial failures, while others have pointed to simple, physical exhaustion. Alexander, as we have seen, was a staunch believer that Jackson hedged his advance due to religious convictions — and there is certainly a case to be made for this — but that case fails to take into consideration Jackson's obvious physical symptoms. These cannot be ignored.

The truth of the matter may actually lie somewhere between the two. As we have seen with Stonewall's promotion of Major Dabney to chief of staff, Jackson's religious beliefs could certainly trump his common sense at times to the detriment of his command, and he had a record of preferring not to fight on the Sabbath if at all possible. These facts, however, do not explain away his obvious symptoms of extreme fatigue, episodes of which were repeated, and became increasingly more apparent as the campaign wore on. Thus it may be fair to say that Jackson, in the throes of exhaustion, made increasingly less sensible judgments, some of which may have found their genesis in his religious beliefs. But it certainly appears that exhaustion alone finally reduced him to a sort of unconscious stupor that afternoon, more and more incapable of thought or communication, until sleep was all he could manage.

With Jackson's orders delivered and hopefully understood, General Lee began his ride back around toward the Darbytown Road to await the assault that morning. That he was confident his orders had been understood, and would subsequently be obeyed, we can only presume.

The initial attack that morning was to be delivered by Huger's columns, straight down the Charles City Road. The night before he had marched to within approximately three miles of Glendale before going into bivouac,[12] thus he had the shortest march to the enemy. Longstreet and Hill had marched to within striking distance of Glendale, and had gone that evening into bivouac on the Darbytown Road, a few miles west of Glendale.[13] It was expected they would be up by noon and prepared for action. South on the River Road, General Holmes had moved his column out to the vicinity of New Market,[14] some four miles east of Malvern Hill. His job was to march his command down the River Road and attack whatever Federals he encountered, hopefully disrupting the Federal retreat in that area, perhaps even securing Malvern Hill if unoccupied. He was in ready position to do so.

The great assault, indeed the assault intended to bag McClellan's entire army and hopefully end the war that very day, was now only a few miles and a couple of hours from commencement. It was understood that all commands were to go in on the sound of Huger's guns. As the sun rose higher in the clear, blue morning sky, anxious heads turned, waited, and listened.

CHAPTER 6

Delay on the Charles City Road

While all ears waited anxiously for the sound of Benjamin Huger's initial assault that morning, soon expected to billow up like thunder from the woods bordering the Charles City Road, events in that sector had actually begun to devolve into an odd sort of melodrama that would over time develop either tragic or comedic overtones, depending upon one's sensibilities. For the ground traversed by the Charles City Road was tight, heavily wooded, and bordered to the north by farm roads leading to the various fords that crossed the White Oak Swamp. For the cautious mind this narrow, dark, wooded scene trembled with visions of surprise, entrapment, and potential disaster. And there is little question that Benjamin Huger's mind had been tuned to an extraordinarily cautious pitch.

What Federal detachments and in what numbers might be lurking out there in those trees unseen? Might they come pouncing down one of the roads off on the left to crush the Confederate column by the flank? These were serious questions worthy of careful consideration, and General Huger had every intention of considering them carefully before budging an inch.

Then again there was that name that kept cropping up, just as it had the day before, a name that suggested caution to even the most aggressive soul. A full Federal division was said to be lurking somewhere nearby, maybe just off on Huger's flank in the swamp, or perhaps dead ahead toward Riddell's Shop or, worse yet, behind. And a full Federal division was nothing to toy with when the name attached to that division was Phil Kearny. No, this advance would require care and prudence of the most intricate, indeed, delicate variety.

Benjamin Huger was a fifty-seven-year-old South Carolinian of aristocratic lineage, best known as an ordinance officer in the army prior to the war.[1] Appointed colonel in 1861 at the outbreak of hostilities, due to his record and prior experience, by 1862 he had risen to the rank of major general. Like many of the officers on both sides of the conflict, however, Huger's capabilities in the field were entirely unknown, and like his colleagues he would have to learn the ropes, so to speak, while on the job. So far for Benjamin Huger, that task had not gone well. Much of the blame for the Confederate fiasco at Seven Pines had been pinned on Huger for not coming up quickly in support of Longstreet and, rightly or wrongly, those accusations had stuck. Sadly, he would do little this day on the Charles City Road to dispel this newfound reputation for dullness, sloth, and incompetence.

Benjamin Huger — From an aristocratic family in Charleston, South Carolina, Huger failed in his assigned role at Glendale and was later transferred from the Army of Northern Virginia (Library of Congress).

The day before Huger's column had barely covered five miles on the march, although the road before them had been essentially open and uncontested. That morning Huger had been called off to assist General Magruder with that general's peculiar fantasy of a Federal assault on his front, only to return then to his own division by mid-afternoon. He found his troops halted at Brightwell's Farm, about three miles west of Glendale, the lead brigadier, Billie Mahone, perplexed regarding the situation before him. On the march they had encountered a small Federal cavalry detachment that had fled almost immediately upon contact, but by then Mahone had become fully aware of the other fords off to his left in the swamp, and was concerned as to the Federals' true location. Were they behind him, directly on his flank, or in front of him? Or were they now moving, intent on causing mischief? All this was cause for considerable concern and caution, and that caution soon begot delay.

Mahone then sent a party out to reconnoiter north toward Jordan's Ford, and there they had a brief splash with Federal pickets.[2] This, for Mahone, apparently had the feel of significant power, and he reacted accordingly. Sensing that the Federals were crossing in strength in that direction, he deployed troops to block any movement his way from Jordan's, and there the matter rested for the remainder of the afternoon. Thus had Huger's entire column come to little more than sitting on their arms in the shade at Bright-well's Farm on the afternoon of the 29th. But wait, there's more.

By late afternoon Huger himself had returned from the confused situation on Magruder's front to the now equally confused situation on his own. Even more reports had been received by then of Federals in strength at Jordan's Ford. Their intent, however, remained unclear. Moreover, it was determined that this Federal force was in fact Phil Kearny's division of the Union III Corps, and Huger knew that, if it was in fact Kearny, then in all probability Huger had trouble on his hands. A critical mistake made in front of Kearny could easily lead to disaster and doom. Thus confusion led to still further delay as Huger pondered the situation, and it would not be unfair to say that through little more than reputation alone Phil Kearny had managed to bring General Huger's entire advance to a sudden, perplexed halt.

Yet this was no rare event. The upper levels of the Confederate army and political structure were familiar enough with Phil Kearny, and it is no surprise that his name struck fear in both Mahone and Huger that June 29th. During the war with Mexico, for instance, General Winfield Scott, in command of American forces at that time, had ordered a team of engineers out to survey the best route of advance toward the Mexican capital. That group of topographical engineers was headed by Robert E. Lee, and Lee would earn top honors for his work in the field and the routes he would endorse. To safeguard those engineers while making their survey, Scott then turned to his finest cavalry, the First United States Dragoons. Company F of the Dragoons accompanied Lee across the Mexican landscape on his topographical mission, and Phil Kearny was then in command of Company F.[3] So Lee knew Kearny by far more than reputation alone, and Kearny knew Lee, and neither doubted the ability of the other.

But after the battles at Williamsburg and Seven Pines on the Virginia peninsula that spring, even the fighting men in the Confederate ranks had developed a sincere respect for the combative Union general. As one of the general's biographers points out, "By 1862, the daring one-armed General had become a legend among both Northern and Southern soldiers."[4] One captured Rebel wondered in open amazement, "Who's that one-armed officer? We've been plugging at him all day and never came close. That's the luckiest man in the world! And what a soldier! What a soldier!"[5]

So as Mahone and Huger went into bivouac that evening, the nagging question of Kearny's true location and intentions hung over their heads like the proverbial Sword of Damocles. Was Kearny now simply toying with them, or was he planning on sweeping down from behind in the dark? What might he be up to? What were they to do?

The decision was finally made to send artillery north to cover the ford crossings — lest Kearny slip back behind them and take the Confederate column from the rear — and go into bivouac at the farm until morning, hopeful that new information would clarify the situation with the coming dawn. Thus did this five mile march and early bivouac of Huger's column represent one-third of the "bootless" pursuit to which Alexander previously referred. Worse still, it serves to underscore not only the lack of initiative, but also the seeming absence of any sense of urgency on the part of General Huger that afternoon for pressing the pursuit that was the very object of General Lee's orders that day. Indeed, it would appear from Huger's actions that, while he may have understood the general substance of Lee's orders, he could have in no way understood their true intent, which was to deliver a lethal blow to the fleeing Federal foe.

Dawn failed to clarify the situation. Huger and Mahone continued to fret and debate, just as they had the night before. Was Kearny now dead ahead down the Charles City Road, awaiting their approach? Or was he still on their flank, or perhaps sneaking off behind them? Lacking this critical information, the decision had been made the night before to send an entire brigade off to the left to scour the White Oak fords for any sign of Kearny's command, or any other Federal troops, for that matter, still lurking in the area. That would at least relieve them of the specter of a flanking attack, and perhaps fix both the Federals' position and intent.

Wright's brigade had been selected for the task. Rans Wright's job was to re-cross the swamp with his entire brigade, then move east along the road that traversed its northern boundary, covering Huger's flank as he did so, while simultaneously locating the slippery Kearny, should he still be north of the White Oak Swamp.

Significantly, this deletion reduced Huger's overall strength by one-quarter, a decision that greatly impacted his division's potential striking power. Here again, Huger's grasp of the true nature of his mission must be called into serious question.

To begin with, a reconnaissance in force is in fact an ancient martial tactic generally used in order to determine an adversary's general position and overall strength, or to demonstrate one's own strength for some tactical purpose. But to simply reconnoiter, a reconnaissance in force is often a poor use of resources. For Huger this job could easily have been accomplished by a much smaller unit (perhaps a single regiment, or better yet just a few scouts) while leaving the power of the division essentially intact. It is hard to understand the assignment of an entire brigade for this task. Indeed, if Wright had in fact run into Kearny's entire division he would have been flattened had he stood and made a fight of it, so what exactly was the point? Worse still, Wright's brigade, once it had crossed the swamp would be essentially cut off from the rest of the division as it moved east toward Glendale, thus unable to cooperate as events were expected to evolve that day.

The answer to all this seems to be that Benjamin Huger, a career staff man, had no idea how to best handle troops in the field, and that his decision, while not technically incompetent, was certainly unnecessary, and greatly reduced his capacity to fulfill his fundamental mission. It is probably safe to presume that the reason Huger historically received little if any criticism for his handling of Wright's brigade that morning was the simple fact that it paled in comparison to the rest of the poor decisions he would make that day, decisions that will soon be examined.

Wright set out at first light. He crossed the swamp, and subsequently moved up the New Road — which paralleled the swamp, thus covering all the fords in that area — throughout the remainder of the morning. He found empty fords and deserted Federal camps, but he found no Federal troops,[6] and he did not locate Phil Kearny's division because Phil Kearny had marched to Glendale the night before and was already in position awaiting attack. Indeed, the only major concentration of troops Wright would bump into were those of Stonewall Jackson as Wright emerged at the White Oak Bridge later that day. Thus, while Wright had accomplished one aspect of his assignment — that of determining whether or not the Federals were still in force in White Oak Swamp — the occupation of these troops to this purpose must be regarded as both a terrible waste of time and resources, resources that had been carefully marshaled by General Lee in a design to overwhelm the Federal retreat at Glendale.

After dispatching Wright on his fool's errand that morning, Huger, with Mahone in the van, set off slowly down the Charles City Road, still convinced for some reason that Kearny was on their left on the north side of the swamp. Later they received information that Fisher's Ford was now clear of the enemy, and still later Huger was the recipient of some interesting news. It seems a Federal courier had been shot and killed by Confederate pickets, and the contents of his dispatch brought in and laid bare before both Huger and Mahone. This dispatch was a direct order for Kearny to retire while maintaining a battery with the Federal rear guard.[7] Mahone and Huger were mystified. Was Kearny the rear guard? And if Kearny was now the rear guard, where in the world might he be?

In time it dawned on both generals that Kearny was in all probability *ahead* of them, guarding the passage of the Federal trains as they wound their way down toward Malvern Hill, not behind them or off to the left. With a sigh, one can imagine, Huger's column was again put into slow, plodding motion down the Charles City Road, only to soon stumble upon yet another perplexing obstacle, this hardly a mile south of Brightwell's Farm.

General Huger's own report explains the sudden dilemma: "The troops bivouacked in their position while it was dark, and resumed the march at daylight (Monday, June 30). Mahone advanced cautiously, captured many prisoners, and killed some cavalry scouts, one bearing an order to Kearny to retire and keep a strong battery of artillery with his rearguard. After passing Fisher's house, we found the road obstructed by trees felled all across it."[8]

The long column was halted; what else could they do? The road was full of cut timbers, trees dropped by the retreating Federal pioneers. The roadway was blocked. The men could no longer march, and the artillery could no longer roll. What was to be done? What *could* be done? Benjamin Huger could not have been more baffled had the trees themselves been hurled from the heavens by the very hand of God, only to pile like a disheartening miracle on the roadway before his eyes. How was one to deal with such an uncommon problem? General Huger did not know. Only two miles now from his objective, with the entire Army of Northern Virginia waiting for the sound of his guns to initiate the great assault, Benjamin Huger stared out at a sea of cut timber as if mystified, and had not the slightest inkling as to what to do next. Nothing in his training or past had prepared him for dealing with such a bewildering obstacle. He was both literally and figuratively stumped.

CHAPTER 7

The Rearguard
of All God's Creation

Just two miles south and east of the baffled Benjamin Huger, General Philip Kearny waited at Glendale, his division deployed for what he probably realized might well be the fight of his life.

Kearny's division consisted of three brigades. On the left, with his left flank near the Long Bridge Road, John Robinson's First Brigade was posted, while on the right David Birney's Second was deployed with his right flank near the Charles City Road. Hiram Berry's Third Brigade was placed behind in close reserve, while James Thompson's two batteries of artillery had unlimbered to the left and front of Robinson's position, covering the approaches down the Long Bridge Road and along Robinson's front. No doubt Kearny had a reasonably good idea as to the Confederate strength that was approaching that day and few illusions as to what that meant for his division.

It is said of Kearny that as his division deployed for battle that day, he remarked to one of his junior officers that they were all, in fact, "the rearguard of all God's creation."[1] While we may never know exactly what Kearny had in mind by that remark, it is reasonable to assume it a rueful acknowledgement of a difficult fact, and as such a remark that opens a brief window into not only Kearny's thoughts that morning, but also the very manner in which the war was conceived by many Northern volunteers.

Indeed, if we want to truly understand the American Civil War — that is, the passionate motivations of the men who marched off to fight it — it may be wise to first appreciate why a forty-seven year old one-armed man of substantial wealth had tossed aside love, comfort, peace, and prosperity to enter the war as a brigadier of volunteers. Why in the world, it might fairly be asked, had a man like Phil Kearny even bothered to assume that day at Glendale the position of "the rearguard of all God's creation"? And then, what exactly might he have meant by that remark?

To begin with, Phil Kearny was not simply a man of wealth, but in fact the son of one of the founders of the New York Stock Exchange,[2] and as a consequence had over the years come by a fabulous inheritance that allowed him to live without even the slightest concern for personal finance. He traveled the world freely, lived wherever he pleased, purchased anything he wanted. As a youth he had been raised in the very lap of luxury. "At Gouverneur [the Kearny estate] Phil had a string of his own thoroughbred horses. An Italian fencing master was hired to coach him in foil and saber. A British middleweight boxer taught him to use his fists. His riding instructor was a former French cavalry captain. He had a tutor for dancing, another for etiquette. At fifteen the younger Kearny had all the manners, comportment and social poise of a wealthy young aristocrat."[3]

Yet despite all the wealth and training, something intrinsically American had emerged in the young Phil Kearny. Specifically, he yearned to prove himself, to be respected for what he might achieve in life on his own terms, not admired simply for the status his family and wealth provided. In fact, in later life Kearny would come to see his enormous wealth as a mixed blessing. "I have wealth that I did not earn ... I have never known a moment without money.... In a way I envy those men who must daily struggle for economic survival ... they can savor the smallest pleasures ... while those born rich are dulled ... by an overabundance of everything."[4]

As a young man, however, Phil Kearny's passion for establishing his own identity became increasingly focused on soldiering, an occupation his father disapproved of, and in fact considered beneath the family. That disapproval did not deter young Philip, however. At school near West Point, Kearny became utterly enthralled by the martial spectacle the academy represented and went to lengths to gratify his curiosity. "An observer had an unobstructed view of the Academy's parade ground from Highland's riverbank. Kearny bought a folding telescope, and at every opportunity was perched high in a tree on the shore, peering through his glass at the cadets at drill."[5]

Kearny's father, however, would not allow his son to pursue a military career, and insisted instead that Phil attend Columbia College (today Columbia University) and pursue a career in law and business with an eye toward eventually taking over the family's financial ventures. Reluctantly Phil agreed, but then quit the practice of law to join the cavalry when he received the first installment of his inheritance. Kearny rapidly established himself then as a leading young officer, was sent to France to study cavalry tactics, fought with the French in Algeria, and eventually emerged from the Mexican War with a reputation second to none. But he had lost his left arm in the fighting, and his first marriage began to wither and eventually fail. In the peacetime army Kearny soon became disenchanted with endless duties of little significance and in 1851 ultimately resigned his commission.[6]

For years Kearny traveled and grew increasingly despondent, but then while in Paris during the spring of 1853 he met a young American girl named Agnes Maxwell. Though almost twice her age, Kearny was swept away, and when his first wife eventually agreed to a divorce in 1858, the couple was married. But the long affair with Agnes had caused such an uncomfortable stir that the new couple left for France and was living in Paris when the prospect of civil war in the United States became increasingly apparent. Despite his distance, Kearny had been following events closely and was convinced that the escalating animosity between North and South could not be halted short of war, and further that any civil conflict would be long and costly.

Phil Kearny was a staunch believer in the Federal Union, and he despised the institution of slavery, yet when the Southern states actually seceded en masse, it shook him to the core.[7] From far off Paris Kearny's grasp of the surging tide of history seemed remarkably clear. "My country needs me," he told his wife. "The Government will want experienced officers to train and lead the raw troops. This will be a long war. I know the Southerners. They will fight to the death. Every city, town and village will have to be taken at the bayonet point. The South has gambled its traditions, its past, its future — its very life — on this adventure. Either they or we shall triumph, and no matter who wins, America will never again be as we have known and loved her."[8]

There was no question that Phil Kearny would return to the United States and fight for the Union. He had once scolded a Southern officer, "No man has the moral right to own another human being. I say slavery is despicable! I would see it damned to hell! It is a stain on the American flag!"[9] Yet he also seemed to comprehend just how catastrophic war between the various states would be, and he predicted a grim affair: "The hatreds between North and South can only be washed away in blood," he said.[10] But, just as with citizens all across the land, Phil Kearny saw his duty clearly: "When the hour comes I shall fight to preserve the laws, the integrity and the existence of my native land."[11]

Phil and Agnes packed for New York, just as thousands of Americans began to take up sides in the dawning conflict. For Kearny there seemed no question — he would fight to destroy slavery and preserve the Union, and so it was for many Northern households. But to truly understand the Civil War, and the passions that motivated men into the fight, it is necessary to understand that in 1861 notions of preserving the union, "the existence of my native land," as Kearny put it, went far beyond the simple physical structure of the government and the arrangement of states as it then existed.

For many of us today both freedom and democracy seem so integral and permanent a part of our way of life that even the thought of their sudden absence — their potential loss — seems incomprehensible. But not so in 1861. At that time the democratic institutions of the United States were still more or less in their infancy, the country itself barely eighty years old. Today what seems permanent to us was then still a novel experiment. It was therefore understood, indeed, deeply feared, that the remarkable good that had been accomplished through the Revolution of 1776 might be easily undone through a civil conflict in 1861.

Surely men flocked to the Union cause for varied reasons, but many fought to preserve the very integrity of the democratic experiment itself, and for those men that was what the cause of Union truly represented. It was not just for the sitting government in Washington they marched — a sort of changeless constellation of states that had to be preserved at all costs — so much as to defend the democratic spark itself, and the grim possibility that it might be snuffed out in the turmoil of civil conflict. This deep seated concern, the fear that democracy itself was on trial during the American Civil War, was captured poignantly by Abraham Lincoln himself in the last line of his Gettysburg Address, when he insisted that the dead at Gettysburg had not died in vain, but rather to insure "that government of the people, by the people, for the people, shall not perish from the earth." That it *might* perish from the earth was precisely the motivating factor that caused many men to volunteer for the cause of Union.

It is impossible to understand the passions of the Civil War without understanding this central truth, for it was a truth that moved millions. One young volunteer from New Hampshire expressed this in his own, unique way: "The women called loudly for a chance to do something in the way to save the Country.... People now realized that war was at their door.... I was in my twentieth year, five feet ten and a half inches in height, in sound health, full of life and martial spirit. I had hoped the North would not compromise or make any concession to the South, for it seemed to me these things had been tried too often already and I, for one, was ready to volunteer, yea, fight for the preservation of the unit of the states and integrity of the Nation."[12]

At the outbreak of war in 1861, this need to respond in democracy's hour of crisis was felt and expressed in numerous ways. For Oliver Wendell Holmes, Jr., who had enlisted just after graduating from Harvard College, the need was felt as a deep sense of historical obligation. At Harvard Holmes had been the class poet. In the army he would wear the uniform of an infantry officer, yet for Holmes the transition seemed natural. "There was no pressing need on his part to join the Union Army; no special social stigma attached to those young men of his generation who did not enlist. A great many Harvard graduates did join the fight; not a few of his social class did not. Those who shunned military service were not stirred by the same noble impulse that stirred Wendell Holmes. His avowed purpose, to help in the destruction of slavery, placed his decision in the context of values.... The call to arms came not alone from Lincoln but from across generations of Puritan forbears."[13]

For Phil Kearny, as with Wendell Holmes, the long arm of family effort and obligation stretched back across the entire span of the young republic. "Kearny's had fought in the Revolution, the War of 1812, and the Seminole War."[14] His uncle, Stephen Kearny, had been a hero in the War of 1812 and was the man who had secured Phil his initial commission with the cavalry. Interestingly, at Yorktown during the initial stages of the Peninsula Campaign, Kearny had come upon an old slave on a nearby farm who clearly recalled hearing the sound of cannons rising once before from the same direction when he was just a young boy, that being George Washington's siege of Cornwallis' British army in 1781.[15] For Kearny it had been a disquieting moment. No, the country was hardly so old nor its institutions so firmly established that they could not be gutted or overthrown.

So the Kearnys rushed back to New York, but it would take a while for the forty-seven-year-old, one-armed soldier to secure any sort of military commission. The scandal of his marriage, his age and his affliction played heavily against him, until he finally was able to wrangle a commission as brigadier of a New Jersey brigade of volunteer infantry.

Phil Kearny took over command of the brigade in late summer 1861. He found the troops one of the worst outfits he had ever encountered, but with hard work, tough discipline, and fair rewards, over the weeks he managed to turn the unit completely around. He grew in respect for them, and they came to love their famous, dashing brigadier. Promotion came after Williamsburg and Seven Pines for Kearny, but he would not forget his New Jersey boys, nor would they ever forget him (in fact, on this very day at Glendale the New Jersey brigade, hearing that Kearny's division was in trouble, would come running to his aid[16]). Kearny was also the first to strike upon the idea of having a scarlet diamond patch sewed onto the uniform of every man in his division, allowing for quick identification on the battlefield, and a boost to esprit de corps. The patch, called the Kearny Patch thereafter, would be emulated later by other commands, and was the forerunner of the division patch used by modern armies.

Phil Kearny had come to Glendale to fight for abolition and Union, but make no mistake, he was still very much a man of his time. A wealthy aristocrat, he was a Democrat serving a Republican administration, a man of fine tastes in an army that lived on hardtack and salt horse. As was the custom of the time, he opened his own wallet to live well, but he spared no expense to insure that his men were taken care of as well. The arrival of his headquarters wagons often turned many a curious head. "The General lived well in the field. A luxurious wagon, its interior completely carpeted and upholstered, followed him everywhere. It had an ice chest filled with French wines. A field kitchen, supervised by a Parisian chef who prepared his meals, was part of his entourage. He paid for all this himself, of course. It was rumored that he had twenty tailored uniforms and two dozen pairs of hand-made riding boots."[17]

In some ways Phil Kearny's life had the feel of destiny about it. When, for instance, at the outbreak of the war with Mexico, he was ordered to recruit a company of dragoons, Kearny headed west to Springfield, Illinois, in order to recruit men and purchase horses. There he met a tall, lanky lawyer by the name of Abraham Lincoln who knew the better horse breeders in the area.[18] Neither man would forget the other. When Phil was seriously wounded at Churubusco and taken in for the amputation of his arm, his head was held in place by Franklin Pierce, who would one day be elected president of the United States.[19] He rode with the French in the great cavalry charge at the battle of Solferino, and was rewarded the Legion d'honneur by Louis Napoleon for his efforts. His life was in many ways a catalogue of valor, and a case could be made that Providence itself had nurtured him for this one critical moment; to understand precisely the position in which his country had been placed, and what would be required to preserve it.

So as Phil Kearny took to the field that morning not far from Riddell's Shop, perhaps after finishing a fine cup of French coffee, it is hard to imagine that the long Federal train slowly rumbling its way south behind him did not serve as an uncomfortable reminder of just how desperate the situation had become. For the cause of Union and democratic institutions, it did not bode well. A learned man with a soldier's keen eye, surely Phil Kearny grasped the grim fact that the Army of the Potomac and, as a consequence, the United States of America, were both that morning at the crossroads of calamity. It had taken the human race thousands of years to develop democratic institutions, but they could be swept aside in the blink of an eye should secession triumph and the nation disintegrate as a result.

Thus as Kearny and his staff watched the Army of the Potomac rumble through the dust south toward Malvern Hill — its herds of beef, miles of wagons, battery after battery of rolling artillery, and its tired, marching troops — it seems entirely understandable that he would have turned to a fellow officer and remarked that they were now "the rearguard of all God's creation." Because, all things considered, that's exactly what they were.

CHAPTER 8

Dithering at White Oak Swamp

As Phil Kearny sipped his morning coffee, then carefully inspected the deployment of the "rearguard of all God's creation" in the farm fields surrounding Glendale early that June 30, no sound or trace of the Rebel onslaught that was gathering in the woods and roads off to the west had yet to be seen or heard from. General Lee's great assault, meant to explode like a thunderclap and sweep the Federals posted at the crossroads into oblivion, had so far fizzled like a defective Roman candle. General Huger, out on the Charles City Road, had been stumped dead in his tracks by a sea of felled trees across his path, his column subsequently frozen in place as if mesmerized by a witch's spell. But what of Stonewall, who just hours earlier had been stomping his boot on a figurative etching of McClellan's army in the dirt, and declaring triumphantly "We've got him"?

When last seen Stonewall Jackson had called for his horse, leaped upon the animal rather awkwardly, and then "was off!" One might presume from this description that Stonewall Jackson, animated by his early morning meeting with General Lee and perhaps with freshly aroused visions of Southern independence dancing in head, had ridden off in a blaze of emotion to rejoin his Valley Army intent on wreaking havoc upon the Federal rear guard. Not so.

In fact, General Jackson would spend a good part of the morning at Savage Station, inspecting the remains of the Federal camp and hospital, sifting through the charred and broken debris left behind by the fleeing Union divisions. McClellan had, of course, in his haste to make safe haven upon the James, abandoned a field hospital there with some 2500 sick and wounded soldiers[1] to the Confederates. Anyone, in fact, who could not walk, ride, or crawl their way south with the retreating army had been left behind to suffer capture and imprisonment. The abandoned hospital was immense, and Jackson toured the facility in wonder, finding the tented grounds "remarkable, for the extent and convenience of its accommodations."[2]

Many a Confederate observer seemed stunned by the extent and quality of the debris and equipment left behind. "The whole country was full of deserted plunder, army wagons, and pontoon-trains partially burned or crippled; mounds of grain and rice and hillocks of mess beef smoldering; tens of thousands of axes, picks, and shovels; camp kettles gashed with hatchets; medicine chests with their drugs stirred into a foul medley and all the apparatus of a vast and lavish host; while the mire under foot was mixed with blankets lately new, and with overcoats torn from the waist up. For weeks afterward agents of our army were busy in gathering in the spoils. Great stores of fixed ammunition were saved, while more were destroyed."[3]

Here at Savage Station there was abandoned booty to be had, the dead of the previous days fighting to be buried, and numerous Federal stragglers to be gobbled up by the pursuing Confederates, and all this required Stonewall's time and energy. Somewhere between the convenient accommodations of the hospital and the leftover Federal supplies, Jackson seems to have forgotten entirely the vigorous pursuit discussed with General Lee just hours before. Perhaps he believed that the Valley Army was making ample progress that morning on its march toward White Oak Swamp under the capable eye of Major Dabney, but the truth was the Valley Army had reached the swamp that morning only to stall in its pursuit for lack of direction.

General Wade Hampton, whose South Carolina brigade was in the van at the time, explains the advance in a post-war letter: "We left the Chickahominy on Monday morning, June 30, though my impression is that the Grapevine bridge could have been used on Sunday, and at any rate there was a good ford of the stream not far below the bridge, near the road by the retreating enemy. Early on the morning of Monday we reached the White Oak crossing, my brigade being in advance; and about the same time the 2d Va. Cav. under Col. Munford came up.... We found a large hospital tent on the brow of the hill overlooking the crossing of the small stream over which a little bridge of poles had been made. The enemy had pulled off the poles and thrown them in the stream above the bridge, and a battery of four guns on the opposite hill commanded the causeway and the ford of the stream."[4]

A battery of four guns was all the force Hampton observed at the time opposing the crossing of the entire Valley Army. Was further reconnaissance conducted? No. What was done? Nothing. What were Major Dabney's orders? There appear to have been none. Where was Stonewall Jackson while all this dithering was taking place? Remarkably, Jackson had stopped en route to White Oak Swamp, only to sit along the side of the road and pen a letter to his wife. This is what he wrote:

> Near White Oak Swamp Bridge.
> An ever-kind Providence has greatly blessed our efforts and given us great reason for thankfulness in having defended Richmond. Today the enemy is retreating down the Chickahominy toward the James River. Many prisoners are falling into our hands. General D. H. Hill and I are together. [D.H. Hill was Jackson's brother-in-law.] I had a wet bed last night, as the rain fell in torrents. I got up about midnight, and haven't seen much rest since. I do trust that our God will soon bless us with an honorable peace, and permit us to be together at home again in the enjoyment of domestic happiness.
>
> You must give fifty dollars for church purposes, and more should you be disposed. Keep an account of the amount, as we must give at least one tenth of our income. I would like very much to see my darling, but hope that God will enable me to remain at the post of duty until, in his own good time, He blesses us with independence. This going home has injured the army immensely.[5]

Obviously, this does not sound like a general occupied with notions of imminent battle, or even of an aggressive pursuit of the enemy. As previously discussed, this letter does, however, stress aspects of Jackson's growing fatigue, and his religious sensibilities, both of which seem to be increasingly occupying his thoughts and perhaps mitigating against his better judgment. The letter, therefore, certainly serves as an insight into Jackson's frame of mind that morning, and a frame of mind that seems oddly tranquil for a man supposedly on a mission to end the war that very day.

It should be noted here, as well, that on the previous day, Sunday the 29th, Jackson had in fact been ordered by Lee to cooperate with Prince John Magruder in that officer's action at Savage Station. This order had been sent forward with Major Taylor of Lee's staff and later delivered to Jackson by one Chaplain Allen, who was better acquainted with the roads in the vicinity than was Taylor.[6] At that time Magruder informed Major Taylor that he had previously received word from Jackson that he would not be cooperating with any assault that day as he had "other important duty to perform."[7]

At the time, of course, Jackson was motionless and in camp. This fact had already been confirmed by Henry Kyd Douglas of Jackson's staff. So what, might be asked, was the other important duty Stonewall had to perform that day that was contrary to his orders from Lee?

Porter Alexander is confident he knows the answer: "The explanation of Jackson's message to Jones [Jones was Magruder's subordinate] is clear in the light of his regard for the Sabbath and from the particular expression used. He mentions no physical obstacle nor any other demand upon his troops, who, indeed, are all resting quietly in their camps, but the '*important duty*' to be performed seems to concern himself rather than his command, and to be entirely personal in character.... He confidently believed that marked regard for the Sabbath would often be followed by God's favor upon one's secular enterprises."[8]

Could it be that Jackson, his thought process somewhat numbed due to fatigue, had concluded that his solemn observance of the Sabbath would bring forth immediate and material rewards from a grateful deity? Did he now presume that victory would be awarded the Southern cause as almost a matter of divine intervention on Monday, June 30, due to his piety on Sunday, June 29? Quite possibly. From this perspective, Stonewall's letter to his wife penned on the way to White Oak Swamp, and his seeming indifference to military necessity that morning would begin, at least, to make some sort of sense, no matter how distorted that logic might appear to us today. Jackson would have hardly been the first, nor would he be the last individual on the world's stage, to be motivated by a very strict or fundamentalist conception of a divine being.

Writing years later, and after much time for consideration, Porter Alexander would again endorse this explanation of Jackson's behavior: "Indeed, I never thoroughly understood the matter until long after, when all the official reports were published, & I read Gen. Jackson's own statements of times & things, & those of the officers under him & compared them with what I knew of the whole situation."[9] Alexander continues: "He [Jackson] believed, with absolute faith, in a personal God, watching all human events with a jealous eye to His own glory—-ready to reward those people who made it their chief care, & to punish those who forgot about it. And he specially believed that a particular day had been set aside every week for the praise of this God, & that those who disregarded it need expect no favors, but that those who sacrificed all other considerations, however recklessly, to honoring Him by its observance, would be rewarded conspicuously."[10]

General Jackson would not join his command at White Oak Swamp until almost noon.[11] A good six hours or more had subsequently passed that morning with nothing of substance being accomplished, and this on a day when aggressive pursuit was critical to the success of the Southern cause.

Earlier that morning Colonel Stapleton Crutchfield, Jackson's chief of artillery, had arrived at the swamp, where he selected a good position on a ridge to the right and overlooking the bridge to place a significant battery of guns. From this high point Jackson observed the Federal position across the swamp, spotted open ground on the left, the hospital tents previously noted by Hampton, and the guns of three or four batteries of artillery.[12] Behind the guns long lines of infantry could be seen on the ground, perhaps asleep, and moving off in the distance behind the infantry an enormous line of wagons, disappearing over a hill toward Glendale — the enemy was escaping! But the hills were high, the trees and brush thick, thus there was no way of knowing for sure in what strength the Federals were posted without a more vigorous reconnaissance.

To deceive the Federal gunners on the opposite hill, and to avoid counter-battery fire, Crutchfield had his guns loaded below the rim of the hill. The intention was to run them up and open fire once all the artillery was in place, thus taking the Yankee rear guard — and specifically their artillery — by complete surprise. To accomplish this task a road had been hacked through the swamp to allow the guns to be placed effectively, and by early afternoon this had all been completed.

But, might be asked, what of the reconnaissance? Up to this point, there seems to have been almost none, and this is difficult to explain. Every account of the Valley Army's arrival that day, of the observations of its various officers, of the depth and degree of difficulty involved in negotiating White Oak Swamp, indicate clearly that no one in Jackson's command had even the foggiest grasp at the time of the strength of the Federal opponent on the opposite hills. Yet no attempt was made to develop an understanding of the strength and parameters of the position, of the various Federal commands that might be involved, or of potential reserves and artillery. Observations had been made of the Federal wagons pulling out in large numbers but, here again, no effort was made by Jackson to try and clarify just what that might mean. Were the Federals in the midst of an evacuation, and if so, why attempt to take by assault what they were about to hand over freely? The logic then would have been to wait, cross over the swamp, and attack any depleted rear guard in full force.

Instead, what occurred was a sort of jumbled catalogue of inadvertent miscues. At around 2:00 P.M. the Confederate guns were run up the hill and all opened a heavy fire on the original battery of Federal artillery Hampton had spotted guarding the bridge crossing earlier that morning. These guns were immediately battered, a gun completely disabled, and the battery forced to abandon its position.[13] Good enough.

Then Jackson ordered Munford's cavalry — which had arrived much earlier that morning but had been put to no practical use — to cross over the creek and try and capture the disabled gun. For some unknown and unexplained reason, both Jackson and his brother-in-law, General D.H. Hill, decided to accompany this cavalry foray across the swamp, only to ride head-

Jackson's artillery position at White Oak Bridge by artist Alfred R. Waud. The artillery action during the fighting at Glendale would last into the evening but would be termed little more than a "farce of war" by Porter Alexander for its lack of meaningful affect (Library of Congress).

first into a storm of Federal fire delivered from heavy cover to their right, a position which, of course, had not yet been detected by the Confederates as there had been no attempt to do so.

The fire was so heavy and well directed that both Hill and Jackson came close to being struck by an artillery shell.[14] Munford's cavalry was forced a quarter of a mile east down the swamp in order to escape, while Jackson and Hill scrambled back across the creek, discretion, at this moment, apparently being the better part of valor. The attempt proved a complete fiasco, and Hill and Jackson were lucky to escape with their lives. Hill would later admit as much. "Fast riding in the wrong direction is not military," he said, "but it is sometimes healthy."[15]

There is an obvious question here. Why, after hours of apparent indifference to common military practice — basic reconnaissance — had two senior officers decided to accompany a single regiment of cavalry on a foray into the teeth of an unknown enemy position, not to mention a position that was already conceived to be a powerful rear guard? Yes, Jackson had ridden before in the Valley with a small contingent in pursuit of a clearly beaten and retreating foe, but this was not that. Moreover, if Stonewall firmly believed that God alone would ensure the Southern effort that day, what, exactly, had changed between 10:00 A.M. and 2:00 P.M. to suggest that he go riding off on such a foolish errand? Unfortunately, there is no good answer to this question, but the situation may best serve to underscore what can only be described as the muddled state of Jackson's thinking that day — exhausted minds make inconsistent decisions.

Yet some good had been gleaned from the attempt, no matter how ill-conceived the effort. For in the course of flying downstream to avoid the Yankee onslaught, Munford had inadvertently discovered another ford just a quarter of a mile lower on the creek that was undefended, and had also as a mere consequence of his route located some of the Federal positions on the opposite bank.

Here is a portion of a post-war letter from Munford regarding the situation:

> At the battle of White Oak Swamp, after Col. Crutchfield's artillery had disabled one gun and driven the cannoneers from the battery which commanded the crossing at the old bridge at White Oak Swamp, Gen. Jackson directed me to cross the creek, with my regiment, at the ford, and secure the guns in front of us. The enemy's sharp-shooters were stationed in rear of the building overlooking the ford; and as soon as we neared the abandoned battery of the enemy, these sharp-shooters, and another battery stationed in the road at the edge of the woods, and commanding the road and the ford over which we had passed, opened a furious fire upon us, and I was forced to move a quarter of a mile lower down the creek, where I found a cow path which led me over the swamp. But *en route* I found where Gen. Franklin's [Federal] troops had been located, having now changed front. They had left a long line of knapsacks and blankets, from which I allowed my men to take what they pleased; and among their things were many late newspapers from Washington, which I dispatched by a courier to Gen. Jackson, giving him full information of what I had seen and *how* and *where* I had crossed.[16]

Not only Munford claimed to have located another nearby crossing point, and relayed that information clearly to Jackson, but D. H. Hill would later confirm that very report: "Our cavalry returned by the lower ford & pronounced it perfectly practicable for infantry."[17]

Thus is it clear that slightly after 2:00 P.M. General Jackson had received reliable information that White Oak Swamp could be crossed uncontested by infantry, and further of the Federal deployment on the other side. As has already been written, Franklin's position was strong, but both flanks were in the air, thus the Yankees here were vulnerable to attack from either side. Here, clearly, was one of the best opportunities of the war, a chance to send the Federal rear guard reeling, flying back down the road toward Glendale in utter confusion as the Valley Army cleared the opposite ridge, then crossed the swamp and swept forward like a sledgehammer toward Glendale.

What would Stonewall do with this invaluable information? We shall see.

CHAPTER 9

The Long Wait

The sun continued to climb into a clear sky that morning, the heat rose accordingly, and through the dust and heat Robert E. Lee rode with the van of Longstreet's column as it wound its way east toward Glendale. They turned from the Darbytown Road onto the Long Bridge Road which ran both north and east into the small hamlet ahead. The absence of Federal troops on this avenue verified the route of McClellan's march for sure, as only two potential routes ran south, and this one had now been proven vacant. Thus it had been made manifestly clear — McClellan was on the Quaker Road heading south toward Malvern Hill, and if the Quaker Road could be taken and held, the Army of the Potomac could be cut in two. Here then, directly before them, was the great opportunity, no longer merely a theory on a map or a glimmering hope in Robert E. Lee's imagination, but a real, tangible enemy moving on a real, discernable road, not more than a mile or so distant. The Rebel army still appeared to hold all the aces.

For Southern leadership hopes were high that steamy Monday morning, and why not? Yes, word had been received from General Huger that he had been delayed, but just what sort of delay had not been specified, and it seemed a trifle at the moment. Surely he would be along soon enough with his 9,000 men to "start the ball," as they sardonically liked to phrase it.

And everything else was now in place: Longstreet and Hill advancing directly on Glendale, Holmes on the River Road, and Jackson surely soon to press the Federal rear at White Oak Bridge. Of the wayward Jackson Lee had now to be certain. Just that morning, after all, he had met with Jackson, and Stonewall had drawn that picture with his boot and stomped it with conviction, and Lee knew then that Jackson understood — "We've got him!" Yes, everything had been brought together as Lee had imagined and planned it, and now it was only a matter of time and execution. General McClellan had left himself vulnerable to envelopment and destruction, and today Lee intended to both envelop and destroy him. If everything went reasonably as planned, by nightfall the Army of the Potomac would not simply be defeated. It would no longer exist.

As the long column edged closer to Glendale the advance struck Federal pickets posted west of the crossroads, and the sudden crack of rifle fire could be heard in the distance, sporadic, but distinct. The meaning was clear. The enemy was near, but just who and in what force remained uncertain.

Officers rode quickly up and down the dusty lines, shouting orders, moving the gray and butternut troops into the trees bordering the road. The light jangle and slap of canteens, knapsacks, and bayonets filled the air, the simultaneous pounding of thousands of feet producing a low, steady rumble. Dust rose in the sky. The Army of Northern Virginia was deploying, moving into position for what was hoped to be the great and final assault of the war.

As the men were slowly enveloped by the trees, Lee tried to get a look, a peek at the enemy in the distance, to form some inkling as to what force lay ahead, how and where they were deployed, how and where they were moving.[1] The two great armies appeared very near to one another, that much was clear, perhaps too near, as random shells began to fall nearby and bullets whistled overhead. Lee paid them no mind. He moved off to a slightly higher elevation, a "field of broom-grass and small pines,"[2] where the view was better. There, much to Lee's surprise, he was suddenly joined by President Jefferson Davis.[3]

Davis had himself graduated from the United States Military Academy with the class of 1828, had served for seven years as an officer in the army, and had been named secretary of war in the cabinet of President Pierce in 1853. He served in that capacity for four years where he helped to thoroughly modernize and upgrade the nation's army.[4] Thus he had as good a background as anyone in the country when it came to martial affairs and, as president of the Confederacy, was often mired "knee deep" in even the most mundane of military questions. Davis had appointed Lee to the command of the Confederate army in Virginia and had to be pleased by the sudden and unexpected turn of events that had the massive Federal foe stumbling away from the very gates of Richmond toward the James. In just a matter of days Lee appeared to have flipped the calculus of victory and defeat completely on its head. Now it was the Federals who were staring down the proverbial barrel of a gun, no longer Jefferson Davis and his government in Richmond.

Constance Harrison had often spotted the president in Richmond, journeying to and from his office: "During all this time President Davis was a familiar and picturesque figure on the streets, walking through the Capitol square from his residence to the executive office in the morning, not to return until late in the afternoon, or riding just before nightfall to visit one or another of the encampments near the city. He was tall, erect, slender, and of a dignified and soldierly bearing, With clear-cut and high-bred features, and of a demeanor of stately courtesy to all. He was clad always in Confederate gray cloth, and wore a soft felt hat with wide brim. Afoot, his step was brisk and firm; in the saddle he rode admirably and with a martial aspect."[5]

The president was obviously concerned by Lee's exposed position so near the front, and immediately questioned him as to his safety. The general countered with the same concerns for the president's well being, but neither apparently would admit to a problem and neither would budge. The obvious danger suddenly forgotten, the two began conversing about the situation as each understood it. The conversation went on at some length, shells occasionally cracking overhead or landing nearby, bullets slapping through the leaves.

On the Long Bridge Road Longstreet's division began moving off to the right, deploying on a line opposite Glendale. Facing the Federals opposite, four brigades formed the front line, from north to south — Wilcox, Jenkins, Kemper and Branch, in that order. A.P. Hill's division filed off to the left of the road, the brigades of Pryor, Featherston, and Gregg shifting off to the north. The men moved into position, took what little shade they could find, and waited for the order to move forward.

In the open field of broom grass Lee, Davis, Longstreet, and Hill — along with all their various staff members — continued to talk, and plot, and reconnoiter until Colonel Edward Porter Alexander arrived with his report, fresh from his early morning balloon observations.[6] The news he shared with them was not so heartening. Alexander reported that he had made ascensions both the night before and again early that morning, and had spotted Federal activity on and about Malvern Hill. This could only mean that McClellan's army — and perhaps a large portion of it — had already escaped, or was near escaping, and that the opportunity to inflict a death blow to the Federal cause might be slipping through their fingers with each tick of the clock. Time and speed were becoming critical. Hopefully, those elements were not running out.

General A.P. Hill, in charge of that quadrant of the field, finally could no longer abide the thought of so many high level officers, both military and civilian, gathered so near harm in his sector, and thus twice ordered them further to the rear.[7] Finally bowing to military protocol, Davis and Lee moved back beyond the range of the Federal guns, and again took up their discussion and anxious wait for the sound of Huger's guns. The hands of the clock were now moving close toward noon, but no sound had been heard from the north, although both Huger and Jackson were known to be only a few miles distant. Where were they? When would they attack?

Alexander, writing years later recalled the moment clearly.

> He [Lee] was so close in rear of his line of battle that men and horses among the couriers and staff, were wounded by random shots. For quite a time, too, President Davis and his staff were present, in conference with the generals, while missiles grew more frequent, and wounded men began to come in from the front.
>
> For hours we stood there waiting — waiting for something which never happened. Every minute that we waited was priceless time thrown away. Twelve o'clock came and the precious day was half gone. One o'clock, two o'clock, three o'clock followed. Even four o'clock drew near, and now, whatever was started, would be cut short by night. Our great opportunity was practically over, and we had not yet pulled a trigger. We had waited for either Huger or Jackson to begin, and neither had begun.[8]

Where, it would be fair to ask, was the general commanding through all of this? Why had so many hours been allowed to dissolve in profitless waiting? This is what Alexander had to say: "As Beauregard, at Bull Run, had sent word to Ewell to begin, and then had gone to the centre and waited; as Johnston, at Seven Pines, had given orders to Hill and Longstreet about beginning, and then gone to the left and waited; so now, Lee, having given orders beforehand to both Jackson and Huger, had passed on to the right and was waiting; and in every case the opportunity passed unimproved."[9]

The account of this tale, from Yorktown to Glendale, has examined and found wanting the actions of any number of general grade officers, both blue and gray. We have, for instance, pointed out the rather serious command failures of George McClellan, and have spent considerable time cataloguing the numerous instances in which Thomas Stonewall Jackson's actions have fallen short of satisfactory. Likewise, generals Magruder and Huger have come under particular and reasonable criticism for their bungling and delay.

But what of General Lee? Yes, it is clear that Lee was present, and of course Lee was dutifully waiting for the sound of Huger's guns to come rumbling down from the north to initiate the great assault. And there is no question that Lee's plan had been well conceived, and that the various commands, by hook or crook, had been brought to their proper jumping off points that morning. That much had been achieved, and that much alone had placed the Army of Northern Virginia in a posture to quite possibly destroy their adversary by day's end — no small accomplishment in and of itself. But what now? Would it be unfair to suggest that Lee could have done more, perhaps much more, to coax movement from his dormant columns? Let's examine the facts.

To begin with, it is inconceivable to presume that Robert E. Lee could have in any way perceived his Army of Northern Virginia to be something

akin to what today we might term a well oiled machine on the morning of
June 30. Absolutely *nothing* in its past performance would allow for such a
judgment, for the plodding, inept, confused opposite had been just the case.
And Lee had to have known this, and thus rationally, logically, had to have
been prepared for it.

The battle at Seven Pines serves as a good starting point. While General
Lee had no hand in the planning of that engagement, and he had little if
any foreknowledge of events as they were to soon unfold, he was there, nevertheless, as events took place, observed the scene at Joe Johnston's headquarters, and had to have formed a reasonably good idea that Johnston's plan
of battle had unraveled, and had unraveled early. Johnston, much like Lee
himself at Glendale, had expected Longstreet to attack at an early hour, but
Longstreet had become tangled in a mire of wrong roads and confused orders,
and the battle did not commence until late afternoon. Then Johnston had
ridden too far forward and was cut down by both musketry and shrapnel,
and for the Confederate effort that day, the wheels came off the wagon. In
all probability Lee did not know what exactly had gone wrong at Seven Pines
for some time if, indeed, ever, but that is not important. He certainly had
to have grasped the obvious fact that the job had been botched, that command coordination had been either confused or nonexistent, and that the
operation had therefore devolved into fiasco.

It can sensibly be presumed that General Lee planned on avoiding the
same stumbling performance at his own operational debut at Mechanicsville,
thus he had all the major players attend a briefing at the Dabb House in
June prior to the action. Longstreet, Hill, Lee, and finally Jackson were all
there. At that conference all roles were agreed upon, and a time schedule put
in place. Jackson was to start the offensive with his arrival on June 26 on
the Federal right, but Jackson never posted, Hill went in impetuously anyway,
and the battle turned into a bloody nightmare for Southern arms. McClellan
fled anyway, but Lee cannot be congratulated for that. Only McClellan would
have fled a *victory*.

The very next day at Gaines's Mill Jackson would once again stumble
late into the action, units would attack without coordination, and only a
magnificent and massive assault at day's end would finally move a single, and
greatly outnumbered, Federal corps from the summit of Turkey Hill. Here
again, command and control issues were abundant and almost undermined
the day's effort. The victory that was obtained at Gaines's Mill had been
obtained at a very high cost in killed and wounded, and there was little question that victories such as that would over time bleed the South dry of its
limited manpower. Where was everyone and what were they doing? For much

of the day General Lee did not know. Importantly, however, it would be Lee's own handiwork late in the day that put together the final push that carried the Federal position. Thus the only true victory the Confederates would claim during the entire Seven Days Lee owed to his own handiwork.

As also detailed, Magruder's efforts at Savage Station on June 29 while on McClellan's tail were inept and half-hearted. Again, Lee knew little of this until the results were in, and McClellan's rear guard had been allowed to slip south across White Oak Swamp. For that entire day Jackson and his command had been content to remain in camp.

There is a single thread that winds its way through all these misbegotten efforts, and that thread is General Lee's lack of not only hands on control of his lieutenants, but even a basic understanding of where they were and what they were up to at any given moment. New to high command himself, he can certainly be forgiven for the confusion that befuddled his army that first day at Mechanicsville, but it seems nothing of value was learned from that disjointed venture, and the *same* sorts of failures would literally plague the Army of Northern Virginia throughout the Seven Days. Jackson fails repeatedly and nothing comes of it. Huger marches a mere five miles and goes lamely into bivouac, and no adjustments are made. Magruder, like Don Quixote, spends much of his day on the 29th tilting at windmills, and Lee knows nothing of it until it is far too late to take corrective action. Only late at Gaines's Mill would Lee intercede, and that intercession ended in victory, but for some odd reason that sort of generalship would not again be repeated.

From all reports, it appears Lee's grasp of the overall situation he faced was excellent, and his plans were certainly well conceived. But there it ends. Like a boxer, generals are not graded on their plans and conceptions, but rather their knockouts, and during the Seven Days the Army of Northern Virginia appeared either to be throwing wild haymakers, or else sitting in its corner and refusing to come out at the bell. As commander it was Robert E. Lee's job to correct these disjointed efforts. Now, it has been well documented that Lee conceived his job as commander to be one of bringing all the various elements of battle into their proper starting positions, then letting his lieutenants do their jobs.[10] If this works it is a fine approach, but only if it works. When it does not work, something must be done to correct what is broken.

By morning of the anticipated engagement at Glendale, General Lee *had* to have realized that some of his lieutenants were not functioning up to the level he had anticipated, and that something was needed to right the situation — why else would he have ridden off to meet with Jackson and Magruder that morning? Yet after days of fighting and constant failure, General Lee on June 30, as Alexander notes, remains waiting in a field of broom grass for *hours*, while knowing nothing of the movements of Huger, Jackson, and Holmes, movements which were at the time going nowhere. If those officers are to be properly criticized for their numerous failures, in fairness shouldn't Lee be criticized for his, for in retrospect his may have been the worst of all. Lee, more so than anyone else, appears to have let the day slip away, apparently committed to a concept of command that had already been proven painfully deficient.

The answer to this problem was, for the times, neither novel nor innovative. It was to have placed staff officers with numerous couriers with each of the columns to report back at sensible intervals to another staff officer at Lee's side. If and when a problem was detected, Lee could have been informed immediately so that a reevaluation of the situation might be performed, and correcting orders issued. But reevaluations and corrections require *information*, and it was this critical lack of information that left Lee in the dark for most of that day, and a situation Lee himself made no effort to alter. Insisting on nothing, he got nothing.

In analyzing Lee's life and military career, his biographer, Douglas Southall Freeman, suggests two reasons for this deficiency. The first was Lee's upbringing as a Southern gentleman, an upbringing that placed inordinate emphasis on politeness and amiability. "Capable always of devising the best plan, he had, on occasion, been compelled by the blundering of others to accept the second best. He had not always been able to control men of contrary mind. His consideration for others, the virtue of the gentleman, had been his vice as a soldier."[11] The second, Freeman continues, was Lee's conception of the command role itself, a theory that oddly removed the commander from center stage once combat was initiated. "To this theory Lee steadfastly held from his opening campaign through the battle of the Wilderness. Who may say whether, when his campaigns are viewed as a whole, adherence to this theory of his function cost the army more than it won for the South?"[12]

Adherence to this theory would certainly cost the Southern cause this day at Glendale. That does not appear debatable. That said, in fairness General Lee must be judged on the totality of his career, not simply one deficient afternoon, and in that regard he certainly remains one of the finest military officers ever produced on North American soil. Moreover, it can be said with certainty that Lee, unlike George McClellan, would be either near or within shouting distance of the front lines at almost every battle fought during the Seven Days, while McClellan did not see a single soldier go into action, and would actually flee the field as his army prepared to fight for its life at both

Glendale, and the following day at Malvern Hill. We will leave the student of military history to judge the two on their individual merits.

As the hours twiddled away that morning at Glendale to no discernable profit, Longstreet resolved to at least feel for the enemy and determine the Federals' strength and position. The order went out to a young colonel of South Carolina infantry, an officer Longstreet had already called "the best officer he ever saw,"[13] to advance a regiment of sharpshooters against the Federals posted just east near a farm of approximately two hundred acres owned by a family by the name of Nelson.[14] That twenty-seven-year-old officer was Micah Jenkins, and while no one knew it at the time, it would be Micah Jenkins' South Carolina brigade, through a hail of fire and almost unimaginable carnage, that would break the Federal line that afternoon and take the Quaker Road, thus splitting the Army of the Potomac in two, and providing the Confederacy — despite all the bungling, delay, and ineptitude — with the greatest opportunity for Southern independence it would ever know.

CHAPTER 10

A Perfect Model
of a Christian Hero

As General Lee and President Davis waited long and impatiently in a field along the Long Bridge Road for the sound of Huger's guns to announce his arrival on the field, at approximately 2:00 P.M. the sound of heavy cannonading finally roiled up from the north.[1] This came suddenly and clearly, crashing over the now eager officers like the resounding waves of a distant sea, and for a moment all drew hope that the great assault had in fact been initiated. Eager to respond, Longstreet had a battery of his own answer with a volley. The response, however, was not what had been hoped for.

The Federals opposite, apparently waiting impatiently all day for the first signal of a Confederate assault, were understandably trigger-happy and unleashed a furious response of their own. Well in front of McCall's position, five batteries of the division artillery had been posted, dangerously exposed, yet painfully close to the Confederates waiting on and around the Long Bridge Road.[2] Having had the better part of the day to observe the Rebels deploy, the fire from McCall's twenty-six guns was not only hot but accurate, and soon the shells began to rain down on the waiting Confederate infantry. As if accidentally stumbling upon a hornets nest, Longstreet had inadvertently triggered a storm of fire against his own lines. It was at this point that General A.P. Hill rode up to Lee and Davis and declared, "As commander of this part of the field, I order you both to the rear!"[3] and the two were forced further rearward in order to escape the avalanche of metal that came crashing all around them.

While Longstreet's first impulse was to prepare to cooperate with what he presumed to be Huger's assault on his immediate left, the roar of guns had in reality not been Huger at all, but rather Jackson's artillery, run-up and unleashed against the Federal battery posted opposite at White Oak Swamp just after 2:00 o'clock that afternoon. The initial report of those guns had been loud and impressive but soon trailed off noticeably as Jackson's gunners returned to a more normal firing sequence. Additionally, after consideration, the noise from the north seemed too far away to be Huger—who was supposed to be by now just a mile or so from Longstreet's position and moving toward Glendale on the Charles City Road—and, moreover, there arose no rattle of musketry, the one sure indicator of a full fledged assault in progress. With that Lee determined to hold Longstreet back until Huger and Jackson were clearly in action, as had been the original tactical formula for the day.

Yet the Federals in front of Glendale had now been mistakenly seduced into action, and the situation along Longstreet's lines had become as a result extremely uncomfortable. One Federal battery, Cooper's Battery B, 1st Pennsylvania Light Artillery,[4] was so close to the Confederate front line hidden in the woods that it simply had to be silenced. As this battery was situated just a few hundred yards west of Mr. Nelson's farmhouse, and closest to the South Carolina brigade commanded by Micah Jenkins, he was ordered to move forward and subdue those guns.

Jenkins was not new to command. "Since he was in charge of the attack, Longstreet had placed his own division under R.H. Anderson, who had in turn given the command of his own brigade to Jenkins, his senior colonel. Anderson's brigade still consisted of the Second South Carolina Rifles, the Fourth South Carolina battalion, the Fifth South Carolina, the Sixth South Carolina, and the Palmetto Sharpshooters."[5]

The young colonel ordered the Sixth South Carolina forward as skirmishers, and they did an admirable job, pushing back the Federal pickets posted to their front, and determining the strength of the Yankee position west of the Quaker Road.[6] But the Federal artillery had been posted so near the Confederate line, and was in turn supported by such a stubborn skirmish line, that the advance of the Sixth South Carolina soon devolved into a hot contest all its own. Rather than silencing the Yankee guns, the volume of fire appeared to actually increase. Like a forest fire ignited by a single, foolishly tossed match, the fight in front of Glendale had heated up, not by design, but by random circumstance.

Thomas J. Goree, then an officer on Longstreet's staff, observed the unfolding of events. "After waiting some time we heard Huger's artillery [Jackson's actually] open quite briskly. Genl. Longstreet thinking that he (Huger) was well engaged with the enemy, sent forward to make the attack in our front. As soon as we fired the first gun, the enemy, who had selected a very strong position, opened on us with 4 batteries of 6 guns each—24 guns. At this time Huger stopped (nor did he do anything more that day) and we found ourselves in a fight with an overwhelming force opposed to us. There was but one way to get out of the scrap and that was to fight out. And here I believe occurred the hardest fight of the war."[7]

Micah Jenkins was no stranger to combat, and despite his youth, he was very highly regarded by Southern leadership. At Seven Pines he had distinguished himself along with his South Carolina command. Douglas Southall Freeman offers this assessment: "Col. Micah Jenkins of the Palmetto Sharpshooters, a youngster of 26 years, had received command of one column when R.H. Anderson had divided the Brigade. In leading successively two regiments, then three and, for a time, four, his conduct had been above all praise. Often his men had fought at 100 yards and sometimes at a third of that distance. One of his companies, forty-seven strong, had bagged 139 armed prisoners, or more than a third of all those taken South of the York River Railroad. Hill estimated that Jenkins had gone more than a mile beyond the main Federal works at Seven Pines.... The camps rang with his praise, which was welcome to the young soldier."[8]

T.J. Goree would go even further in his praise for Jenkins' performance: "Genl. Anderson's S.C. Brigade under Col. Jenkins (Genl. Anderson being temporarily in command of a Division) *immortalized* itself.... Col. Jenkins carried the brigade into action about 3 o'clock P.M., a little further to the left of where Genl. D.H. Hill was engaged. From this time until night he fought unsupported and alone, and advancing all the time. He fought 5 separate & distinct lines of the enemy, whipping each one. He whipped the whole of Genl. Couch's Division, consisting of 12 or 15 regiments, with a little brigade of 1900 men. He passed over several abatis of felled timber, 2 lines of breastworks, captured three pieces of artillery, 250 prisoners, & several stands of colors."[9]

Micah Jenkins had been born in December 1835, and raised in Edisto, South Carolina, an offshore island not far from the city of Charleston.[10] He was raised in relative prosperity in a family that owned three plantations on or about Edisto Island, and Jenkins entered The Citadel as a cadet at the age of only fifteen. As such, Jenkins would soon join a fairly unique group of graduates, those schooled in a military atmosphere but not as career soldiers.

Prior to the Civil War numerous Southern states had established military colleges of their own, most of these founded on the West Point model. Contrary to popular opinion, these schools were not enclaves for the well-to-do, but rather were created with the express purpose of offering an education to "the poor boy at the plow handle, the apprentice at his work bench, and in general all those whose circumstances in life had denied them the advantages of the usual preparatory training in the classical schools of the South."[11]

In that sense these schools were, for their time at least, expressions of a progressive ideal, and an egalitarian form of education. By and large, their format was military, but their purpose was civilian. "Unlike West Point's mission to educate soldiers, these state-supported military colleges existed to produce educated citizens within a framework of soldierly discipline. Each aimed to produce a productive citizen who, when necessary, could take up arms in defense of his state or country. Consequently, there was less emphasis on the military subjects in favor of a more broad-based curriculum. But like West Point, and unlike many of their civilian counterparts, these schools tended to concentrate on technical rather than classical subjects."[12]

Most often these schools had been created during that period after the great clash of 1832 between President Andrew Jackson and the state of South Carolina, when that state attempted to impose a right to nullify any Federal law it deemed unacceptable. South Carolina failed at the point of military intervention, but the crisis left its mark on Southern politicians, along with a deep and abiding distrust of Federal authority. Should such a crisis occur again, many Southern states were determined to be prepared to resist what they deemed the Federal government's meddlesome ventures into their own internal affairs.

There were eleven of these schools located in the South at the outbreak of hostilities, the two most famous being the Virginia Military Institute in Lexington, Virginia, and The Citadel in Charleston, South Carolina.[13] In the aggregate, these institutions would offer the South a ready pool of educated, trained, and motivated officers at the war's inception, and go a long way toward explaining the clear edge in battlefield superiority the South enjoyed during the first year or two of the conflict. While these officers may not have initially filled the ranks of high command — although many would rise to that level — their contributions tended, at least initially, to be in training, then in regiment, brigade, and division command. When need required the cadets themselves were mustered for duty, at times even battle.

The initial raising of an army was no simple chore. Indeed, the conversion of what was generally a rural and undisciplined mix of volunteers into soldiers was no easy job, and the younger cadets from these military schools, who were generally used to teach close order drill, often had their hands full. One rather humorous note home from a Virginia recruit exemplifies the difficulty of the task for both teacher and pupil alike: "I was three and thirty years old, a born invalid whose habit had been to rise late, bathe leisurely and eat breakfast after everybody else was done. To get up at dawn to the sound of fife and drum, to wash my face in a hurry in a tin basin, wipe on a wet towel, and go forth with suffocated skin, and a sense of uncleanliness to be drilled by a fat little cadet, young enough to be my son ... that indeed was misery. How I hated that little cadet! He was always so wide awake, so clean, so interested in the drill; his coat-tails were so short and sharp, and his hands looked so big in white gloves. He made me sick."[14]

Of course, like most colleges at the time, these military institutions were small, and their graduating classes, as a result, tended to be limited. It is estimated, for instance, that in 1861 The Citadel had graduated perhaps no more than 225, but these men "were well trained and, with few exceptions, were quick to enlist. They rendered for South Carolina a service similar to the Virginia Military Institute."[15] As was to be expected, however, the price paid by the alumni of these institutions for their war-time service was high. "Of 193 South Carolina Military Academy [The Citadel] graduates in Confederate service, 29 were killed in battle, 4 died of war-related causes, and another 29 were wounded. Of the 1,781 VMI alumni who served in the South's armed forces, 249 of them died."[16]

In 1854 Micah Jenkins was graduated first in his class from The Citadel[17] and soon thereafter moved to Yorkville, South Carolina, where in conjunction with his Citadel classmate Asbury Coward, he helped found the Kings Mountain Military School. There Jenkins thrived, was married, became a father, and ran the academy until secession came to South Carolina. Soon thereafter contingents of the state's troops were called north to fight with the Army of Northern Virginia, and Jenkins went along as a colonel in the South Carolina Volunteers.

Jenkins fought well at the first Battle of Bull Run, but had his first real test at Seven Pines. There he found the price of glory high indeed: "This brigade went into action with 1900 men. It lost 700 killed & wounded, & among this number was more than half of its field officers, and near one third of the line officers. But, it never faltered, nor even stopped. It advanced slowly but steadily for more than two miles, all the time in the face of a galling fire, and nearly all the way over felled timber & the enemy's breastworks."[18] Jenkins emerged from the carnage uninjured and a virtual celebrity in the Army of Northern Virginia for his actions. T.J. Goree had this to say: "Col. Micah Jenkins is a great friend of mine and he is a favorite with the army. Gen. Longstreet thinks him the best officer he ever saw. He is only 27 years of age & is a perfect model of a Christian hero."[19] Micah Jenkins had already experienced a great deal of war, but by nightfall this day, he would be tested far beyond anything he had ever experienced or dreamed of before.

As the volume of fire began to rise that afternoon between the front lines near Glendale, senior officers strained to hear the sound of Huger's guns rise up from the Charles City Road, but hour after hour passed, and nothing came of it. General Longstreet, as noted previously, turned to Jenkins' brigade to try and silence the Federal artillery across the way.

Years later Longstreet would recall the moment vividly.

> The ground upon which I approached was much lower than that occupied by General McCall, and was greatly cut up by ravines and covered with heavy timber and tangled undergrowth.... By 11 o'clock our troops were in position, and we waited for the signal from Jackson and Huger. Everything was quiet on my part of the line, except occasional firing between my pickets and McCall's. I was in momentary expectation of the signal. About half-past 2 o'clock artillery firing was heard on my left evidently at the point near White Oak Swamp where Huger was to attack. I very naturally supposed this firing to be the expected signal, and ordered some of my batteries to reply as a signal I was ready to cooperate.... Instantly, the Federal batteries responded most spitefully. It was impossible for the enemy to see us as we sat on our horses in the little field, surrounded by tall, heavy timber and thick undergrowth; yet a battery by chance had our range and exact distance, and poured upon us a terrific fire.... Colonel Micah Jenkins was in front of us, and I sent him an order to silence the Federal battery, supposing that he could do so with his long-range rifles.[20]

The day and opportunity were dwindling down to but a few precious hours of daylight, and still nothing had been heard from either Huger or Jackson. For Lee it must have been maddening. What had gone wrong?

Then around 3:00 o'clock General Lee received a troubling note from Colonel Thomas Rosser of the 5th Virginia Cavalry, who was out reconnoitering the ground on the far right of the Confederate line in the area just west of Malvern Hill.[21] Rosser had spotted long columns of the Federal Army scrambling over that hill on their way toward the James. The Federals, it appeared, were escaping in both great confusion and haste, but escaping nevertheless. The great opportunity for Southern independence, like the sands running out of an hourglass, appeared to be disappearing through General Lee's fingers. Now it seemed the Federals were scrambling over Malvern Hill with no opposition at all. What of General Holmes? Why had there been no attack in that sector?

Lee had to go see for himself, to try and salvage something of the day. There was still time enough to strike a decisive blow if he could get someone, *anyone,* to follow an order. Just why he decided to go check personally on Holmes when Huger was just a few miles away, and the entire assault had been hanging on that officer's next move for hours, has never been explained. Alexander was equally perplexed: "It seems strange that Lee, though at no great distance on the next day (the 30th), should have still failed to see Huger, and either to bring him to the battle, which was waiting for his arrival, or to order it to proceed without him. But there is no intimation in the reports, of any communication; nor, in Huger's proceedings, of any consciousness that important action was waiting upon him."[22] Regardless, General Lee left the field at Glendale to Longstreet, and galloped off south toward Malvern Hill.

CHAPTER 11

A Battle of Axes

While Richmond initially reverberated with a sense of relief after McClellan's army had been driven from the very doorstep of the city, it would not be long before that relief had been tempered by a strong dose of reality. For what immediate comfort had been provided by the sudden absence of the Federal legions had been purchased in blood, and it would take only days before the cost of the city's deliverance began slowly to be tallied in the most painful and apparent way. Soon carts of the dead, wounded, and dying began slowly rumbling up Richmond's streets to unload their gruesome cargos.

In Northern cities like Philadelphia, New York, and Boston, the headlines in the papers had been read, the number of casualties vaguely digested, but in the end the war remained in those Northern climes a dreamlike conception in far off Virginia, something still perceived as a noble, perhaps even glorious, endeavor. In those cities the heat of the early summer did not carry on the breeze the cries of the wounded, nor the grim, disturbing odor of death as it did in Richmond. Indeed, in Richmond the sound of the guns only so many miles away could be heard plainly during the fighting of the Seven Days, often rattling doors and windows, a drumming reminder of the harm so many friends and loved ones daily faced. Battlefield medicine, historically a primitive art to begin with, had been at the outset of the Civil War simply overwhelmed by the sheer scope of the carnage, and it would never truly catch up. Richmond, situated more or less in the center of the cyclone, would almost overnight become a vast hospital and factory of burial.

Constance Harrison experienced this disturbing metamorphosis of her home and capital city first hand: "Ambulances, litters, carts, every vehicle that the city could produce, went and came with a ghastly burden; those who could walk limped painfully home, in some cases so black with gunpowder they passed unrecognized. Women with pallid faces flitted bare-headed through the streets searching for their dead or wounded. The churches were thrown open, many people visiting them for a sad communion — service or brief time of prayer; the lecture — rooms of various places of worship were crowded with ladies volunteering to sew, as fast as fingers could fly, the rough beds called for by the surgeons. Men too old or infirm to fight went on horseback or afoot to meet the returning ambulances, and in some cases served as escort to their own dying sons."[1]

Death, grim and conspicuous, had come now to haunt Richmond like a vulture, a reality that would not depart the city until the end of hostilities and the collapse of the Confederacy years later.

> Day by day we were called to our windows by the wailing dirge of a military band preceding a soldier's funeral. One could not number those sad pageants: the coffin crowned with cap and sword and gloves, the riderless horse following with empty boots fixed in the stirrups of an army saddle; such soldiers as could be spared from the front marching after with arms reversed and crape-enfolded banners; the passers-by standing with bare, bent heads. Funerals less honored outwardly were continually occurring. Then and thereafter the green hillsides of lovely Hollywood were frequently upturned to find resting-places for the heroic dead. So much taxed for time and for attendants were those who officiated that it was not unusual to perform the last rites for the departed at night. A solemn scene was that in the July moonlight, when, in the presence of the few who valued him most, we laid to rest one of my own nearest kinsmen.[2]

Days and nights, for Constance Harrison, were spent feeding soldiers and tending to the wounded, yet despite the heat and toil, in wartime Richmond wondrous joy could still be discovered in the most simple of pleasures. "From one scene of death and suffering to another we passed during those days of June. Under a withering heat that made the hours preceding dawn the only ones of the twenty-four endurable in point of temperature, and a shower-bath the only form of diversion we had time or thought to indulge in, to go out-of-doors was sometimes worse than remaining in our wards. But one night after several of us had been walking about town in a state of panting exhaustion, palm-leaf fans in hand, a friend persuaded us to ascend to the small platform on the summit of the Capitol, in search of fresher air. To reach it was like going through a vapor-bath, but an hour amid the cool breezes above the tree-tops of the square was a thing of joy unspeakable."[3]

Roughly nine miles south and east as the crow flies from where Constance Harrison had taken fresh air atop the capital building, Benjamin Huger was on the 30th of June still mired in doubt and confusion along the Charles City Road. It had taken him the entire morning and then some to advance his column but a single mile, then only to be stymied dead in his tracks by the sight of a forest of cut timber laid directly across his path.[4] For this he had no answer.

Huger met with his lead brigade commander, "Little" Billy Mahone, and together they surveyed the situation. Mahone, a graduate of the Virginia Military Institute in the class of 1847, had been at the war's inception the president of the Petersburg and Norfolk Railroad and was a man of intelligence and drive. Little Billy "was so short of stature and so frail that he seemed insignificant,"[5] but he also had a solid reputation as an engineer and in the spring of that year had been assigned the construction of the river battery at Drewry's Bluff overlooking the south bank of the James.[6] That work had been completed with such speed and expertise that Mahone's finished product was precisely what had stopped the Federal naval flotilla from advancing up river to Richmond in May with a withering fire that had pummeled the *Galena* and forced the remaining boats to retire. Mahone would one day rise high in the ranks of the Army of Northern Virginia and become known as a capable fighter, but today would hardly prove a feather in Little Billy's cap.

The situation facing the two generals was such that imagination, or at least at bit of innovation, was called for, but the solution they arrived at seems to this day somewhat absurd. The most important aspect of their mission at the time surely was speed, for Lee's entire offensive operation was hanging on their division advancing soon into battle down the Charles City Road. While the column's artillery and trains were obviously impeded by the sea of felled trees, those trees did not necessarily prohibit infantry from moving ahead.

In fairness to Mahone, his orders would have come of necessity directly through Huger, and if Benjamin Huger did not grasp Lee's overall mission for his column, then it is doubtful that Mahone would have on his own — it was not within the commanding general's nature or function to outline his plans to brigade commanders. What Lee actually imparted to Huger in terms of orders is not on record, thus we can only surmise that General Lee attempted, at least, to impress upon him the necessity of speed and striking power. Did General Huger understand that the entire operation rested on his opening performance? Maybe yes, maybe no. It is hard to say from the meager facts available and most certainly the column's humble performance as recorded that day. At any rate, if even the roughest outline of what was expected of him by General Lee was grasped by Benjamin Huger and, as a consequence, General Mahone, then the need to push forward rapidly, it seems, would have been at that moment of paramount consideration.

War, as in life in general, at times requires rapid improvisation. If, after all, Constance Harrison and the other good citizens of Richmond could suddenly, and with no prior training, mobilize the entire city to feed, clothe, nurse the wounded, and bury the dead, would it have been asking too much of General Huger to use a little imagination and initiative to move his column beyond some cut timbers? In trying situations such as these those who can think on their feet are often rewarded, while those who cannot often fail. This generally requires an open and flexible mind, unfortunately something historically frowned upon or even penalized by almost all military operations, from the Persians to the Prussians. War requires order, discipline, and a prompt — at times virtually unthinking — response to commands, but General Huger's dilemma on the Charles City Road required quick improvisation, not a rapid response to any sort of command, and something he appears to have been entirely unprepared for. Thus had Huger been entirely stumped, and in the throes of his confusion, he apparently turned to Little Billy for guidance.

In hindsight — which, of course, is always twenty-twenty — the most sensible course of action would have been to push forward a strong reconnaissance directly down the Charles City Road toward Glendale. The purpose of this force would have been fourfold. First, the reconnaissance could have located and driven off the Federal pioneers who were busy cutting timber in front of the Confederate column, and thus endlessly exacerbating the Rebels' dilemma. In that sense the bleeding could at least have been stopped and a solution fashioned for the problem as it existed, and not a problem with no end in sight. Secondly, the reconnaissance could have scouted, and perhaps even lightly cleared, simple paths along the side of the road or through the woods nearby in order for Confederate infantry to pass that portion of the roadway that had been compromised, while reforming on the road south of the impediment where it still remained clear. Thirdly, this force could have pushed on toward Glendale to actually feel out the Federal position on Huger's front while establishing a perimeter in advance of the column. Finally, word could have easily been sent via courier from this advanced position to Longstreet and Lee, advising them both of Huger's problem and anticipated time of arrival. Lee then could have reconsidered his options.

While this reconnaissance was taking place, efforts could have begun to clear the timbers from in front of the column. To do this it seems that the most obvious design would have been to un-hitch numerous teams of artillery horses, and use those teams in an efficient pattern — which any sensible farmer could have prefigured — to drag the logs from at least one side of the road to the other, while at least some of the infantry began working its way through the woods toward Glendale. The horses were already in harness, and with the application of simple chains or ropes, could have been outfitted quickly to do the job (teams of infantry, of course, could also have been organized to clear the road, but this would have been exhausting work, and far less efficient than teams of horses). If the horses could pull limbers and guns, why not timbers? This, perhaps, may not have been the most ideal solution, but it would have been a sensible response employing the equipment at hand, and a solution far better than what the two generals eventually agreed upon.

If the Federal pioneers had been run off from the road as suggested by a strong reconnaissance, and the original obstruction cleared with teams of horses, it is entirely feasible that Huger could have had infantry in front of Glendale by mid-afternoon, and the road cleared shortly thereafter. With that the remainder of his infantry, and all his artillery, could have been pushed rapidly toward the front, which would by then have been established and scouted by his other advanced units. Not only that, but General Lee would have been made aware of the situation, and thus capable of sensibly reevaluating his plans. In this scenario, Lee would no doubt have opted to remain with the plan as originally outlined, only delayed now by time and events.

What of this was accomplished or even contemplated by General Huger? None of it! Huger, apparently befuddled beyond reason, appears to have demurred to Little Billy, and Mahone, being an engineer — and perhaps not understanding General Lee's need for rapid advance — decided to cut an entirely new road parallel to the one now obstructed. Mahone, a railroad executive, no doubt had an abundance of experience cutting tracts for new railbeds through woods, but probably *none* at all in clearing them. His decision, therefore, while appearing odd from the outside looking in, was not especially foolish, but it was hardly practical in terms of accomplishing the division's mission.

The greater problem with this decision, moreover, was that the Confederates lacked the necessary tools to rapidly accomplish the task, and thus the effort slowly devolved into a "battle of axes" as it has been termed ever since. In essence, with an abundance of tools and manpower, the Federal pioneers, unhindered in their efforts by Confederate sharpshooters or infantry, in all probability were able to fell two trees that afternoon for every one felled and cleared by the Confederates. Porter Alexander offers this exasperated critique: "It seems incredible that this division, within four miles of Lee, could have been allowed to spend the whole day in a mere contest of axemen, wherein the Federals, with the most axes, had only to cut *down*, and the Confederates, with the fewest, to cut *up* and remove. The result could scarcely have been doubtful."[7]

Slocum's artillery north of the Charles City Road, in action against Benjamin Huger's column as depicted by John R. Chapin (Library of Congress).

Why General Huger failed to notify Lee of the precise nature of his predicament remains unclear. Why Lee did not demand an explanation remains even more curious. General Huger eventually filed a report of the troubles he encountered that afternoon, and his report seems utterly devoid of even the slightest grasp of the fact that any sort of urgency had been required that day on his part. "Gen Mahone found it best to cut a road around the obstruction [felled trees]. For such work we were deficient in tools. The column was delayed while the work was going on, and it was evening before we got through and drove off the workmen who were still cutting down other trees. As we advanced through the woods and came to an open field on high ground (P. Williams on map), a powerful battery of rifled guns opened on us."[8]

Eventually, as written, General Huger was able to move his column approximately one mile farther down the road by late afternoon, to a position — as he puts it, near the Williams farm — where he advanced some guns and tested a Federal battery opposite. These Federal guns were, in fact, a number of batteries unlimbered by Slocum on Kearny's far right flank, and they easily out-dueled Huger's meager deployment late in the day. General Huger goes on then to conclude his report with the following, less than inspirational, observations: "I withdrew most of our guns, and only kept up a moderate fire. On our left the White Oak Swamp approached very near. The right appeared to be good ground, and I determined to turn the battery by moving a column of infantry to my right. It was now dark."[9]

Benjamin Huger accomplished absolutely nothing that entire day. In the great assault to gain Southern independence, his infantry fired not a shot, and his artillery achieved almost as little. "It was now dark," as Huger put it, a statement that was in reality, not only a fair description of the conclusion of his operational day, but an apt assessment of the future prospects of his military career.

CHAPTER 12

For the Nonce Below
Their Wanted Tension

Unknown to General Lee, but of utmost significance, General Huger, by means of sheer inaction, had removed his entire command, some 9,000 infantry and artillery, from the force that was to strike the Federals at Glendale that day. This represented a decrease in overall striking power of almost one-quarter, and a reduction that would eventually prove critical for Southern success. Moreover, Huger's column, had it continued directly down the Charles City Road as planned, would have come in almost directly on the gap between Slocum and Kearny's divisions and, if driven hard, had the potential of breaking through and wrecking the Federal defense in that northern sector. But it was not to be. Thus Lee continued his planning throughout the afternoon hours as if Huger's pieces were still on the board, when in fact they had been swallowed whole by sheer incompetence.

As if penning the introduction for Benjamin Huger's book of inertia, Stonewall Jackson continued on that afternoon at the White Oak Bridge as if nothing at all had had been expected of the Valley Army. The Stonewall who had just that morning stomped his boot on the dirt etching of McClellan's army with such emotion seemed to have evaporated like a phantom during the heat of the day. Nothing beyond a desultory and ceaseless cannonading had been attempted, and that of questionable value.

Alexander, considered by many the premier artilleryman in the Army of Northern Virginia by war's end, was less than impressed: "The cannonade, which was kept up during all the rest of the day, was not only a delusion, but a useless burning both of daylight and ammunition, for it was all random fire. The Federal and Confederate artillery could not see each other at all. They could scarcely even see the high-floating smoke clouds of each other's guns. They fired by sound, at a distance of three-quarters of a mile, across a tall dense wood, until they exhausted their ammunition.... The noise was terrific, and some firing was kept up until nine o'clock at night, but the casualties on each side were naturally but trifling."[1]

Jackson had received word directly from Colonel Munford that a perfectly usable cow path over the creek a mere quarter mile farther down from the bridge had been discovered during the course of their ill-fated reconnaissance into the teeth of the Federal position. The meaning of this was clear. Infantry could advance across the swamp in large numbers and, once the scope of the Federal position had been determined, attempt a turning movement. What did Stonewall do with this information? Nothing! Indeed, he made no attempt whatsoever to follow up and seems to have literally ignored Munford's report.

Munford, writing years later, recalled the moment: "Thirty-nine years is too long a time to attempt to say what I wrote him [Jackson], but I know that I thought, all the time, that he could have crossed his infantry where we recrossed. I had seen his infantry cross far worse places, and I expected that he would attempt it. We remained near where we recrossed all day, with a vidette on the other side of the swamp. He put his sharp-shooters in on the right of the ford, and made no attempt to cross where we recrossed. Why, I never understood."[2]

While Stonewall Jackson remained inert, his brother-in-law, Daniel Harvey Hill, aware of the critical nature of the situation, took it upon himself to try and press the matter. "Without asking orders, he threw his skirmishers into the fringe of the swamp West of the crossing, pushed some of them across the stream and kept them there. By threats and scoldings, he got a fatigue party forward to the site of the broken bridge."[3] But the men would not work under constant shellfire, and Jackson would seemingly do nothing to push the effort. Hill became frustrated. "Our cavalry returned by the lower ford, and pronounced it perfectly practicable for infantry. But Jackson did not advance. Why was this? It was the critical day for both commanders, but especially for McClellan."[4]

At around 2:30 that afternoon, Rans Wright emerged from the White Oak Swamp having completed the mission ordered by General Huger the night before, to scour the swamp fords in search of Kearny's division, or any other Federal troops lurking out there in the darkness and undergrowth on Huger's left flank. Wright had marched his brigade the length of the swamp, had found hundreds of Federal stragglers and many deserted camps, but no Union forces in strength. He reported the facts to Jackson and asked for orders. Jackson had none.[5] In fact, he simply told Wright to return from whence he had come, and to try and rejoin Huger's division. The fact that Wright had marched across the swamp and had located crossing points within easy marching distance of Jackson's troops was of no interest to Stonewall. But why should he have been interested? Old Jack had already ignored the report of his own cavalry officer that a serviceable cow path was open and available only a quarter mile away. That considered, why should the availability of a ford farther away have turned his head?

It is apparent that by this point in the afternoon, Stonewall Jackson either would not, or could not, force himself to action. As most senior officers in Lee's army readily understood, this was the critical hour, yet Jackson, with multiple opportunities dancing before him, appeared incapable of any movement at all. If he had had any intention of crossing White Oak Swamp in force, would he have sent Wright — a full, fresh brigade of infantry — back to Huger? No, the Stonewall Jackson of the Valley would have kept Wright at hand and used those troops to his advantage. But then that Jackson would have had a strong reconnaissance across Munford's cow path at the first mention, this followed in turn by half the Valley Army.

Make no mistake about the opportunity that was slipping away. Across from Jackson at White Oak Swamp was the Federal force under William Franklin, and Franklin understood perfectly well the ugly predicament he was in. Here is what he had to say: "Jackson seems to have been ignorant of what Gen. Lee expected of him, and badly informed about Brackett's Ford. When he found how strenuous was our defence at the bridge, he should have turned his attention to Brackett's Ford, also. A force could have been as quietly gathered there as at the bridge; a strong infantry movement at the ford would have easily overrun our small force there, placing our right at Glendale, held by Slocum's division, in great jeopardy, and turning our force at the bridge by getting between it and Glendale. In fact, it is likely that we should have been defeated that day, had Gen. Jackson done what his reputation seems to have made it imperative he should have done."[6]

Franklin's statement is compelling, but wrong in one important detail. Jackson was not "badly informed" regarding Brackett's Ford. In fact, he knew nothing of it, this due to the fact that it had not been reconnoitered. Old Jack did not know about Brackett's Ford simply because he did not care to know about that ford, or any other crossing point, for that matter.

An attack directly across the White Oak Bridge was entirely unnecessary. The opportunities simply abounded for Confederate success that afternoon at White Oak Swamp, but Jackson seems to have been either entirely disinterested or too mentally exhausted to think them through. Alexander continues the drama: "Wright started back, and at one and a half miles came to Brackett's Ford, a well-known road, across which a large part of the Federal forces had crossed during the night, and which they had then obstructed by cutting down trees and destroying a small bridge. Pushing two companies of skirmishers through the swamp, Wright captured the enemy's picket force on the south side, but saw, beyond the picket, a force of the enemy with artillery too strong for his brigade; so he withdrew."[7] But Jackson had not been interested enough in Wright's intelligence to send back a staff officer to report back to him any interesting possibilities, or supply reinforcements, should Wright require them.[8]

The strongly posted force Wright had stumbled across on the south side of the swamp was actually Slocum's division (as discussed in Franklin's narration above), posted north of the Charles City Road, and in essence the extreme right flank of the Federal Glendale defense. Wright could do nothing with his one brigade against an entire division consisting of three brigades, and sensibly moved off, but Jackson had four full divisions under his command, fourteen brigades (fifteen, if he had held on to Wright's), more than 25,000 men. Here, then, is one — and just *one*— of the opportunities Porter Alexander lamented so many years later when he wrote that "when one thinks of the great chances in General Lee's grasp that one summer afternoon, it is enough to make one cry to go over the story how they were all lost. And to think too that our *Stonewall Jackson* lost them."[9]

Opportunities abounded for Stonewall Jackson and the Confederacy that afternoon, any one of which could have ended the war in a matter of hours, but the opportunity described by Franklin at Brackett's Ford was so remarkable that it simply requires further elaboration. To begin with, Rans Wright with a few companies of infantry had forced the ford and overwhelmed the meager Federal picket located there, thus the task of taking and securing the ford for a large scale movement of Confederate infantry had already been accomplished. The ford itself was only a little over a mile from Jackson's location at the bridge, a simple stroll in the park for Stonewall's famous foot cavalry. Yes, it would have taken Old Jack some few hours to move most of his force to that location, then get them into proper alignment to overwhelm Slocum, but it was only 2:30 in the afternoon when Wright had made his initial report, thus there was still ample time to complete the movement, and certainly enough daylight.

Three features stand out regarding the Brackett's Ford crossing. First, and most significantly, any force crossing at that location would have emerged immediately on the extreme right (and exposed) flank of the Federal Glendale defense. Secondly, there were roads leading down to the ford from behind Jackson's position at White Oak Bridge which would have made the assembly there fast and simple. Finally, and as William Franklin pointed out, a large force could have been assembled in the cover near the ford without being

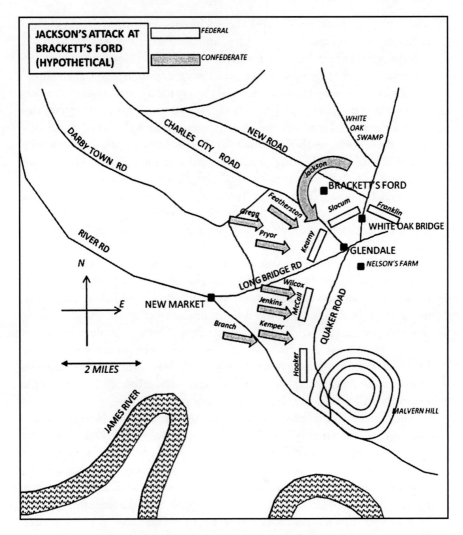

Map — Jackson's Hypothetical Assault at Brackett's Ford

observed. These three ingredients simply cried out for action, and had Jackson been aware enough to have taken advantage of them, the result could not possibly have been in question — the Federal defenders at Glendale would have been routed from the field! Why?

Leaving a small body of troops behind at White Oak Swamp to screen his movement and hold Franklin in place (artillery alone could have sufficed), Stonewall could have easily shifted the bulk of his force to Brackett's Ford undetected within a few hours and had it arrayed for assault. Jackson would have had a full fourteen brigades (fifteen had he retained Wright) going in at full throttle against Slocum's three, and Slocum's flank was in the air. It is inconceivable that Jackson, even half asleep, would not have routed any defender from the field with such an overt advantage in manpower. At Chancellorsville, as a comparison — where Jackson made his most famous flanking movement, providing Lee with what many argue was his most masterful victory of the war — Stonewall had more troops at his disposal, but assaulted a full Federal corps, with the remainder of the Army of the Potomac fully arrayed behind it. Still, that assault resulted in pandemonium and sudden rout, and had night not fallen on the fleeing Federals, the Army of the Potomac might well have been cut off from any avenue of retreat. That was, after all, exactly what Jackson was attempting to divine — the roads to the U.S. Ford — when he was mistakenly cut down by his own troops in the darkness.

At Glendale the rout would have been far more lopsided. Unlike at Chancellorsville, the force behind Slocum consisted of only three divisions, all disconnected, and all facing west. Jackson's force would have come down on their exposed right flank like a lightning bolt out of the blue, sweeping Slocum's frantic refugees before it. Regardless of what capable officers men like Kearny, Meade, and Hooker were, none would have been able to stand up to such an onslaught. There would have been precious little time to change front and face up to the Confederate avalanche, and there is little doubt that all would have been swept away.

Moreover, this maneuver would have put Jackson immediately in Franklin's rear, thus cutting off the Federal rear guard at White Oak Swamp by maneuver alone. Under the circumstances, Franklin would have had no option at that point — virtually surrounded on enemy ground, and with no hope of reinforcement — but to surrender his command. Had Longstreet then, on the sound of Jackson's guns (and regardless of the fumbling Huger), launched his frontal assault at Glendale, the rout would have been accelerated by a factor of two. The Federal blocking force (Slocum, Kearny, McCall, and Hooker) would have been swept aside with ease, and the meager portion of the Army of the Potomac that had managed to race to what was conceived a safe haven on the James eventually surrounded and either destroyed or forced to capitulate. The Army of the Potomac would have ceased to exist.

Here now, we can get at least a sense of what General Lee had in mind that day at Glendale, and this was only *one* potential out of many, although it was surely the best. *This* is the reason Alexander years later would still insist, "But never, before or after, did the fates put such a prize within our reach."[10]

This, surely, was the greatest opportunity for victory and independence the Confederacy would ever have. Every conceivable element was in their favor — Jackson, their most proven field commander with the largest contingent of troops only a mile from his jumping-off point with open roads to take him there; a passable ford already secured; good cover to conceal his deployment, and an unsuspecting foe one-fifth his size offering an uncovered flank for the taking.

Had General Huger, by means of some magical potion, been able to complete his assignment, or just deployed infantry along the Charles City Road at Glendale, the rout would have been even that much more catastrophic. Turning to face Huger, Slocum and Kearny would have been utterly blindsided by Jackson's overwhelming assault, blown away like leaves before a cold winter wind.

This conception is hardly a new or theoretical invention. The remarkable opportunity at Brackett's Ford was sitting literally right in front of Jackson's *nose*, and it is impossible to believe that on any other occasion he would have failed to both find and force it. Franklin certainly understood it, and a simple reconnaissance would have painted the picture for Old Jack in a heartbeat. The Stonewall Jackson of Shenandoah Valley fame would have surely spared no effort to take advantage of such an incredible opportunity. But there had been no reconnaissance simply because there had been no effort, as Alexander ruefully acknowledges: "No reconnaissance had been made for other crossings, even of Brackett's, over which much of the Federal force had passed."[11] Thus this, the most advantageous opportunity of all, would not merely be squandered. It would never even be considered.

Still, opportunities were aplenty. What of the other swamp crossings that had been discovered and reported to Jackson? Was not there potential there? These too offered Stonewall wonderful possibilities to advance infantry across the swamp and strike a concealed blow. While these possibilities may not have been as favorable as the circumstances at Brackett's Ford — few *could* have been! — various schemes still could have been utilized to fashion an overwhelming Confederate success that day.

The crossing Munford discovered, for instance, was also reported as unguarded and led to Franklin's unprotected flank. Thus Franklin could have possibly been turned by several brigades, then swept away by Jackson's others, but even if that had not worked to perfection, Stonewall could surely at least have forced Franklin's command into serious combat, thus causing the Federal rear guard to stay put above White Oak Swamp in a fight for its life. But this, too, was apparently not a consideration.

What, perhaps, had gotten into Stonewall Jackson that afternoon to make him so resistant to action? Douglas Southall Freeman, writing of Lee's army, believed he had the answer: "Incredibly, almost mysteriously, and for the first time in his martial career, he quit. His initiative died almost in the moment of his return from the south side of the swamp. The alert, vigorous Jackson of the early morning grew weary, taciturn and drowsy. Marshy approaches, destruction of the bridge, and the fire from the new Federal position made a crossing impossible. This he concluded and then, exhausted, went to sleep under a tree."[12]

Alexander, obviously unsympathetic to Jackson's actions during the entire Seven Days, voiced a slightly different point of view: "His failure is not so much a military as a psychological phenomenon. He did not try and fail. He simply made no effort....[13] Apparently, he was satisfied to remain where he was and to do only what he was doing — nothing."[14]

Clearly, Stonewall Jackson at this point appeared to be in a downward physical spiral. Major Dabney, writing years later, offered his own unique diagnosis of Jackson's seemingly odd malady: "The labor of the previous days, the sleeplessness, the wear of gigantic cares, with the drenching of the comfortless night, had sunk the elasticity of his will and the quickness of his invention for the nonce below their wonted tension."[15]

Daniel Harvey Hill, desperate to accomplish at least something of value that afternoon, urged General Huger to engage on Jackson's right, but this proved entirely futile. "Huger, on the Charles City road, came upon Franklin's left flank, but made no attack. I sent my engineer W.F. Lee, to him through the swamp, to ask whether he could not engage Franklin. He replied that the road was obstructed by fallen timber. So there were five divisions within sound of the firing, and within supporting distance, but not one of them moved."[16]

The greatest opportunity the Confederacy would ever enjoy — the potential attack across Brackett's Ford — would slip away into the shadows of late afternoon, much of it due to the fact that, as the good major points out, Stonewall Jackson's elasticity of will and quickness of action had slipped, no doubt, for the nonce below their wanted tension. As Harvey Hill points out, five full divisions of Confederate infantry would simply sit on their arms.

History is often stingy with second chances for those who fumble away their first, but on this day Old Jack would defy the odds, and be given chance after chance to make good on his early morning promise to crush McClellan's army under the heel of his boot. His junior officers would remain game to the task. The question was would Stonewall Jackson ever rise to the occasion?

CHAPTER 13

Riot on the River Road

It would seem that by the grinding mathematics of statistical probability alone, something should have gone right for General Robert E. Lee on the afternoon of June 30, but that was not to be the case. Of the four columns giving chase to McClellan's army and supposed to engage at various points that day, by 3 o'clock not one of the four had achieved anything of substance, and two had hardly moved at all. While Lee himself had held Longstreet in check until the sound of Huger's guns could be heard, the other three had — for varied and indefensible reasons — done nothing. Jackson appeared benumbed and beyond willful progress, Huger was checked by a band of axe wielding Federal pioneers, and General Holmes — like Huger and Magruder before him — for some inexplicable reason awaited attack on ground overlooking the River Road.

To this day some confusion seems to surround the orders Holmes actually received from Lee, and thus as a matter of course the role his column was to play in the day's advance. For instance, Douglas Southall Freeman states that "Gen. T.H. Holmes was to proceed down the New Market road from Cornelius Creek and to engage the enemy where found. The length of his march obviously was not computable, but it probably would be about nine miles with no material obstruction."[1] This seems straightforward, and reasonably aggressive, as might be expected in the four pronged convergence Lee seemed to have in mind. Daniel Harvey Hill, on the other hand, insists that "Holmes was to take possession of Malvern Hill"[2] and not simply probe forward and engage targets of opportunity, as Freeman suggests.

Alexander is somewhat ambivalent on the subject, stating that "Holmes division, under the excellent but super annuated & deaf old general of that name, was sent down the river road towards Malvern Hill, a magnificent amphitheatrical position commanding all the principal roads, & over which the enemy would have to pass.... Holmes might easily have taken & occupied this hill, but his troops were all green, & they were a good deal demoralized

113

by some shelling of the woods by Federal gunboats in the James & he remained quiet."[3] Historian Stephen Sears, to complicate matters more thoroughly, asserts, "At the farthest extreme, moving toward the head of the Federal columns by way of the River Road, was the division of Theophilus Holmes, 7,200 men of all arms and six batteries of artillery. These were new troops, and Lee originally intended them simply to act as a reserve on his right flank and perhaps to interrupt and damage the Federal supply trains if opportunity arose."[4]

Which of these interpretations is correct? Oddly, they vary from remaining behind in reserve (essentially doing nothing), to moving forward somewhat aggressively, to marching hard and taking Malvern Hill as a direct objective.

Holmes' command was the smallest by far of the four converging columns, and with only 6,000 to 7,000 (estimates vary) infantry, he could not have taken on a large element of the Federal Army. But if Malvern Hill were unoccupied, or at least nearly so, had Holmes moved rapidly on the morning of the 30th, he in all probability could have taken Malvern Hill, and with six batteries of artillery, quite possibly brought the head of the Federal retreat to a confused, frantic halt.

Six batteries of guns and 6,000 infantry would not have been able to snatch the summit of Malvern Hill from even a division or two of stubborn Federal infantry, but early that morning no Federal infantry had as yet arrived. According to reports, John Fitz Porter would not arrive at the head of the Federal V Corps until about 9:00 A.M.,[5] thus giving Holmes ample early morning hours to have worked with, had he so desired. So it is entirely conceivable that Holmes *could* have taken Malvern Hill had he moved with dispatch, and bolstering this interpretation, at least, are Alexander's thoughts on the subject. As has been written, Alexander had been up in the *Gazelle* for a trip down the James River overnight, then again early in the morning. So if anyone had a good idea as to the situation at Malvern Hill in the early hours of the 30th, it would surely have been Alexander, and, again, he states emphatically that Holmes "might easily have taken & occupied this hill." With dispatch, that is.

Did General Holmes move with dispatch? No. In fact, he hardly moved at all. That morning he marched from New Market, where he was reported to have gone into bivouac overnight, east down the River Road to New Market Heights, a ridgeline not far from the river that commanded the local roads and lowlands, and a distance of not more than a mile from where he'd broken camp that morning. "These constituted a position of great natural strength and of strategic value. From New Market Heights a Federal column advancing on Richmond, nine miles to the West, could be hurled back easily. Moreover, directly East of the Heights, the highway forked. The New Market Road or River Road continued to parallel the James, but the diverging Long Bridge road turned left and put Holmes within easy supporting distance of Longstreet."[6]

Does this appear to be an officer moving "hell-bent-for-leather" to secure an important objective? Hardly! Interestingly, the record indicates that Holmes reported to Lee that he was in position at New Market (Heights) at 10:00 A.M. on the 30th.[7] Now, if Holmes knew that he was expected to move aggressively and seize Malvern Hill, would he have simply gone into position three miles from the objective, then informed the commanding general that he had marched a mere mile and not have expected some sort of immediate, perhaps even harsh, rebuke? It is very doubtful. Even more interesting, there seems to be no indication whatsoever that General Lee was upset at the reception of this information.

So was Holmes simply a reserve on the far right, or an active player who, like Huger and Jackson had come up painfully short of his intended mark? It may never be known for sure. As previously discussed, Lee preferred, as commanding general, to bring all the disparate elements of battle together, then leave the actual fighting to his lieutenants, presuming, of course, that they were fully aware of his plans and objectives.

To accomplish this task, General Lee generally provided his officers with orders that were discretionary in nature, that is, specific in terms of their objectives, but general in terms of how those objectives were to be achieved. This was intellectually commensurate with Lee's conception of his role but would prove operationally deficient. Why?

This system required officers of a very high caliber, not only capable of understanding a wide range of variables, but officers who could negotiate those variable — whatever they might be — to a successful conclusion. This operational mode provided Lee's officers with a great deal of latitude, and for subordinates who understood the general scheme and what was expected of them within that framework (as Jackson would later prove to be) this worked fine. But many officers, used only to rigid, specific instructions, could not cope with the many "what ifs" discretionary orders naturally entailed. They became overwhelmed in Lee's system of command, and failed, often dramatically.

A number of factors, taken as a whole, suggest that this was the sort of order Lee gave Holmes for his responsibilities on the 30th. To begin with, Holmes was an old school officer, now 57 years old, and thus Lee, despite his unfamiliarity with him, may have given Holmes the sort of deferential treatment due his age and rank, but not necessarily his abilities. Lee would have gone over the situation as he conceived it, then given Holmes a string of potential "what ifs," from storming Malvern Hill if opportune, to simply sitting back in reserve if, perhaps, the other columns had achieved their goals rapidly. This makes sense from Lee's perspective, and provides an answer as to why there remain so many varied opinions as to what Holmes was supposed to accomplish that day — they were all potential roles for General Holmes but all also dependent upon circumstances.

Thus Lee's command structure required men who could understand and fulfill his tactical schemes, in short, lieutenant officers who thought and acted as he did, and Theophilus Holmes, "a stiff and deaf representative of the Old Army,"[8] certainly does not appear, when viewed through the narrow aperture of time, to be one of those men. Holmes had handled the administrative duties of a department head in North Carolina and, "as far as the records show, he did creditably in reorganizing the defenses of his State, though he may not have been aggressive."[9] Lee first extended Holmes' department jurisdiction to the south bank of the James River, then ordered him north with his force as McClellan's threat to Richmond grew more ominous.

A staff officer who could hardly hear, Holmes may not have understood what Lee truly wanted of him at all, and Lee may have been too decent to press the matter. The facts do not prove this, but they tend to confirm it. From this perspective, then, Holmes moved his force to New Market Heights, and waited in accordance with the one aspect of his orders that appealed to him, while Lee, receiving a message of that column's location at 10:00 A.M., perhaps presumed Holmes to be on the move. Thus Holmes had no problem sending the message, and Lee, although perhaps disappointed with the overall progress, did not respond negatively to its reception. The fact that Alexander was on Lee's staff and presumed that Holmes could have, should have, and probably had been ordered to take Malvern Hill, tends to support this interpretation. Moreover, Holmes — like Magruder and Huger — would be quietly reassigned by Lee to other duties after the Seven Days fighting, a sure sign that he had been displeased by Holmes' performance. Lee was not punitive by nature, and always seemed to have aspired to fairness with his officers. Why would he have reassigned Holmes if he had simply been obeying orders? There must have been more to it than that.

Holmes had cavalry at his command and could easily have sent out a reconnaissance party to scour the roads ahead and the situation near Malvern Hill on the 30th. But he made no attempt to do so, or to reconnoiter the situation on his front, so it is safe to conclude that he had no intention other than to hunker down and await further instructions.

Be that as it may, it shines a light once more on the ineffectiveness of General Lee's approach to overall command at that point in his career. Where was Holmes and what was he up to? For most of June 30, the most critical day of maneuver for the Confederate Army, Lee did not know. He let events play out in the hands of his lieutenants, and those lieutenants consistently let him down.

For the better part of the day Theophilus Holmes sat at New Market Heights and did nothing. He requested no orders, and appears to have received none. Then suddenly around 4:00 P.M. an engineering officer arrived at his headquarters and reported the Yankees escaping across Malvern Hill, their enormous train of wagons and artillery potentially vulnerable to artillery fire from a heavily wooded area that extended on both sides of the River Road. Holmes, in no apparent hurry to comply, directed Colonel James Deshler, his chief of artillery, to take three sections of two rifled guns — six pieces in all — forward and commence the bombardment.[10]

Here again, the fact that Holmes readily agreed to this deployment with no confirmation from Lee, suggests yet again the fact that his column was not simply being held in ready reserve, and that a move to strike the Federal retreat at Malvern Hill was well within the scope of his orders, as Holmes already understood them. If true, why had he done nothing at all for the entire day but sit atop New Market Heights facing east. Holmes had made no effort whatsoever to divine the situation at Malvern Hill, or anywhere else, for that matter, and this certainly suggests an officer either utterly devoid of imagination and vigor, or one swimming in waters suddenly far beyond his depth. Or perhaps both.

General Holmes' reaction — to send forward six rifled guns — was in itself a trifling response when considering the critical issues confronting Confederate arms that day. He had almost thirty pieces available, and while these may not all have been of the same quality, surely something more substantial could have been cobbled together if a severe disruption of the Federal withdrawal was in fact what he actually had in mind. As Alexander points out, "No target is more attractive to an artillerist than his enemy's wagon train,"[11] because it is long, slow, and prone to pandemonium once the shells begin to find their range.

Was General Holmes holding back due to fear of a Federal thrust down the River Road toward Richmond and, if so, how could such a conclusion be justified when he had made no attempt to reconnoiter the ground in his front and uncover the facts? The sad truth is, Theophilus Holmes appears to have had no idea what he was doing on the afternoon of the 30th, nor what the situation was anywhere along his front, thus his actions seem entirely consistent with an officer determined to *avoid* action with the enemy, and not seek it, as was expected.

It was about this time poor Major Brent — who had been dealing with General Magruder's odd confusion for days now — appeared on a mission at Holmes' headquarters with a message for the general. Magruder had for some reason been ordered by Longstreet (a situation to be explored in the next chapter in some detail) to march in support of Holmes, and Brent asked politely if the general had any suggestions in terms of the proper placement of Magruder's division.

Holmes had none.

Brent then inquired if Homes might "inform him where the enemy was and in what probable strength?"[12]

"No," was the tart reply.

Brent continued politely, and inquired one last time if Holmes had any message for General Magruder?

"No," again, was all General Holmes could manage.

Major Brent had been virtually stunned by the performance, and he would not forget it soon. Years later he could still recall it distinctly. "The impression made upon me was that General Holmes found in some way a cause of resentment at receiving a message from General Magruder. His bearing was the most singular I have ever seen, and was marked by the absence of even a simulation of ordinary courtesy."[13]

Holmes had no reason to be upset with either Magruder or the unfortunate Major Brent, and he certainly had no cause to be rude with a member of another officer's staff. Most likely he was simply upset with being asked a basic military question by a junior officer — "where the enemy was and in what probable strength?" — for which he had no answer. And General Holmes had no answer because he had done nothing all day to try and discern the answer to this, one of the most basic of all military questions. Rudeness is simply a form of ignorance, and ignorance is a charge Theophilus Holmes would have had to have pled guilty to that June 30. He had done nothing, so he knew nothing. It was as simple as that.

At any rate, General Holmes started down the River Road, artillery in trail, but then decided to have a look forward himself in case the guns needed more in the way of infantry support than he had allotted. On the road west of Malvern Hill he ran into General Lee, who had ridden south from Glendale to reconnoiter the area, and determine the condition of the Federal retreat. By all means, Lee told Holmes, bring up his guns and his entire division. Then Lee turned and rode off toward Glendale.

Holmes brought up his six rifled pieces and had them placed in the woods, but the dust cloud kicked up by his entire division hurrying to their support caught the eye of the Federal gunners waiting on Malvern Hill. The only open avenue of approach to Malvern Hill at that time was the River Road, and the Yankee defenders had prepared their position accordingly. First one shell cracked over the marching Confederates, then suddenly a shower of shells began to rain down like a storm of hail. The shells came from not only the Federal artillery ranked hub to hub on Malvern Hill, some thirty rifled pieces, but also from the gunboats lying just offshore in the James.

The massive naval shells crashed through the trees and exploded overhead with thunderous concussions. The Federal gunboats "opened fire on them, throwing those awe-inspiring shells familiarly called by our men 'lampposts,' on account of their size and appearance. Their explosion was very much like that of a small volcano, and had a very demoralizing effect upon new troops, one of whom expressed the general sentiment saying: 'The Yankees throwed them lamp-posts about too careless like.' The roaring, howling gun-boat shells were usually harmless to flesh, blood, and bones, but they had a wonderful effect upon the nervous system."[14]

General Holmes had stopped to go inside a nearby home to conduct some business when the shells began to fall and burst all around, and was seemingly unaware — due to his deafness — of the cacophony overhead. The cavalry panicked, stampeding their mounts into a nearby fence, and crushing infantrymen crouched along the rails. Several infantry regiments broke and ran, heightening the panic. The advance rapidly devolved into a riot. A reserve battery of guns got cut off. The panicked gunners cut the traces, grabbed their horses, and left "two guns and three caissons"[15] behind, never having fired a shot. Horses were falling, men screaming, shells cracking overhead with thunderous explosions, or cutting angry swaths through the trees. In the midst of all this, and adding a final, somewhat comical flourish to the riot on the River Road, General Holmes stepped outside the small home, "stopped abruptly, and cupped his ear suspiciously. 'I thought,' said he, 'I heard firing.'"[16]

Colonel Deshler opened against the Yankee guns on Malvern Hill, but only received a mighty salvo in return for his efforts. Entirely outgunned, and receiving counterbattery fire from two directions, he nonetheless dueled valiantly if vainly until darkness descended upon the field. Deshler then removed what remained of his battered pieces, and returned with the infantry to New Market Heights, the point from which the madness had emanated in the first place.

Theophilus Holmes was done for the day. Three men lay dead, some fifty wounded,[17] and absolutely nothing beyond folly had been accomplished.

CHAPTER 14

Misfortune's Plaything

While Theophilus Holmes sat his division atop New Market Heights to no practical purpose, as Benjamin Huger got nowhere at all cutting a new road to Glendale with what few axes his troops could locate, and then as Old Jack curled up under a tree and went to sleep at White Oak Bridge, Prince John Magruder had once again been put into motion. Prince John, who had slept but a pitiful few hours over the past few days, would today find himself fatigued and perplexed all that much more, marched in meaningless circles as if he and his exhausted command had, by means of some sorcerer's prank, been reduced to little more than misfortune's own plaything.

Ordered by General Lee from Savage Station that morning to make the roundabout march to Timberlake's Store in rear of the Glendale front, Magruder had already experienced nothing but confusion, error, and delay all morning due to a critical lack of knowledgeable guides.[1] After a trek of some seven to eight hours through the heat and dust, he had finally managed to bring his division stumbling up to its appointed destination between 1:00 and 2:00 that afternoon,[2] exhausted, but at least in position to support the effort at the crossroads, should that support be needed. Unfortunately, this would prove the high mark of Prince John's day as, from that point forward, things would go rapidly downhill. In a day of confused officers and confused orders, Prince John's long day's journey into darkness would prove the most confusing of all.

Halted to allow the rear of Hill's division to pass on the Darbytown Road, Magruder received a note from General Lee inquiring of his progress[3] (just why Lee would pursue Magruder's status while ignoring Huger and Jackson is one of the enduring mysteries of this engagement). Lee seemed to have presumed that Prince John was still on the march, and also that Magruder's division was well east of its actual location, and this misconception would apparently play into Lee's tactical thinking later. At around 4:30 that afternoon, and in Lee's absence, Longstreet ordered Magruder south in

120

support of Holmes along the River Road, and this is where the story begins to get interesting.

To begin with, it is not entirely clear whether the order for Magruder to move to Holmes' support had been conceived by Longstreet alone (who was then in command of the field at Glendale in Lee's absence), Longstreet in consultation with Lee, or Longstreet at Lee's direction,[4] but one way or another, the attempted redeployment of Magruder's division would have a profound effect on events later that day. Lee was at this time off on his mission to reconnoiter the Federal retreat over Malvern Hill and would not run into Holmes along the River road until well after 4:00 P.M. The order issued for Magruder to move south seems not to have been for that division to support and bolster Holmes in an attack, but rather to cover Longstreet's own right flank. "This order, it appears, was not intended by its author to strengthen Holmes for attack, but was designed to cover Longstreet's own flank in the event the enemy should drive Holmes."[5]

This explanation, however, creates more questions than it answers. General Lee had ridden off for Malvern Hill after receiving a message from Thomas Rosser that the Federal train had been seen coursing over that hill in great confusion. Based on that observation, Lee's concern could hardly have been that of a Federal attack on Holmes. Rather his concern was that the Yankees were *escaping* unharmed, and *that* was what he rode off to reconnoiter. Rosser, fresh from the area, had not observed or reported any sort of massing of infantry or artillery which would have signaled a Federal advance. He had reported the opposite — a hurried retreat in great confusion. So why, all of a sudden, was there concern for a Federal advance up the River Road toward Holmes? It makes no sense.

Moreover, it is hard to understand why Lee would have compromised his striking power at Glendale. That road junction was *the* critical point, indeed the hub around which the entire day's offensive had been centered. To take Glendale (or the Quaker Road which ran south to Malvern Hill) was to split the Army of the Potomac potentially in half, thus creating a scenario in which the remaining parts could be devoured in detail. Magruder's division was a significant portion of the power Lee had deliberately assembled to make that assault an overwhelming one, while the reduction of Magruder's division diminished that power by a whopping 27 percent — and that includes Huger's division which was in reality already off the board. It is difficult to imagine that General Lee would have decreased that critical power in order to address a phantom enemy on his far right flank when all the reports indicated nothing of the kind.

Is there another possibility? Is it more likely, for instance, that Longstreet, in Lee's absence, felt the sudden need to cover his right flank which was, in fact, dangling in the air? It had been Longstreet, after all — and much to his credit — who had had the Union forces opposite his line reconnoitered even if incompletely, and as a consequence surely understood the fact that he was facing three Federal divisions. Moreover, a thorough reconnaissance would have revealed the fact that Hooker's left extended well below Longstreet's own right, a situation that created the troubling, although somewhat theoretical, possibility that once Longstreet's forces started forward, they might be taken in the flank by Hooker. The order, after all, to redeploy Magruder had come directly from Longstreet, and Longstreet was in charge of the field in Lee's absence. So the most sensible answer to the question of who moved Magruder and why appears to be Longstreet with the intention of covering his own right flank.

Or is it? Because the truly puzzling thing is that when Magruder finally arrived along the River Road, he was met not by General Holmes or a member of his staff, nor by a member of Longstreet's staff, but by Colonel R.H. Chilton, General Lee's chief of staff. "Then 'Prince John' dashed off and met the Chief of Staff, who conducted him to a position in the forest on the right of Holmes. There, Chilton explained, Lee wished Magruder to place his troops. Magruder did not wait for more details. He dispatched officers to find his Brigades and to bring them up. In person he spurred away to locate Holmes."[6] Yet the position selected by Chilton was not on Longstreet's right, as the original order indicated, but rather to the right of Holmes, and a location from which Magruder could not have supported Longstreet at all. But seeing that Lee's own chief of staff had placed Magruder, it must be assumed that the final order and placement had come from Lee himself, and not Longstreet after all.

Why would General Lee have moved Magruder from the reserve at Glendale to the right of Holmes? It can only have been to cooperate with Holmes in an assault on the Federal position at Malvern Hill. That is the only thing that makes sense. Lee must have issued the order immediately after hearing from Rosser, not in fear of a Federal assault up the River Road at all, but to launch his own assault against the confused Federal retreat Rosser had reported crossing Malvern Hill. There is no other reason for Chilton to have placed Magruder to the right of Holmes, yet by the time Prince John had arrived in the area, the riot on the River Road had already taken place, and Holmes was struggling backward toward New Market Heights.

At any rate, by around 4:30 that afternoon Prince John had received his orders, and thus began one of the most confused and useless treks in the annals of the Army of Northern Virginia. Surely this was not what John Bankhead Magruder had in mind when he graduated from West Point in the class of 1830. He had served in the infantry, earned the brevet rank of lieutenant colonel in the War with Mexico, and afterward settled down with a number of satisfactory posts in the artillery.

"In particular he had served at Fort Adams, Newport, Rhode Island, and had won a great name as a *bon vivant* and as an obliging host. Whenever celebrities were to be entertained, Colonel Magruder — 'Prince John' — would tender a dress parade, with full trappings and gold-braided pomp, and this he would follow with a flawless dinner. From Fort Adams he had been transferred to far-off Fort Leavenworth, but there, too, he had held dress parades and reviews, though the spectators might be only Indians or frontiersmen; and when the troops had marched off the parade ground, he had entertained his brother officers, *mutatis mutandis,* no less lavishly than at Newport. In the serious work of his profession he had succeeded Colonel Dimick in direction of a new artillery school at Leavenworth and had convinced interested juniors that he knew his ranges as thoroughly as his vintages."[7]

Tall, handsome, and always immaculately uniformed, Prince John had been well known in the "Old Army," where he affected an urbane, theatrical air. Professional as well as genial, "Lieutenant Colonel Magruder was acknowledged to be the centerpiece of the social season in fashionable Newport. No one could match Prince John at stretching limited resources into plausible illusions."[8]

When secession carried Virginia into the Confederacy, Prince John resigned his commission and offered his services to his native state. Soon he was made a colonel of Virginia Volunteers in Richmond and not long thereafter given command of the Confederacy's operations on the lower portion of the Peninsula.[9] It was there at Yorktown where Magruder captured the imagination of all the South as McClellan's giant army crawled close to the small town then began an investment and siege of Magruder's mere 13,000 effectives. "A dozen or so miles from Fort Monroe Magruder had drawn what he called his advanced line across the Peninsula, made up of infantry outposts and artillery redoubts."[10] Creating the line would be one thing, manning it quite another. Prince John had so limited a garrison that he was forced to make up for what he lacked in true manpower by means of the art of illusion, and this he accomplished with great panache.

Promotion to major general came swiftly after Prince John gained victory in the war's first minor clash at Big Bethel near Fortress Monroe, a contest that years later would hardly have been styled even a skirmish, but in 1861 was hailed openly as "one of the most extraordinary victories in the annals of war."[11] For his role in the action Prince John became an instant celebrity across the South. "His every word was applauded; he himself was described as all that 'fancy had pictured of the Virginia gentleman, the frank and manly representative of the chivalry of the dear Old Dominion.'"[12]

Thus did Prince John Magruder early establish himself as one of the founding luminaries in the emerging pantheon of Southern heroes, and at Yorktown he did little to tarnish that shining image. By repeatedly marching his small command back and forth where they could be spotted by Federal pickets; by the beating of drums, the parade of artillery, and the repeated shouts of officers — often to no one at all!— Prince John had bamboozled George McClellan into laying siege to an objective he could have taken in an afternoon. With that sublime performance Prince John's star rose to its zenith, but then with the abandonment of Yorktown, and the absorption of the Peninsula Army into the greater forces guarding Richmond, Magruder's once shining star had begun to decline. Fussy and exhausted, never quite in the right place at the right time, Prince John was, by the 30th of June, grasping for the esteem the South had once so lavishly bestowed upon him. And it wasn't going well.

At around 4:30 in the afternoon of June 30, Magruder galloped off for the River Road, determined to shine with this, his newest set of orders. The expedition ran into immediate difficulty, however, as guides were unfamiliar with the roads, and the maps were insufficient to the task. There was this mysterious Darbytown Road, for instance, where no one could locate an actual Darbytown either on the map or on the road. Guides rode hither and yon, yet with no guiding lights, one road became easily confused with another. Which turn was the right turn? Which way was the right way? No one knew.

Stephen Sears explains one of the more exotic oddities faced by the woe-begotten column that afternoon: "It seemed that at some time past, back in England, in an inheritance dispute, the family Enroughty had grudgingly agreed to call itself Darby but perversely retained the old spelling. The maps showed numerous Enroughtys living in this part of the Peninsula, but every one of them answered only to Darby — thus the Darbytown Road — all of which thoroughly befuddled Prince John."[13] The Darbytown Road led, not to Darbytown after all, but to Mr. Enroughty's front door, and by this point some of the tired guides and officers must have thought the situation utterly diabolical.

Thus in confusion and misadventure the column was headed off, not south, but southwest toward New Market, as Prince John bounded ahead to locate the proper location for his division's new deployment. "Magruder, the ever-galloping, started immediately by a short route a local guide showed him, and he left his artillery to follow by the road."[14] It was at that point that Prince John received the mentioned notice from Colonel Chilton of Lee's staff, and dashed off to meet that officer south of the River Road. Chilton promptly pointed out the position where "Lee wished Magruder to place his troops" and that was fine enough, except that now Prince John could not locate his misplaced marching columns, which were, of course, off on their own wild goose chase. Magruder sent his staff members off looking for his lost brigades, while he went back to await the troops. Finally the brigades were located and started toward the correct point of deployment, but by now night was falling and Holmes' expedition against the Federal position on Malvern Hill had already ended in fiasco.

Thus by any sensible calculation Magruder's new deployment had already become an exercise in futility (Holmes was gone so there was no one to cooperate *with*), but orders were orders, and Prince John was not about to have his competence questioned yet again. "By that time, the exhaustion, lack of sleep and indigestion probably had brought Magruder to a state of mental confusion. When he met in the woods one of his Brigadiers, Paul Semmes, he ordered the Georgian to move forward his troops. Semmes protested, justly enough, that in the gathering darkness of the forest, he would be certain to have command disorganized and scattered if he attempted to advance, but Magruder would not heed: the effort must be made!"[15]

Then, almost incredibly, Prince John received yet another set of orders from General Lee. Now he was to abandon the position on the right of Holmes, and return his division to Glendale where he was once again to move in support of Longstreet — exactly, of course, from where he had started the afternoon's pilgrimage to begin with.[16] Once again Prince John was in the saddle, bounding off to locate the remainder of his lost brigades, and guide them back to their original staging point. He rode back to Glendale, found Lee, and was told to redeploy his brigades on the front in relief of Longstreet's now battered division. "To supervising this transfer of front-line position, Magruder devoted himself until 3 A.M. and then he slept an hour. It was his second hour of repose in seventy-two. His men, of course, were exhausted. Most of them had marched twenty miles that day and had kept the road for eighteen hours, but not one of them had been privileged to draw a trigger."[17]

Mistakes, of course, are made by even the finest minds, and even under the most opportune circumstances, but this handling of Magruder's division was a critical mistake in a critical situation, and it would have far reaching ramifications. Viewed in conjunction with the other — and seemingly endless — command failures that occurred that day, it makes the field operations of the Army of Northern Virginia on the 30th of June appear something akin to satire. In this instance, however, no satire could possibly be more scathing than the actual performance.

The bottom line was that 12,000 veteran infantry had been taken for no sensible profit from the Glendale front where ultimately they could have been utilized to tremendous advantage. Whether Lee, Longstreet, or both, had deemed that movement prudent is beside the point. Magruder had been removed from the crucial point of attack to accomplish nothing, and the Confederacy would that day suffer the consequence.

CHAPTER 15

A Thing Understood
as It Really Is

In Washington City, as likewise across the entire country, attention turned to the events taking place in the dense, tree covered country of the Virginia peninsula, just east of Richmond. Newspapers were gobbled up, taverns percolated with gossip and rumor, hotel lobbies became crowded with the curious, all anxious for the latest bulletins from the front. So it had been since Lee's first attack at Mechanicsville, and so it would remain until events eventually played themselves out. At first it appeared that McClellan had in fact scored a tremendous victory over Lee along the banks of Beaver Dam Creek near Mechanicsville, as McClellan's reports brimmed with boasts of self-serving hyperbole: "He'd repulsed the rebel attack and won a complete victory against tremendous odds. A complete victory!"[1]

In the White House Abraham Lincoln responded with joy, and for days he virtually lived in William Stanton's office, hanging on every report, but those reports were few and sketchy at best. Something seemed wrong. For a true victory would, it seemed, have put McClellan on the march toward Richmond — the objective, after all — and soon the sad truth became increasingly obvious. McClellan was on the south side of the Chickahominy River moving toward the James. Whether in victory or in defeat, McClellan was in retreat. When it became clear where George McClellan was headed and just what he was up to, Abraham Lincoln became despondent. "I was as nearly inconsolable as I could be and live,"[2] he told a visiting congressman. The Army of the Potomac had been within a mere handful of miles from the Confederate capital. Victory seemed so near at hand. Now this.

Lincoln was by no means alone in regard to his sentiments. The whole North seemed to suffer McClellan's failure. "And when news of the Seven Days' reached the North in a form that magnified the Union defeat, home front morale plunged. A panic on Wall Street sent stocks as well as the value of the new green back dollar ... into a temporary free fall. Newspapers described the public mood as 'mortified' by this 'stunning disaster' which had caused 'misery' and 'revulsion' throughout the North.'"[3]

The nation was counting on George McClellan, of course, to turn and defeat the Rebel Army under Lee, but what no one knew at the time — or *could* have known at the time — was that George McClellan was no longer leading his army either toward or away from the enemy. On June 30 McClellan was aboard the Federal gunboat *Galena* in the river James, soon to shove off on a waterborne excursion.

McClellan, despite the boasts and bombast, was a defeated man. "The truth of the matter is that George McClellan had lost the courage to command. With each day of the Seven Days his demoralization had increased, and each day his courage to command decreased accordingly. By Day Six the demoralization was complete; exercising command in battle was now quite beyond him, and to avoid it he deliberately fled the battlefield. He was drained in both mind and body. Brigadier Andrew A. Humphrey of his staff saw him the next morning aboard the *Galena* and, Humphreys wrote his wife, 'never did I see a man more cut down than Genl. McClellan was.... He was unable to do anything or say anything.'"[4]

What Abraham Lincoln — and the citizens gathered in the hotels, taverns, barbershops, or on street corners — did not know that June 30, was that today the Army of the Potomac had been abandoned by its leader, left to be destroyed by a rapidly closing foe. If their fathers, brothers, sons, and friends were going to survive this day, they were going to have to fend for themselves. How, many wondered, had things come to such a pass?

For months Abraham Lincoln had been dueling with his Potomac Army commander via telegram and dispatch, trying in vain to get him to march, to move, to fight. Yet no words or logic seemed to have an effect. Lincoln had agreed to give his commander every soldier he could spare, just so long as McClellan left behind an agreed upon number of troops to defend the Federal capital. In early April, as McClellan dawdled before Yorktown, the president received a shocking telegram from his general, virtually accusing the administration of willful neglect. Should the vast Confederate legions — estimated then by Allen Pinkerton somewhere between 100,000 and 120,000 men — overwhelm his army in some desperate action, McClellan insisted that he could not be the person held accountable.[5]

To this unfounded and unfair accusation Lincoln responded on April 9 with kindness and calm logic. "Your dispatches complaining that you are not properly sustained, while they do not offend me, do pain me very much," the president began. He then went on to review in detail the most recent troop movements and deployments, and then pointed out that McClellan had not left sufficient troops to guard Washington, as he had previously promised to do. "Do you really think," the president asked, "I should permit the line from Richmond, *via* Manassas Junction, to this city to be entirely open, except what resistance could be presented by less than twenty thousand unorganized troops? This is a question which the country will not allow me to evade."

To McClellan's assertion that he was undermanned, Lincoln responded with simple facts. "There is a curious mystery about the *number* of the troops now with you," he pointed out. "When I telegraphed you on the 6th, saying you had over a hundred thousand with you, I had just obtained from the Secretary of War, a statement, taken as he said, from your own returns, making 108,000 then with you, and *en route* to you. You now say you will have but 85,000, when all *en route* to you shall have reached you. How can the discrepancy of 23,000 be accounted for?"

Finally, the president closed with a heartfelt recommendation that his general put his army into motion and get after the enemy. "The country will not fail to note — is now noting — that the present hesitation to move upon an intrenched enemy, is but the story of Manassas repeated.

"I beg to assure you," the president went on, "that I have never written you, or spoken to you, in greater kindness of feeling than now, nor with a fuller purpose to sustain you, so far as in my most anxious judgment, I consistently can. *But you must act.* Yours very truly."[6]

When Yorktown was eventually found abandoned by McClellan's Confederate adversary, he of course hailed the seizure of this now undefended city as a stroke of military genius. "Our success is brilliant," he proclaimed, then promised to "push the enemy to the wall."[7] But that push never came, and over the ensuing weeks and months the plodding general accomplished little except badger the president for time, men, and every form of supply imaginable. The excuses for not moving, at first a trickle, became a torrent. "Once again he dug in and called for reinforcements. Once again he upbraided the administration for not supporting 'this Army.' When Lincoln and Stanton sent him one of McDowell's divisions, McClellan found other reasons for delay. Continuous rains had lashed the marshy plains east of Richmond. McClellan reported that his artillery and wagon trains were bogged down in muddy roads, his army immobilized. Before he could move against Richmond, the general must build footbridges, must corduroy the roads."[8]

Then, June 25, on the eve of Lee's initial assault at Mechanicsville, McClellan began to become unhinged. He telegraphed Washington, now asserting the enemy's strength at an unfathomable 200,000, announced that he intended to die with his troops in combat, and again accused the administration of willful misconduct. Shortly thereafter, now with his army in full retreat toward the James — a "change of base" as McClellan would thereafter describe it — the general accused the Lincoln administration of something remarkably close to treason. "I have lost this battle because my force was too small. The government must not & cannot hold me responsible for the result.... I have seen too many dead & wounded comrades to feel otherwise than that the Government has not sustained this army.... If I save this army now, I tell you plainly that I owe no thanks to you or any other persons in Washington. You have done your best to sacrifice this army."[9]

Lincoln had sacrificed his own army? To what possible purpose? Fortunately for General McClellan, the last two sentences of his telegram had been deleted by the military telegrapher, and neither Stanton nor Lincoln ever saw the full text.

These were dark days for the United States and for Abraham Lincoln in particular. In a storm of failure and controversy, he had to keep his head while others around him lost theirs. Later he would remark to his secretary, "Thus often I who am not a specially brave man have had to sustain the sinking courage of these professional fighters in critical times."[10] It was not an easy job.

On June 28, the day after the bloody Confederate victory at Gaines's Mill, as Lee was searching for McClellan's fleeing army in the Chickahominy swamp east of the Confederate capital, and as Richmond awoke to rejoice in its newfound liberation, Lincoln sat down at his desk and penned this conciliatory note to his shaken general. "Save your army at all events," he implored. "Will send re-enforcements as fast as we can. Of course, they cannot reach you today, tomorrow, or next day. I have not said you were ungenerous for saying you needed re-enforcement. I thought you ungenerous in assuming that I did not send them as fast as I could. I feel any misfortune to you and your army as keenly as you feel it yourself.... If you have had a drawn battle, or a repulse, it is the price we pay for the enemy not being in Washington.... Less than a week ago you notified us that reinforcements were leaving Richmond to come in front of us. It is the nature of the case, and neither you or the government that is to blame. Please tell at once the present condition and aspect of things."[11]

Then on the same day Abraham Lincoln turned and wrote William Seward a note outlining his thoughts on the war, and in particular the fact that he now thought it critical to raise another 100,000 men to complete the task — no small increment, considering the defeat the nation was in the midst of absorbing. Despite the ruin and failure of McClellan's Peninsula Campaign, and his own profound disappointment, the president's unshakable determination still shined through his words. "Then let the country give us a hundred thousand new troops in the shortest possible time, which added to McClellan, directly or in directly, will take Richmond, without endangering any other place which we now hold — and will substantially end the war. I expect to maintain this contest until successful, or till I die, or am conquered, or my term expires, or Congress or the country forsakes me; and I would publicly appeal to the country for this new force, were it not that I fear a general panic and stampede would follow — so hard is it to have a thing understood as it really is."[12]

George McClellan, however, would not, apparently could not, refrain from his incessant demands, regardless of the facts, and no matter now how painfully obvious those facts were. From behind Malvern Hill the general telegraphed again for more reinforcements, to be sent, he hoped "very promptly."[13] This, despite the fact that the president had already advised him on the 28th that what reinforcements he might be able to cobble together could not possibly reach him soon. Later that day the general telegraphed again, requested 50,000 reserves "instantly"[14] as if the president could simply snap his fingers and make a division or two of veteran troops appear atop the summit of Malvern Hill to McClellan's delight.

McClellan, throughout the Seven Days as, in fact, throughout most of his Civil War career, exhibited such egotism, paranoia, self-inflation, bouts of martyrdom, and moments of delusion that, were he alive today, he might seem a candidate for professional counseling. Historically, his apologists have pointed to his concern for his troops, and his revulsion of the hideous nature of the Civil War battlefield, as a sort of panacea for these glaring character flaws, and his persistent refusal to act. True, McClellan felt for his men, but most officers felt for their men, as were most officers horrified by the human debris scattered behind in the wake of 19th century combat. Yet running like a rabbit from the field of battle while abandoning his entire army to the jaws of an approaching foe hardly has the feel about it of an act of compassion, nor a gesture born of devotion. The notion, insinuated, that George McClellan could not bring himself to fight because he was a man of modern, 21st century sensibilities stuck somehow in a 19th century war holds no water. Perhaps it is time to bring General George McClellan into clearer focus.

To McClellan's absurd demand that reinforcements be rushed to him "very promptly" (and 50,000 instantly), Lincoln again responded with kindness and common sense. "It is impossible to re-inforce you for your present emergency," he tried to explain. "If we had a million men we could not get them to you in time. We have not the men to send. If you are not strong enough to face the enemy you must find a place of security, and wait, rest, and repair. Maintain your ground if you can; but save the army at all events, even if you fall back to Fortress Monroe. We still have strength enough in the country, and will bring it out."[15]

For the time being, at least, the Army of the Potomac was on its own. There could be no immediate reinforcement. Washington could not help the beleaguered McClellan as Lee's army attempted to close the trap around Glendale that June afternoon. Across the North people waited in fear and gloom. In Richmond the mood remained grimly apprehensive. Constance Harrison recalled the times. "When on the 27th of June the Seven Days' strife began, there was none of the excitement that had attended the battle of Seven Pines. People had shaken themselves down, as it were, to the grim reality of a fight that must be fought."[16] The "grim reality" understood now by the citizens of Richmond was the reality imposed by thousands of dead and wounded in their midst. Just to the east the guns were booming again. Soon there would be more.

On the 30th of June 1862, as on all the days preceding it during the Seven Days, Abraham Lincoln waited impatiently for news from the front. Would the nation's principle fighting force find safe harbor, be mauled during its retreat, or perhaps even be destroyed?

These were not inconsequential questions. They spoke to the future of the United States, indeed, if there was still to be one. To a very great extent, the nation's future marched with the Army of the Potomac, and that army had now been led into harm's way, then abandoned, by its commander. Surely it was better by far that Abraham Lincoln did not know the truth that day; that the nation's principle fighting force and all its wagons, supplies, and reserve artillery was then being pursued and entrapped by four converging Confederate columns. For a "thing understood as it really is" can at times be a hard pill to swallow.

CHAPTER 16

The Gallant Jenkins

At Glendale the heat was still rising in the late afternoon, shadows were beginning to lengthen, and time, which had seemed abundant for the task at hand only hours past, was for the Confederacy now beginning to slip away. Lee returned from his reconnaissance south toward Malvern Hill around 4:30 P.M. to the sound of cannonading and musketry ringing in the air above Riddell's Shop.[1] He had given orders to hold Longstreet back until all the various commands might go in together, but now it was clear that something was afoot. What was happening?

For hours, of course, Longstreet's two divisions had been deployed in the woods across a narrow front, exposed to enemy fire, and nerves were no doubt beginning to fray. As told, the fire from several Federal batteries along McCall's line opposite were playing havoc with the Confederates, front and rear, and Longstreet sensibly ordered Jenkins to try and silence those guns.

Douglas Southall Freeman describes the situation: "When Lee reached the troops on the Long Bridge road he found the artillery blazing away but the infantry not yet fully engaged. Magruder had been ordered by Longstreet to march to the support of Holmes. Nothing further had been heard from Huger and nothing from Jackson. Neither of them could be attacking successfully, if at all, because such reconnaissance as could be made by Lee showed that the Federal right and centre, which would have been exposed to assaults by Jackson and Huger, were standing staunchly, apparently inviting the Confederates to attack."[2] Kearny on the Union right remained in position unfazed, while McCall's batteries in the center were defiantly belching metal at the Confederates like bullies on a playground. What was Lee to do?

The main assault that was delivered that day at Glendale is today presented in most texts as a classic advance, ordered by Longstreet, delivered in turn by his forward three brigades, but on close examination that seems not necessarily to have been the case. While the situation remains somewhat

133

sketchy, it is more likely that the fighting escalated from what was initially a spat over artillery, to an all-out engagement, much as a string of fireworks goes off once the fuse is lit. Longstreet ordered Jenkins to take out Cooper's battery, but this task seems then to have evolved into an all out struggle for the crossroad involving everyone at hand.

Longstreet explains, "I sent orders for Jenkins to silence the battery, under the impression that our wait was understood, and that [his] sharpshooters would be pushed forward till they could pick off the gunners, thus ridding us of that annoyance; but the gallant Jenkins, only too anxious for a dash at the battery, charged and captured it, thus precipitating battle."[3]

With all that in mind, when General Lee returned to the Long Bridge Road, the fight appears to have already been at least partially in progress, and perhaps on the verge of careening out of control. Freeman, for instance, is careful to note that Lee "found the artillery blazing away but the infantry not fully engaged." Not fully engaged hardly means dormant, and in all probability what Lee found was Jenkins' brigade already hotly involved, and the entire front around him about to explode. As with the rest of General Lee's army, events, and not his orders, were ruling the day, and on the 30th of June General Lee had not once been able to take control of those events and bend them to his will.

James Longstreet — Called "my old warhorse" by Robert E. Lee, Longstreet rose to corps command in the Army of Northern Virginia, and proved to be one of Lee's most consistent lieutenants (Library of Congress).

Whether Longstreet's orders to Jenkins were clear or ambiguous is not known, but Jenkins appears at least to have interpreted them as silencing the aggravating Federal battery by whatever means at his disposal. To the young colonel this apparently meant an all-out attack by his entire brigade, not merely the deployment of his sharpshooters, as Longstreet later claimed he actually had in mind. Whether this all-out assault was a function of military necessity, direct orders, personal ambition, or simply a logical combination of all three, will never be known, for Jenkins was well known in the Army of Northern Virginia as an extremely brave and capable officer, yet one also with designs on high command.[4]

Alexander, who was watching at the time, recalls the moment: "Between three and four o'clock the enemy, aware of their proximity [Hill's and Longstreet's troops], unwisely increased the fire of one of their batteries [Cooper's]. Longstreet ordered Jenkins, second to none in either courage or ambition, to charge it. This brought on the battle at once, though not in the best shape; for, instead of one simultaneous attack by the whole force, more time was wasted, and the brigades came in piecemeal."[5] Thomas Goree, then on Longstreet's staff, seems also to support Alexander's explanation: "As soon as the enemy opened on us so heavily Genl. Longstreet at once ordered forward his infantry. The So. Ca. Brigade under the gallant Col. Jenkins commenced the attack."[6]

Longstreet claimed — years after the war in his *Memoirs*, it should be noted — that the order had gone forward for Jenkins to utilize his sharpshooters (or at least that's what Longstreet claims he intended), but Alexander appears to confirm the fact that Jenkins was given orders directly from Longstreet to charge the battery. It is highly unlikely that Jenkins would have disobeyed orders, soldier that he was. It is far more likely that Longstreet's orders were either ambiguous, or were in fact to charge the battery, as Alexander claims, and Jenkins actually did. In any case, Micah Jenkins deployed his entire brigade to the task, and as Alexander confirms, the fighting soon spun out of control, all of this contrary to Lee's desires.

This is no trivial matter. Longstreet's and Hill's divisions were the last two available to Lee that afternoon to break the Federal defense at Glendale. A coordinated, powerful attack, using these last two divisions to their maximum striking potential — "one simultaneous attack by the whole force," as Porter Alexander puts it — was therefore a matter of the highest priority, but that opportunity, like all the other Confederate opportunities that day, appears to have been squandered. The "more time" which was "wasted" as Alexander notes, was the time it took Longstreet, and perhaps Lee, to ready the three other brigades under Longstreet's control that afternoon, to move to Jenkins' support (this included Branch's brigade of Hill's division). Thus the attack made across the front at Glendale that afternoon was an assault made "piecemeal," the various brigades going in, if not helter skelter, at least lacking anything approaching optimum coordination.

As a result, this proved an attack that vastly compromised the offensive power of the two divisions, and therefore their potential for success. Here again, the Confederate high command had simply shot itself in the foot, and it appears Longstreet's name should be added to the long and growing list of command failures for the day. He either ordered a foolish assault, contrary to Lee's wishes, or gave orders that were so obtuse that the assault proved a natural result. Perhaps this is why, years later, when penning his memoirs, Longstreet fudged his memories a bit, knowing that the "gallant Jenkins," long in his grave, could not possibly rise and object. For one reason or another, it seems the fighting at Glendale had foolishly gotten away from Longstreet, and the repercussions, while hardly as extreme as those forged by Jackson or Huger, would still be dire.

"To charge the battery, Jenkins positioned the Second South Carolina Rifles on the right, the Palmetto Sharpshooters on their left, the Fifth South Carolina next, and the Fourth South Carolina Battalion on the left of the brigade."[7] The ground over which the brigade had to advance was open farm fields, Mr. Nelson's farmhouse (previously owned by a family named Frayser) visible but a few hundred yards to the south and east. With him that day was his young adjutant, John Lee, only twenty-one years old, and just graduated from The Citadel the year prior, along with Jenkins' brother-in-law, John W. Jamison, whom Jenkins had convinced to leave South Carolina and join him as an aide-de-camp for the Virginia campaign.[8]

The South Carolina brigade had seen heavy action during the Peninsula Campaign at Seven Pines, and more recently at Gaines's Mill. There they had been involved in a sharp clash with Federal infantry at dusk near the base of Turkey Hill after Porter's Federal corps had been finally routed from the crest of the hill, leaving their dead, wounded, and dying behind. When the firing finally faded away, Jenkins' exhausted troops slept where they might. "After the fighting had ended that day, Jenkins and his two regiments slept in the woods among the abandoned Union fortifications near Turkey Hill. According to one soldier, they used discarded Federal knapsacks as pillows, covered themselves with Union blankets, 'took a smoke from Yankee cigars ... and slept soundly amid hundreds of the dead and dying.'"[9]

While the fighting that spring had turned those who had survived into veterans, that gain in experience had come at a fairly steep price. Micah Jenkins, for instance, would never forget the losses suffered at Seven Pines. "We never fought twice in the same place, nor five minutes in one place, and steadily on the advance; were under fire from 3 P.M. to 7:40 P.M. The service we did will be evidenced by our list of killed and wounded. In my two color companies out of 80 men who entered, 40 were killed or wounded, and out of 11 in the color guard 10 were shot down, and my colors, pierced by 9 balls, passed through four hands without touching the ground."[10]

Now heavily depleted, the brigade formed in the trees just west of the Quaker Road and readied themselves for the job at hand. The Federals across the way were known to be deployed in heavy force, and covered by numerous batteries of artillery all across the front. The sight could not have been terribly appetizing, even for an officer such as Jenkins, focused on duty and advancement as he was, and with a well deserved reputation for hard fighting.

"Posted squarely in front of this advance was George McCall's division of Pennsylvania Reserves, facing their third battle in five days. McCall's line ran in a shallow concave curve west of the Glendale crossroads, George Meade's brigade straddling the Long Bridge Road on the right, Truman Seymour's on the left. John Reynold's brigade, led since Reynold's capture by Colonel Seneca G. Simmons, was in reserve. Of McCall's 7,500 infantry, some 5,000 were in the front line. Out in front of the infantry was the artillery line — five batteries, with twenty-six guns."[11]

Jenkins' objective was Cooper's Pennsylvania battery, directly on his front, and the brigade went in straight at them, Jenkins mounted and leading the way. Across the open farm fields they rushed, flags flying, taking heavy casualties as they moved. Suddenly from their left another battery of Federal artillery located near the crossroads opened a heavy, enfilading fire into the brigade's left flank as it struggled forward. This was Randol's battery of twelve guns, situated in a perfect position to rake the field virtually from the side. The effects were horrid, but Jenkins pressed on. The South Carolina brigade finally reached Cooper's battery, struggled with the gunners, in some cases hand-to-hand, and fought furiously to take the guns.

The artillerymen began limbering up their pieces, trying desperately to save the battery, but Jenkins would not have it. "Shoot down their horses!"[12] he screamed, and as his men shot the horses down where they stood in their traces, the Federal gunners, after a desperate struggle, finally turned and fled. For the moment, at least, the battery had been silenced, the six Union guns now in Confederate hands.

But the fighting had been severe, the toll in dead and wounded already high. Standing behind the advance that afternoon, Porter Alexander observed the carnage.

> As I watched the fight of Jenkins's South Carolina brigade at Frazier's Farm a fine, tall, handsome, young fellow dropped out of ranks & came back toward me. As he seemed weak I went to meet him & found he had been shot through the lungs, the bullet passing clear through. He had been the color bearer. I had a small flask of some of my father's "Old Hurricane" brandy 1811, & I gave him a drink, & helped him on toward where an ambulance could be had. He asked me, rather apologetically, if I thought he had

any chance of recovery. I told him about poor Bob Wheat who was killed at Gaines's Mill only three days before, but who had been shot through the lungs at Bull Run in July '61, & though he was exceedingly stout & thick, so that the hole was fully two feet long through him, had yet gotten well very easily & soon. He was evidently cheered & said, "Of course, I'm willing to die for my country, if I must; but I'd a heap rather get well & see my mother & my folks again." Poor fellow, I hope he did, but I never knew.[13]

The battle for the intersection at Glendale, and the road leading south to Malvern Hill, had begun. Though it would be over by the time darkness finally fell, it would prove to be one of the fiercest of the war. Perhaps both sides knew instinctively just what was at stake; one, the Federals if they lost; the other, the Confederates, should they win.

For Micah Jenkins the next few hours would prove some of the most remarkable and frightening of his life. When the engagement at Glendale was over he would pen his wife a note concerning the events, but no longer writing boldly as he had after his feats at Seven Pines. The horror of what he had seen and endured at Glendale would leave its mark on the young South Carolinian, war changed from a glorious affair to something painfully different. "I write with the most saddened feelings," he said. "God has been merciful, but, oh my God, what terrible trials have we been through. Nearly all my best friends, men and officers, killed or wounded."[14]

Cooper's Federal battery was now in Rebel hands, but it would not remain that way for long. The Federal defenders would at once, and forcefully, respond to Jenkins' attack. The fight along the front at Glendale was about to explode. "And here I believe," Thomas Goree declared emphatically, "occurred the hardest fight of the war."[15]

CHAPTER 17

Go Build a Bridge

As Micah Jenkins' brigade crashed headfirst into Cooper's battery just south of Glendale, there was still ample time for Stonewall Jackson to take action and cooperate in the day's events. For Jackson the point had never been that he had to rout the Federals on his front, nor drive them, nor even defeat them. While the accomplishment of any of those possibilities would have obviously been hailed by Lee along with Southern writers and politicians as proof positive that the Stonewall of the Valley had returned to form — and would certainly have dramatically improved the probability of a significant Confederate success that day — all that was really needed was a vigorous demonstration of strength near White Oak Bridge. What was required was a demonstration convincing enough in its intensity and tenacity that William Franklin would have been obligated to hold his position against it for fear that, should Stonewall actually break through his lines, the collapse of the entire Federal effort behind him would become an instant probability.

Such an effort by Jackson would have as a matter of course kept all of the Union forces largely strung out and beyond communication — from White Oak Swamp in the north to Malvern Hill in the south. It would also have frozen large increments of Federal troops in place, keeping them from active cooperation, and maintaining the possibility — the military planner's fondest dream — of isolating, then defeating those increments in detail. While Stonewall may have, due to sheer exhaustion, lost all sight of this most basic of objectives, many of his subordinates had not, and continued late that afternoon to search for advantageous opportunities.

One such subordinate was General Wade Hampton. Hampton was one of the first to arrive at White Oak Bridge that morning with his South Carolina brigade and was thus witness to the unfolding events of the day. He observed Jackson and Hill make their futile reconnaissance across the creek with Munford's cavalry, their harried return, and the cannonade which began around 2:00 P.M.

139

Porter Alexander recounts the situation at the bridge at the time.

> It appears from subordinate reports that the long delay between the arrival
> of the head of Jackson's column and the opening of his 28 guns was caused
> by cutting a road to enable the guns to be kept concealed while getting
> position. Concealment here was of little value, and the time thus lost by
> the artillery, and the sending across of Munford's cavalry at the road crossing,
> illustrate the prominent feature of Jackson's conduct during the whole Seven
> Days,— to wit: a reluctance to bring his infantry into action. Here infantry
> alone could accomplish anything, but only cavalry and artillery were called
> upon. He could have crossed a brigade of infantry as easily as Munford's
> cavalry [which Munford has already acknowledged], and that brigade could
> have been the entering wedge which would split apart the Federal defense
> and let in the 13 brigades which followed.[1]

Stonewall Jackson, along with numerous historians, later argued (in the
report Jackson filed regarding the engagement) that the Federals' destruction
of the bridge deterred him from acting, but this argument will not bear
scrutiny. "The bridge, whose destruction is mentioned [by Jackson], was not
necessary to a crossing. It was only a high-water bridge with a ford by it
which was preferably used except in freshets. Now the floor of the bridge,
made of poles, had been thrown into the ford, but Munford's cavalry got
through without trouble, and infantry could have swarmed across."[2]

Here Alexander touches upon yet one more reason Jackson was rumored
at the time to have held back his brigades — to spare his infantry — which,
it was hinted, he believed had already done their share of heavy fighting in
the Valley. Porter Alexander admits he was well aware of such rumors at the
time. "This last expression [Jackson's refusal to employ his infantry] is but
another form of rumor which, to my knowledge, had private circulation at
the time among the staff-officers of some of the leading generals. It was
reported that Jackson said that 'he did not intend that his men should do
all the fighting.'"[3] Unfortunately for Jackson, this rumor would have even
greater life breathed into it years later by Daniel Harvey Hill: "I think an
important factor in this inaction was Jackson's pity for his own corps, worn
out by long and exhausting marches, and reduced in numbers by its numerous sanguinary battles. He thought that the garrison of Richmond ought
now to bear the brunt of the fighting."[4]

This is, upon reflection, an astonishing insinuation, and seemingly one
entirely at odds with Stonewall Jackson's remarkably aggressive martial style.
One thing is certain: wars are rarely won by inaction, but they are often pro-
longed. Wars are won by the application of overwhelming force. Thus if
Jackson thought he was doing his command a favor by holding them out of

combat during the Seven Days, history can well testify that he made a terrible mistake. On the 30th of June the war might have ended with Southern independence had he taken action. By not acting the war would drag on almost three more years and finally end with a Confederate defeat and the South's virtual destruction. Beyond that, Jackson had no reason at the time to feel his Valley Army had been any more hard pressed or roughly used than any other Confederate contingent in Lee's army. "Jackson's troops (his own and Ewell's divisions) had had a sharp campaign in the Valley, but the rest of the army at Yorktown, Williamsburg, and Seven Pines had suffered just as many hardships, and done even more severe fighting, as the casualties will attest. There were no arrears to be made up."[5]

Regardless of Stonewall Jackson's reasons for inaction, Wade Hampton would, through his own initiative, provide Stonewall with one final opportunity to put things right late that afternoon. After watching Jackson and Hill routed from the woods by Federal artillery across the creek, Hampton moved his brigade into the woods on the left of the bridge. Years later in a letter to Porter Alexander, he would recount the afternoon's events: "As there were no further hostile demonstrations where we were, I placed my brigade in a pine forest on the left of the road leading to the ford, directing the men to lie down; and, desiring to ascertain the character of the ground in front of us, I rode to the edge of the swamp, accompanied by Capt. Rawlins Lowndes, and my son Wade, who was serving on my staff at that time. The swamp was comparatively open, the ground not at all boggy, and we soon struck the stream."[6]

Hampton, entirely on his own, would perform the very basic sort of reconnaissance that the situation cried out for, and which had been the standard since armies first marched. He discovered that the footing was entirely passable on the northern portion of the swamp, and then he came to the creek. "This was very shallow," he observed, "with a clear sandy bottom, and not more than 10 or 15 feet wide. Crossing this, we soon came in sight of the open land opposite our position."[7] Hampton continued carefully uphill toward the Federal position, then suddenly spotted the Union troops: "We could see a very wide and deep ravine in which was a line of Federals lying down in line of battle, and evidently expecting, if any attack was made upon them, it would be from the open field below the ford of the stream. In this event their position would have been very strong."[8]

What Wade Hampton had discovered, of course, was not only the Federal line of battle facing Jackson across the way, but also the right flank of Franklin's position, in the air at White Oak Swamp. Not only had he found the exposed flank, but Hampton had also found an open and entirely passable route to that flank. The implications were obvious — the Federal position could be turned!

Wade Hampton was himself one of the more interesting stories of the American 19th century, a story that would include savage fighting, remarkable advancement in the Confederate Army, heartbreaking loss (at Petersburg one son would die in his arms while the other was being carried off to a hospital with a bullet in his back), postwar political success, and yet ultimately, virtual destitution. Like Phil Kearny who commanded a division on the line of battle opposite him, at the outset of hostilities Hampton was a man of extraordinary wealth, indeed considered "in some circles as the wealthiest man in the prewar South,"[9] and like Kearny, he had inherited that fortune. Whereas Kearny's wealth had come from the New York Stock Exchange and the Kearny family investments, Hampton had inherited vast land holdings across the South, from South Carolina to Mississippi, and, of course, the slaves that came with them.

Today, armed with a larger and far broader perspective of American history, it is easy to grasp the Civil War as a contest fundamentally about the issue of slavery, the rising tide of the abolition movement colliding head-first with the antiquated, ante-bellum notions of agrarian property rights and the morality of human bondage, like two vast tectonic plates, one old, one newly rising. That perspective provides a larger, far more accurate picture of the war than any 19th century explanations could possibly have achieved, but in expanding the scope of our gaze to include only the largest issues, individuals are often lost, their personal motivations and stories either tossed aside, or unfairly lumped into general categories and stereotypes that strip them of their human individualism and vitality. Human beings are rarely one-dimensional. Often they are complex and convoluted, at times working at cross-purposes, indeed even pursuing contradictory goals while utterly unmindful of the contradictions that drive them.

American citizens of the Civil War era were no different. True, some were highly motivated and intensely focused on the issue of abolition, and just as true some others were highly motivated and intensely focused on the issues of state's rights, secession, and the preservation of chattel slavery. But, just as the spectrum of today's political cosmology spans a wide range, for both North and South during the era of the Civil War, most individuals fell somewhere in between those extremes. Wade Hampton was just such an individual. He was, for instance, considered by many the largest land owner in all the South, yet he nevertheless voiced serious doubts about the institution of slavery, and he was also an eventual Confederate hero, yet one who had originally argued long and strenuously against secession.

As Edward Longacre points out, Wade Hampton's life radiated an odd mix of contradictions: "The quintessential slave owner, he had questioned the ethical underpinnings of the Peculiar Institution and had argued against reopening the African slave trade. A prewar spokesman for sectional harmony, he had become one of the most avid Confederates. A model Christian who condemned violence and abhorred dueling, he personally dispatched more opponents in battle than any other general officer, with the possible exception of Nathan Bedford Forrest. The man who 'redeemed' his state from black rule, he extended more political benefits to African Americans than any other Democratic governor in the postwar South."[10]

Born into one of the most prosperous and influential families in South Carolina, Hampton's life was nonetheless hardly one of idleness or indulgence. A powerful athlete, hunter, and outdoorsman, like Robert E. Lee, and many other Southern males of the era, Hampton was raised with a strict sense of obligation. "At an early age, the third Wade Hampton was tutored in the responsibilities incumbent upon an heir to southern aristocracy. By instruction and example, his father and other family elders impressed on him that he, like they, had certain obligations to his race, class, and region. In every situation, and especially in the face of adversity, he was expected to comport himself as a gentlemen — sober, self-composed, and unfailingly polite. Above all else, he must uphold his family's honor, never allowing shame or disrepute to tarnish the Hampton name."[11]

Graduated from the South Carolina College in 1836, Hampton entered politics in 1852 and won a seat in the South Carolina Legislature. Yet prewar politics represented merely a secondary interest for him, his principle occupation being involved in the profitable operation of "a half dozen plantations in two states, on which more than fifteen hundred slaves produced a variety of cash crops, principally cotton, tobacco, and rice."[12]

Much like Phil Kearny, when war erupted in 1861, Wade Hampton could easily have remained on the sideline. He was forty-three years old, a planter of great reputation with no military experience to speak of, who surely could have sat out the hostilities without raising an eyebrow. But for a man raised with a strong sense of obligation, that would never do. When South Carolina seceded — against all his wishes and admonitions — he never hesitated. Hampton quickly put his efforts and fortunes at the service of the newly formed Confederacy, and raised a full command of his own, named after his family, the Hampton Legion.

At the first battle at Bull Run, Hampton handled his legion with considerable skill in the face of the initial Federal onslaught that overran the Confederate left flank. Fighting and maneuvering for most of the afternoon, he was wounded during the action that finally stymied the Union offensive; the action, by the way, would provide Thomas J. Jackson his more famous sobriquet, "Stonewall," for all posterity. Hampton's skill and valor helped turn the tide for the Confederacy that day at Manassas, and those qualities were recognized almost immediately. "After the shooting stopped on that bloody Sabbath, President Davis, accompanied by the commander of Hampton's army, visited the colonel at his field headquarters near Portici. Beauregard, who was in an ebullient mood ... credited Hampton with much of the success that had been achieved on the left flank. Davis nodded emphatically and added warm praise of his own."[13]

Thus for Wade Hampton it seemed only natural to perform his own personal reconnaissance of the Federal position at White Oak Swamp while Jackson dithered, whether ordered to or not. What he located for the Confederacy was yet another golden opportunity to end the day in triumph, and Hampton knew it at once. He slipped back away from the Union position carefully so as not to alert the enemy of his presence, then went directly to Stonewall with the news.

Porter Alexander takes it from there: "He [Hampton] drew off unobserved & went to Gen. Jackson & told him that it was easy to lead infantry to surprise & rout them, & asked permission to take his own brigade there & attack. Gen. J. asked if he could make a bridge across the branch. H. said no bridge was necessary, but one would be very easy to build. Gen J. said, 'Go & build one.'"[14]

Hampton had just provided Jackson with some of the most significant intelligence of the war. He had discovered an open route to the exposed Federal right flank and he was sure he could turn that flank with but his brigade alone. If the flank could be turned, then the road across the swamp might be opened, and with that the entire Valley army given access to Franklin's rear, and, just down the road, the crossroads at Glendale. Here, surely, was a vision of victory. Jackson's response: go build a bridge.

Thus had Wade Hampton been detailed to build a bridge that was entirely unnecessary; that could accomplish little more than waste precious time, and that would ultimately take him no farther than he could walk. What could Stonewall have been thinking? Was he thinking at all?

CHAPTER 18

A Reckless Impetuosity
I Never Saw Equaled

As Wade Hampton rushed off to build his unnecessary bridge across the creek at White Oak Swamp, General Lee, peering over the Glendale front from the vantage point of the Long Bridge Road, had a serious decision on his hands. As previously discussed, historical accounts have often portrayed Longstreet's attack this afternoon at Glendale as a seamless, organized, and coordinated assault delivered by his division. A 2005 critique of the Peninsula Campaign crafted for essentially a military readership, for instance, offers this assessment: "Longstreet organized his attack into an initial assault line of three brigades led by Richard Anderson. Behind them were three brigades in close support. Lawrence Branch's brigade of A.P. Hill's division was supporting on the right flank, and the rest of Hill's division remained in reserve."[1] This presentation, again, in all probability, suggests the assault as Longstreet would have liked to have launched it, certainly as he would have preferred to have remembered it as he penned his memoirs in later years, it is but not what actually happened.

It has already been established that Longstreet, who launched the assault and therefore should certainly have known what happened, admitted later that "the gallant Jenkins, only too anxious for a dash at a battery, charged and captured it, thus precipitating battle." Alexander, as well, makes it clear that Jenkins had been ordered by Longstreet to take Cooper's battery, and that this action brought on the general engagement. Goree agrees, essentially, with Longstreet and Alexander, and all this has been previously documented. Since all three were eyewitnesses to the action and intimately involved, it would seem safe, therefore, to credit their version of the facts. Again, this may seem an insignificant point, but it certainly confirms an assault launched in spasms rather than a uniform wave. Not only would this have greatly compromised the assault's punch, it confirms an operation far less well-crafted than historians generally portray, and would also have presented General Lee with a different set of variables to consider as he returned from Malvern Hill.

If the sound of Jenkins' assault was what Lee heard as he returned from Malvern Hill — and it is reasonable to assume that that was the infantry he did hear, as no other had yet been committed — then his choice would either have been to pull Jenkins back or move at once to support him. Lee's options for the day were running low at that moment, and surely he understood this. It had to have been obvious to him, as well, that neither Huger nor Jackson were as yet committed (still no sound of battle from up north), and that the critical hours of daylight necessary to follow up a successful breakthrough — should one occur — were fast slipping away.

Everything Lee had planned for had so far fizzled, but here in front of him now was the *one* remaining possibility. He could see that the battle had already been joined — foolishly, perhaps — but joined nevertheless, and apparently successfully, as far as it went. Jenkins, in all probability, had either taken Cooper's battery, or was in the process of doing so, as Lee returned. Thus, in a sense, the decision had already been taken out of Lee's hands. For if Longstreet was ever going to take the crossroads, he would have to do so immediately and move at once in support of Jenkins, who was then an island of gray in a sea of blue. If Jenkins was not at once supported, his assault and initial success would have been in vain, his brigade sacrificed for nothing. In the final analysis, the decision must have been simple — attack!

The order would have been given to Longstreet, and it would have taken him at least some time to put his remaining brigades into position for the advance. This is what Alexander meant when he noted that "more time was wasted," and that the assault, as a result, went in "piecemeal." In terms of the positioning of the brigades, at that moment Jenkins held the center, Wilcox would later advance on his left, with Kemper soon to move on his right. Four other brigades were in support, Branch taking position on the far right and rear to offer cover to the flank.[2] Yet Wilcox and Kemper, with Jenkins already ahead, would not have been able to properly align their movements upon each other's flanks, and this created the spasmodic attack Alexander observed. Thus each brigadier went in by his own lights, and at considerably different times — a very ragged attack. Kemper advanced first, emerging from the covering woods, and moving forward at about 5:00 P.M.,[3] and it would take Longstreet another forty minutes to get Wilcox into the action.

"James Kemper's Virginians had not yet been in any of the Seven Days fighting, and at the command 'Forward' they started ahead without thought to order or discipline, rushing headlong through the woods and underbrush and clearings, hallooing the Rebel yell. Kemper admired their spirit but despaired of keeping them under command. In ragged order or no order at all they burst out of the woods into the open ground in front of two batteries of the German Light Artillery."[4] Thus the assault on the Confederate right, though impetuous and spirited, was, to a great extent, already out of control.

On the far left, Wilcox stepped off, as noted, some forty minutes after Kemper, his left resting on the Long Bridge Road.[5] He advanced directly toward George Meade's brigade arrayed across that avenue, with Randol's battery of six guns and Amsden's Pennsylvania Light Artillery virtually in his face.[6]

Here again, the Confederate reconnaissance and thought process must be called into serious question. For instance, had Wilcox advanced with the Long Bridge Road on his right — north of the road, rather than south — he would have advanced into the gap between Meade's right flank, and Kearny's left, rather than advancing directly into the teeth of a strong position. "The whole Union line was so long that it was unoccupied in portions."[7] In that sense, the Federal position was entirely vulnerable in a number of locations due to these breaks, and these could easily have been probed, identified, and attacked, had the Confederates taken the time and effort to do so. But they had not, so Wilcox, rather than attacking the weak point in the line, would advance directly into its strength.

In that Wilcox was not dressing on Jenkins' flank (Jenkins' brigade was long since involved), there was no need to remain on the right side of the road to begin with, and much to be gained by shifting north. Clearly, the gaps were the places to strike, thus potentially breaking through the Federal position with virtually no resistance, turning the flanks, and possibly gaining the Union rear with the least effort. While Longstreet had sent out a force to reconnoiter the Federal position, it was inexcusable that these areas had not been identified as long as Longstreet had been deployed and as near his division they were located. But it seems that aggressive reconnaissance — the lifeblood of any offensive venture — was utterly missing from almost all Confederate operations that day. For this negligence, they would repeatedly pay a heavy price.

Wilcox's troops moved forward quickly, gingerly passing through timber, crossing over a creek, then through yet more woods before finally gaining open ground in front of the Federal position. Here, as they emerged into the sun and open fields, they were immediately assailed by a strong volley of musketry and a salvo of artillery fire from infantry posted along the Union front and the two batteries previously mentioned.[8] The fight was at once joined, and very quickly heated to a boil.

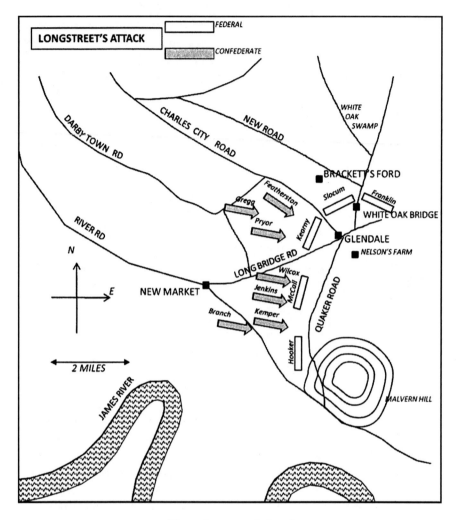

LONGSTREET'S ATTACK

FEDERAL

CONFEDERATE

WHITE OAK SWAMP

DARBY TOWN RD

CHARLES CITY ROAD

NEW ROAD

BRACKETT'S FORD

Featherston

Gregg

Slocum

Franklin

Pryor

WHITE OAK BRIDGE

RIVER RD

Kearny

GLENDALE

N

NELSON'S FARM

LONG BRIDGE RD

Wilcox

Jenkins

McCoil

E

NEW MARKET

QUAKER ROAD

Branch

Kemper

2 MILES

Hooker

JAMES RIVER

MALVERN HILL

Map — Longstreet's Attack

Taking heavy casualties, Wilcox, like Jenkins before him, pushed his brigade into the teeth of the Union position. "The 8th Alabama became engaged with the force in the woods but the 11th Alabama got within 100 yards of the battery before the Federal defense forced it back. The regiment renewed the attack and this time came within fifty yards of the Federal guns. Once more the 11th gave ground."[9] In a battle of wills, for the moment, at least on the Confederate left, the Union force seemed to be holding.

On the far right flank of the assault, however, it was another story. Kemper's Virginians charged ahead, straight into the maelstrom, seemingly oblivious of the fire in their faces, whooping and racing at the double-quick as the left portion of McCall's line of infantry and artillery blasted away at them from behind hastily thrown up breastworks of logs and stone. They stormed through a small wood, across a bog, then square into the Federal line. Here they discovered a log house, temporarily barricaded and refitted as a defensive strong point, but the screaming Rebels surged past it like an unstoppable wave. "Undeterred by the fire from the breastwork, the house, and the artillery, Kemper's men stormed onward, overran the house, captured six of the eight guns, and pushed on to the woods east of the clearing. They had far outrun the brigades on either side of them. Determined to hold their ground, they made the best of their bad position and maintained a vigorous fire."[10]

Kemper's assault had sent the left of McCall's battle line reeling, many of the fleeing fugitives storming through Joe Hooker's defenses to the immediate south. Here, just as with Jenkins' brigade in the center of the assault, the Federal line had been breached, perhaps only minutely, but breached nevertheless. The question then was, could these small breaches be held and if possible expanded? Could the Quaker Road, running only a few hundred yards east of Kemper and Jenkins at that moment, be taken? Could the Federal army, still in retreat, be slashed in half?

As Kemper's brigade held on for dear life on the southern flank of the Rebel assault — Federal infantry was swarming in to repel the penetration — Wilcox forced his command yet again into the heart of George Meade's line of blue along the Long Bridge Road. Here the fighting became close and savage, often face to face, bayonet to bayonet, or even fist to fist — a furious contest! The focal point of the attack became Randol's battery, the six guns that had been spitting hot metal at both Jenkins and Wilcox as they advanced throughout the late afternoon. As Stephen Sears observes, to the Union troops holding McCall's teetering line on the right, the advancing Confederates appeared, like some grim legion dispatched from the underworld, to rise right out of the ground in front of them. "There was some low ground 300 yards in advance of Randol's battery, and the Yankees could see there just the tips of several Rebel battle flags. For a time the flags remained motionless, then they rose and grew larger and behind them men seemed to rise up out of the ground."[11]

Amsden's battery in front of Meade's brigade, suddenly ran low of ordinance, and had to limber up and retire, leaving only Randol's six guns to confront the desperate Rebel charge.[12] Meade's brigade, already weakened from its fight at Gaines's Mill, was suddenly fighting for its life. Now the Federal infantry support sprang to their feet, raced head-long through the flame belching artillery, and collided with the advancing Confederates just in front of the guns. The collision was horrific. "Bayonet crossed bayonet in a fierce melee. Heads were mashed with rifle butts. Primal rage possessed the struggling men. Decimated at last, the Alabamians were driven back."[13]

But they were not driven back for long. The Confederates reformed and attacked again, slamming once more into the line of Yankee infantry in front of the guns. "The color bearer and every man in the color company of the 7th Pennsylvania went down. A Federal captain shot Lieutenant T.J. Michie in the arm with his pistol and slashed him on the head and face with his sword, whereupon Michie, already several times bayoneted, his wounds mortal, ran the captain through with his sword and killed him."[14]

General McCall, who was with his battery at the time, would years later recall the desperate Confederate charge: "On the right, Randall's battery was charged upon by the enemy in great force, and with a reckless impetuosity I never saw equaled. They advanced at a run over a space of six hundred yards of open ground. The guns of the battery mowed them down, yet they never paused. A volley of musketry was poured into them at a short distance by the 4th regiment, in support of the battery, but it did not check them for an instant; they dashed on, and pistoled and bayoneted the cannoniers at their guns."[15]

The Pennsylvania infantry broke, falling backward in front of the guns, streaming wildly to the rear through the battery. The Federal gunners, unable to fire for fear of cutting down their own troops, were suddenly overwhelmed by the Confederate tide, and were either gunned down where they stood, or forced to flee to the rear. Undaunted, however, much of the Federal infantry still stood their ground, and was in turn joined by the 7th Regiment, then coming onto the field from the rear. The contest for Randol's guns was renewed yet again, and the bodies of the dead and wounded began to litter the battery, the dead resting in eternal stillness, while many of their wounded comrades writhed nearby in agony.

Again, General McCall, who witnessed the action, recalled the fighting: "As I was with the battery at the time, it was my fortune to witness, in the bayonet fight that there took place, such a display of reckless daring on the part of the Alabamians, and unflinching courage on the part of the Pennsylvanians, as is rarely beheld. My men were, however, overpowered and borne off the ground."[16]

The fight swayed back and forth, neither side giving an inch. Men were shot down as they grappled over the guns, falling on and around the abandoned caissons and limbers, dying between the dead and wounded horses. Once again the struggle was hand to hand, eyeball to eyeball, savage in its intensity. Smoke filled the air, making it difficult to discern friend from foe. Wilcox's own report bore witness to the carnage: "Capt. W.C.Y. Parker had two successive encounters with Federal officers, both of whom he felled with his sword, and, beset by others of the enemy, he was severely wounded, having received two bayonet wounds in the breast and on in his side, and a musket ball breaking his left thigh."[17]

Few who witnessed the fighting at Glendale ever forgot it, nor failed to characterize it as equal to the most intense and frenzied combat of the entire war. "No more desperate encounter took place in the war; and nowhere else, to my knowledge, so much actual personal fighting with bayonet and butt of gun. Randol's battery, over which it began, was taken and retaken several times."[18]

Finally Wilcox's Alabamians drove through the battery and sent the Federals reeling into a wood behind, where they at once reformed and began pouring a withering fire into the Confederates. The Alabamians had taken the battery but were now far out in front, like Jenkins to their right, unsupported, and still facing a considerable force of Yankee infantry. Wilcox, knowing he could not remain where he was and survive, led his brigade back to the wood opposite and abandoned the battery, at least until reinforcements might arrive in his support. "The enemy," Wilcox explained, "at first repulsed and driven from the battery, retire to the woods, and deliver a terrible and destructive fire upon this regiment. With its ranks sadly thinned, it [the Alabamians] heroically stands its ground. The enemy, now seeing this regiment isolated and unsupported, advance from their cover against it. The sword and bayonet are freely used; many of the men received and gave in return bayonet wounds. There are no supports for them; no re-enforcements come, and they are at length forced to yield and retire to the woods in the rear, having left upon the field and around the battery in dead alone eight officers, of whom seven were captains or lieutenants commanding companies, and forty-nine privates."[19] George Meade, directing his Pennsylvania brigade in the heat of the battle, was twice wounded, and would be down for the remainder of the fight.[20]

At that point in time, both combatants on the Confederate left, worn and seriously depleted, withdrew to the cover of woods on either side of the battery — the dead and wounded strewn in between — and continued a vigorous musketry. Thus, on the far left of the Confederate attack, the Federal line had been breached by Wilcox's brigade, but not broken. On the right, Kemper, his brigade far in the advance, had wrested a temporary lodgment on McCall's left, and scattered that portion of the Federal line, and in the center Jenkins had, temporarily at least, overrun Cooper's battery.

These three furious brigade assaults had been launched independently, bereft of any semblance of coordination, and had evolved rapidly into something remarkably akin to savage brawls, yet despite all the failure and confusion, at that point, much had been accomplished. The Federal center was reeling and near implosion. While much more still needed to be achieved if Lee's plan to cut the Federal army in half was to be accomplished by nightfall, that plan, at this juncture of the battle, was by no means beyond realization.

CHAPTER 19

Nightfall

By 6 o'clock that evening — and just a few miles north and east of Wilcox's confrontation with George Meade's Pennsylvanians — for Confederate aspirations, both time and opportunity were rapidly fading into darkness at White Oak Swamp. Wade Hampton, returning to his brigade, quickly chose a work crew to follow him into the swamp in order to construct for Stonewall Jackson a bridge of no practical utility at a point where it was not needed at all. "Realizing — even if his superior did not seem to — that a golden opportunity might soon slip away, Hampton hastily assembled a fifty-man detail and set it to felling pine trees for construction material. In 'a few minutes,' pioneers and engineers fashioned a rough-hewn but serviceable bridge across the place where Hampton had waded the swamp."[1]

Hampton was confident that he could cross the swamp with his one brigade alone and take the unsuspecting Federals by the flank, turning the position, and perhaps — if the assault were driven hard — run the Union troops off the hill above the bridge, thus opening the road to Glendale for the entire Valley Army. Were that to happen, Jackson's force, driving down the road toward Glendale, would as a matter of sheer circumstance come in directly in front of Wilcox's command, thus pinning the enemy in place, and crushing Meade's Pennsylvanians from both front and rear. Not only that, by swift marching alone, Franklin, Slocum, and Kearny could all be cut off from the remainder of the Federal force en route to Malvern Hill, and McCall scattered to the four winds.

Thus did Hampton hurry to complete his project, and return to Stonewall in high hopes of being given the go ahead to cross over the swamp and attack. Hampton explains what happened next.

> Ordering a detail of my men to cut some poles where they were standing and to carry them into the swamp, a bridge was made in a few minutes. I then again reconnoitered the position of the enemy whom I found perfectly

quiet—unsuspecting. On my return to our side of the swamp, I found Gen. Jackson seated on a fallen pine alongside of the road that led down to the ford, and seating myself by him, I reported the completion of the bridge and the exposed position of the enemy. He drew his cap down over his eyes which were closed, and after listening to me for some minutes, he rose without speaking, and the next morning we found Franklin with the rest of the Federal troops concentrated at Malvern Hill.

While we were waiting at the White Oak crossing we heard the noise of Longstreet's battle at Frazier's Farm, and Capt. for Maj. Fairfax of Longstreet's staff came with a message from the general to Gen. Jackson. Though I heard this message, I cannot recall it.... In speaking to Gen. Lee in 1868 on this subject he expressed the greatest surprise at my account of this matter, and he said that he never had understood why the delay had occurred.[2]

Thus would Jackson's last opportunity vanish in futility at White Oak Swamp, not with a bang, but, as is said, with a whimper. The Valley Army, along with the other infantry at Jackson's disposal that afternoon, would sit on their arms within the sound of the fighting at Glendale, and the effect of this on the Federals opposite would be immediate, as would it have far ranging implications for the remaining combat that day. William Franklin, gauging his movements on the other side of the swamp based on what Jackson either did or did not do, explains his decision: "The enemy kept up the firing [Jackson's cannonade] during the whole day and crossed some infantry below our position [Daniel Harvey Hill's skirmishers], but made no very serous attempt to cross during the day, and contented himself with the cannonading and the firing of his sharp-shooters. Nightfall having arrived, and the wagons having all disappeared, I took the responsibility of moving my command to the James River by a road to the left which had not been much used, and arrived at headquarters safely about daylight."[3]

The point here is clear. Stonewall Jackson's lack of effort at White Oak Swamp would not only fail to carry the position and open the way to Glendale, it would fail even to hold the Federal rear guard in place, allowing Franklin to slip away unnoticed under the cover of darkness. Even more importantly, many of the infantry units that were with Franklin opposing Jackson would find themselves marching straight back into the fighting at Glendale, arriving, not only at the critical point, but at the critical time.

As Stephen Sears notes, once the initial brigades had been consumed in battle at Glendale, the fight would evolve into a contest determined by the arrival of reinforcements; thus, whichever side could feed the contest most effectively would in all probability prevail. In that sense, Jackson's lethargy would play well for the Federal cause. "If the Federal rear guard at White Oak Bridge was too large and too well posted for Jackson to challenge in pitched battle, at least he could hold it away from the larger battle. As it happened, the two brigades sent to Franklin by Sumner were returned in time to play an important role at Glendale, and two of Richardson's brigades also entered that fight. These 11,700 Yankee reinforcements were the literal measure of Stonewall Jackson's failure on June 30."[4]

In that sense, Stonewall Jackson would be indirectly responsible for the Federal reinforcements that saved the Glendale front from destruction late in the day's fighting. Thus, instead of Jackson's Valley Army arriving behind George Meade's brigade to crush it from both front and rear (with Wilcox in front), the troops that came streaming down the Long Bridge Road from White Oak Swamp early that evening would not be Confederate at all but Federal infantry, destined to Meade's support.

But Stonewall Jackson, by the late afternoon hours of June 30, had seemingly slipped far below the physical capacity to either think or function. For all intents and purposes, Jackson was probably asleep on his feet when Hampton last approached, and could probably not even have digested what Hampton was attempting to tell him, better yet compute how best to respond. Like a wounded animal, he simply obeyed his instincts and removed himself from a discomforting situation. Saying nothing, he got up and walked away, dumbfounding Hampton along with historians ever since. "It is said that Jackson fell asleep and either was not or could not be aroused by his staff officers. Night came. The roar of the battle at Frayser's Farm continued to crash over White Oak Swamp. The men prepared to bivouac. The General started to eat supper with his staff but was so weary that he fell asleep with food between his teeth."[5]

Kyd Douglas, on staff with Jackson during the Seven Days, offered something in the way of an analysis of Jackson's odd behavior, but which sounds curiously as much apology as it does explanation: "One thing is certain, General Lee was not supported by the action of his subordinates, as his strategy demanded. General Jackson has not escaped criticism, and he does not seem to have been his very self. There were things, it is true, he could not overcome. He was in the saddle continuously and seemed never to let up. Tired out with work he certainly was and so were his troops. But no one who rode with him on the 29th or 30th can recall a moment when he rested. But after reading the criticism on both sides, A.P. Hill's and W.B. Franklin's, and giving due credit to all explanations, the impression still remains, that if he had been up to the Stonewall standard that he had established in the Valley and kept to ever after the 30th day of June, he would have found the way to do more effective service that bloody day, and it would have been a sad one for the Army of the Potomac."[6]

If Stonewall Jackson ever regretted his performance during the Seven Days battles, and more specifically his sleepwalking ineptitude of the 30th, it is surely not on record. Quick to find fault with his own junior officers, often for even the most petty of infractions, Jackson was not one to offer disapproving critiques of his own efforts no matter how questionable, either publicly or privately. Months later he would prepare his own report of events, and whether this seemingly constitutes a reasonable explanation of events as Stonewall might have honestly recalled them, or an intentional dodge of legitimate criticism — and therefore a willful evasion of the truth — remains, to a large extent, in the eye of the beholder. Either way, the report surely skims lightly over the circumstances of the day.

> About noon we reached White Oak Swamp, and here the enemy made a determined effort to retard our advance, and thereby prevent an immediate junction between Gen. Longstreet and myself. We found the bridge destroyed and the ordinary place of crossing commanded by their batteries on the opposite side and all approach to it barred by detachments of sharp-shooters concealed in a dense wood close by. A battery of 28 guns from Hill's and Whiting's artillery was placed by Col. Crutchfield in a favorable position for driving off or silencing the opposing artillery. About 2 P.M. it opened suddenly upon the enemy. He fired a few shots in reply, and then withdrew from that position, abandoning part of his artillery. Capt. Wooding was immediately ordered near the bridge to shell the sharp-shooters from the woods, which was accomplished, and Munford's cavalry crossed the creek, but was soon compelled to retire. It was soon seen that the enemy occupied such a position beyond a thick intervening wood on the right of the road as enabled him to command the crossing. Capt. Wooding's batteries turned in the new direction. The fire so opened on both sides was kept up until dark. We bivouacked that night near the swamp.
>
> A heavy cannonading in front announced the engagement of Gen. Longstreet at Frazier's Farm and made me anxious to press forward, but the marshy character of the soil, the destruction of the bridge over the marsh and creek, and the strong position of the enemy for defending the passage prevented my advancing until the following morning. During the night the Federals retired.[7]

Yes, the marshy soil and the destruction of the bridge were factors, but what, for instance, of Hampton's report? What of the crossing point Wade Hampton discovered, of the bridge he constructed, and the Federal flank Hampton found floating in the air almost begging to be attacked? What of the crossing found by Munford and reported early in the afternoon? What of the other crossing points located, or of Wright's emergence from the swamp and his report that there was no Federal activity in the swamp to the west? What of Brackett's Ford lying only a mile away and connected to Jackson's position by good roads? Why was there no reconnaissance at all? Of these bewildering questions Jackson says nothing.

Porter Alexander, who analyzed Jackson's activities during the Seven Days in considerable detail, remained less than impressed with Jackson's official report, especially as to his inability to accomplish anything at all on the 30th, and Alexander minced no words. "Considered as an excuse for Jackson's inaction during the whole day," Alexander scoffed, "this report is simply farcical."[8] As previously written, Porter Alexander considered Jackson's delay on the 29th essentially religious in nature, and on the 30th possibly an unwillingness to employ his own infantry due to fatigue and overuse. "And now I shall have to tell," Alexander wrote somewhat bitterly years after the war in a private memoir meant for his family only, but published years after his death, "of how upon several occasions in the progress of the fighting during the next six days, Gen Lee's best hopes & plans were upset & miscarried, & how he was prevented from completely destroying & capturing McClellan's whole army & all its stores & artillery by the incredible slackness, & delay & hanging back, which characterized Gen. Jackson's performance of his part of the work."[9]

Indeed, Porter Alexander placed most of the blame for Confederate failure during the Seven Days, and most certainly for the heartbreaking failure at Glendale on Jackson. "As it was, within a month of taking command he [Lee] scattered all the tremendous forces concentrated for his destruction & practically deposed McClellan, the "Young Napoleon" of the Federals. But think of the moral effect on the country, & the world had he captured this entire army of 100,000 men with all its stores & arms & artillery. And this he would indoubtedly have done had Gen. Jackson of those six days been the same Gen. Jackson who had marched & fought in the Valley but a few weeks before."[10]

But the Jackson of the Chickahominy proved not to be the Jackson of the Valley after all, and through the exertion of, it seems, an odd blend of pity for his own troops, his own profound religious beliefs, and in the end an exhaustion so consuming that it was almost paralyzing, Stonewall Jackson would not only fail at Glendale, he would fail catastrophically.

CHAPTER 20

I Had Gained Command
of the Quaker Road

At the battle of Seven Pines in late May, Micah Jenkins had to push his brigade through and over any number of Federal commands and heavily fortified positions in order to negotiate a bloody and contested advance of almost one mile into the Federal rear. That would prove an advance that would make Jenkins and his brigade an immediate legend in the Army of Northern Virginia, while at the same time striking from the brigade's rolls a significant number of capable officers and men — victory in war, always comes at a price, often heavy. Today at Glendale Micah Jenkins would require all that determination and far more to advance, through a storm of Federal fire and almost fanatical resistance, but a few hundred yards toward the Quaker Road.

No sooner had Jenkins' brigade swarmed through James Cooper's battery of Pennsylvania artillery on McCall's front than they were greeted by a blast of musketry in their faces from supporting infantry concealed directly behind the battery. This was McCall's reserve infantry temporarily hidden behind a breastwork they had recently thrown up,[1] and under command of Colonel Seneca Simmons. Jenkins would soon find the Federal infantry just as desperate to hold and protect the road behind them as he was to take it.

After letting loose a terrible volley into Jenkins' unsuspecting troops, Simmons ordered a charge in an effort to retake the battery, and the blue clad troops poured over the breastwork and back into the guns. Once again, the fight raged back and forth through the battery, often devolving into hand-to-hand combat, wounded soldiers falling everywhere, the dead quickly littering the field. Bullets simply filled the air. "If there was one Ball Whistled past my devoted head," one Pennsylvania infantryman later wrote home, "that day there was thousands. It appeared to me they flew in every Square inch of air around me except the little Space I stood in."[2]

Taken somewhat by surprise, and overwhelmed as a result, Jenkins'

South Carolina brigade was pressed backward, then finally forced to abandon the battery they had fought so hard to initially secure. But the Pennsylvania reserves had suffered dearly for their efforts as well, leaving scores of dead and wounded on the field including Seneca Simmons, their commanding officer. The price of the counterstroke for the Pennsylvania brigade had been steep.

Jenkins fell back but quickly regrouped his command. He had no intention of allowing the Federals to defeat his efforts that day, and with the addition of two Alabama regiments[3] sent as support from Wilcox, he started forward once more. "Those of us left standing," wrote one of Wilcox's men, "poured a volley at a distance of not more than ten paces into the faces of the gunners. They fell across their guns and under the wheels, whole teams of horses plunging about in their mad agony, trampling under foot the wounded."[4] The fighting was again furious, the two lines exchanging heavy volleys at virtually point blank range as they dueled over the now abandoned guns, but this time it was the Confederates who would, for the time at least, prevail. McCall's infantry was pushed back slowly, then fled the battery, leaving their dead behind. Once again, Cooper's battery belonged to Jenkins, but just as with the Federals only moments before, the counterattack had proved costly.

As Wilcox came on the field with the rest of his command to the left of the South Carolina brigade, the fighting across McCall's entire front became both furious and deadly. Smoke swirled around the Nelson farm, north and south along the Quaker Road, guns roared, artillery boomed, and men fell everywhere across a half mile front. Thomas Goree watched as some of Longstreet's finest brigades were chewed to pieces in the maelstrom. "In this fight as in most of the others, our loss was heavy but not so heavy as that of the enemy. In this fight we took a considerable number of prisoners & 18 pieces of artillery. Nearly all of the brigades of Genl. Longstreet's Division lost one third the number carried into action, killed & wounded. The South Carolina Brigade (Jenkins') lost more than half & the Ala. Brigade (Wilcox) lost at least one half."[5]

With the battery taken again, Jenkins pushed his men forward, out beyond the now silent artillery pieces, limbers, and abandoned caissons, toward the Federal infantry still clinging to their position along a breastwork only a few yards behind. "Jenkins and his men then moved through Cooper's abandoned battery and advanced against the breastworks under a galling frontal fire from General Truman Seymour's Federal brigade. Suddenly, two other Federal batteries opened fire about three hundred yards on the left, and from this position were able 'to enfilade [Jenkins'] entire command.' At this point, his men were not only taking murderous musket fire in the face, but were being methodically slaughtered by grape, canister and shells from the twelve Federal guns on their left flank."[6] Caught in a deadly crossfire, the South Carolina brigade was being decimated.

Jenkins, mounted and surely the target of almost every Federal rifle on the field, pressed his men forward into the center of the fury that was explod- ing all around them, with virtually no concern for his own safety. Whole rifle companies of South Carolina troops were torn to pieces with each Federal volley and salvo of canister,[7] but still they swept forward. Twenty, thirty men fell at a time. For a moment the South Carolinians would hesitate, but with a wave of the hand, Jenkins was somehow able to move them on, driving them unceasingly toward the enemy. "He told me," Thomas Goree later recalled, "that at one time when he [Jenkins] saw how fast they were falling around him, he stopped and prayed God to send a bullet through his heart. He says, too, that at times as he would ride up and down the line, his men would turn and give him a look as much as to say, 'We can go no further,' when he would wave his hand to them and they would again dash forward."[8] Somehow the assault continued through a rain of bullets, bursting shells, and exploding charges of canister (cylindrical charges containing round, metal balls) that not only killed, but tore men to shreds.

Forty yards they closed to within the Federal infantry, men falling by the score, red sheets of musket blasts in their faces, then they closed to within thirty yards, and still they pressed on. At twenty yards the Federal infantry- men began to panic. "With 'a single wave of his sword [Jenkins pointed] out the path of duty,' and even though unsupported on the left by the other brigades, his men continued their advance toward the breastworks. Jenkins reported that as they got to within twenty yards of the Union line, many of the Federal soldiers rose and ran, 'and our cool, deliberate volleys prostrated them in hundreds.'"[9]

Micah Jenkins was the first to go over the breastwork, jumping his horse in pursuit of the fleeing Federals, only to have the horse shot out from under him. He tumbled to the dirt, then leaped to his feet to face the remaining Union troopers, but "his men came over behind him and fought the remain- ing Federal soldiers with bayonets and musket butts."[10] Another wild melee, another eyeball-to-eyeball slaughterhouse, as men were shot, stabbed, and bayoneted along the length of the breastwork, until finally the last of the Federal soldiers turned and fled. Hot on their heels, the South Carolinians pursued, gunning the running fugitives down, adding yet another tally of dead to the day's already grisly toll.

In the center of the Federal Glendale defense, McCall's line had been shattered, blown wide apart by the brigade of South Carolinians who were now hot at their heels. Jenkins' men ran toward the abandoned guns of the Union battery, and began turning them around. "As the Union troops abandoned the breastworks, F.W. Kilpatrick, the captain of Company B of the Palmetto Sharpshooters, along with Lieutenant Robert M. Simms of the Sixth South Carolina, then turned the abandoned guns of Cooper's battery on the fleeing Federals 'and handsomely accelerated their "change of base."'"[11]

With that McCall's depleted and battle worn division had been routed, run over in a fight they should never have been asked to make, now scattered behind what had previously been the Federal center. The path to the Quaker Road now lay open. On the far right of the Confederate assault, Kemper's brigade had broken the line, and Wilcox on the left, while not smashing through, had pummeled the Federal position.

"At the center of the union line George McCall's division was wrecked. Along a half-mile front every one of the twenty-six Federal guns had been taken or withdrawn or abandoned, and those of McCall's troops still on the field were disorganized or leaderless. Of his three brigade commanders, Simmons was dead, Meade badly wounded, and Truman Seymour had disappeared."[12] Later that evening Seymour would be discovered walking along the Long Bridge Road, benumbed, shell shocked, and vainly in search of General Franklin. His hat had been pierced with bullet holes, his horse shot out from under him, and, when asked, Seymour readily admitted that he had no idea where his brigade might be.[13] Longstreet's initial three brigade assault had swept over McCall's position like a frenzied, gray wave.

Micah Jenkins — Commanded a brigade of South Carolina infantry at Glendale. His brigade would take the Quaker Road, thus cutting the Army of the Potomac in half (Library of Congress).

On the far right of the Union line corps commander Heintzelman was at the time riding with Phil Kearny, both anticipating Huger's assault down the Charles City Road — which would never be delivered — when the sound of musketry, artillery fire, and the shouts of combatants rolled toward them like a deafening thunder from the Federal center. That thunder grew to a tempest, then suddenly faded as the celebratory cheers of the Confederate attackers could be distinctly discerned.[14] Both Federal officers knew exactly what the cheers meant — the Union center had been broken. Disaster was at hand.

In the center of the storm Micah Jenkins continued pushing his mangled brigade forward. Through Cooper's battery, over the breastwork, and then up and out across the open fields they swarmed, racing toward Mr. Nelson's farm. The fugitives from McCall's shattered line were stampeded in front of the South Carolinians, some in a vague semblance of order, others scattered throughout the woods, still others stumbling up the road toward White Oak Swamp in search of help, relief, or safety.

Thomas Goree, standing in rear of the full advance, recalls the sequence of events as they took place. "One of A.P. Hill's (Branch's Brigade) was ordered as a support to Kemper & Jenkins. Kemper's (which used to be Genl. Longstreet's old brigade) charged & took a battery. The enemy then brought up reinforcements and Branch failing to support Kemper, the battery was retaken and many of the old brigade captured with it."[15]

Thus, while Kemper was being pressed on the Confederate right, Jenkins, in the center, continued pushing his brigade forward. Goree's eyewitness account captures the fearful carnage of the advance: "Jenkins in the meantime had taken a battery and still kept forward. His advance at this time was the most desperate I ever knew. A few hundred yards to the left of the battery he took was one that Wilcox was trying to take. Just in Jenkins' front was a very large force of the enemy's infantry which he immediately engaged, when this battery on his left commenced on him with grape and canister. Thus he advanced in the face of a terrible musketry fire at the same time infiladed by artillery. Notwithstanding, he pushed on, charged the enemy and drove them from their position with terrible slaughter."[16]

Unwilling to stop, indeed unstoppable, Jenkins pushed his brigade east until they reached the day's objective — the Holy Grail, as it were, of General Lee's tactical conception for the day — the Quaker Road. There the young colonel quickly deployed his men in a strong blocking position, prepared to defend what he had taken, while awaiting reinforcements that he knew were close at hand to cement the issue for Confederate arms. Jenkins would later write in his report of the battle: "I had gained command of the 'Quaker

Road' and reinforcing masses [Federal reinforcements] could not advance but in direct fire of our men; I had a very strong position."[17]

Despite all the day's blunders — regardless of Huger's, Holmes', and Jackson's repeated failures — the Quaker Road had been taken by Confederate forces, and at that moment the Federal army had been sliced in two. As Micah Jenkins deployed his battered brigade along the Quaker Road, a stunning Confederate victory passed from the realm of theoretical possibility to attainable reality. The moment simply had to be seized, and Franklin, Kearny, and Slocum's Union commands would all be cut off from possible retreat, while the retreating Federal column on the road to the south, subject to immediate attack and seizure. It was almost everything Lee had planned for, all delivered, not by a well coordinated four pronged envelopment, but rather the almost fanatical assaults of three of Longstreet's brigades.

Yet that success had been achieved at a very high price in both blood and valor. Jenkins's South Carolinians had been purged of nearly one-half their numbers, the field behind them left strewn with their fallen comrades, many writhing in pain, still others torn to pieces. Both Wilcox and Kemper had suffered similarly. In some individual regiments the accounting of the dead and wounded had been truly staggering. "The 11th Ala. (Col. Syd Moore's Reg.) out of 10 officers commanding companies lost 8 killed & two wounded. The Palmetto Sharpshooters (Col. Jenkins Regt.) out of 375 men, lost 44 killed & 210 wounded."[18] Humphrey's Company C of the Palmetto Sharpshooters suffered 80 percent casualties, while the Fifth South Carolina Volunteers suffered 70 wounded and 11 killed at Glendale out of a total of 175 men who had advanced into battle that day.[19] "Like the Palmetto Sharpshooters, the Fifth was now only a shell of what it had been after reorganization in April. Fewer than 100 men and only 6 commissioned officers were left for duty."[20]

But numbers alone could not come close to describing the carnage and human misery wrought that afternoon. Young lieutenant John Lee, Jenkins' adjutant, lay on the field behind his now advanced South Carolina brigade, both legs blown off during the desperate advance. The boy would try hopelessly to recover his legs and bandage the wounds himself, before dying on the field. Not far from Lee, Jenkins' brother-in-law, John Jamison, had also been cut down, a Federal ball puncturing his lung and lodging near his heart. Jamison appeared near death (remarkably, Jamison would recover) when the colonel finally found him later that evening, and Micah Jenkins would break down completely after discovering young Lee not far away.[21]

"The colors of the Palmetto Sharpshooters were borne by several men, all wounded or killed, until the flag was finally carried through the end of the fight by Christopher L. Reid, a private in Captain William Humphrey's Company C. Major William Anderson, who had acted as commander of the Palmetto Sharpshooters, was mortally wounded and died four days later. Jenkins wrote, 'I am much aggrieved at the death of my noble Major.'"[22]

Colonel Jenkins' own performance that afternoon seemed something almost on the cusp of the mythical, indeed, "miraculous," as T.J. Goree would later describe it. "His horse was shot twice. A hole was shot through his saddle blanket, his bridle reins cut in two near his hand. An India rubber overcoat tied on behind his saddle has 15 holes through it made by a musket ball & piece of shell. His sword was shot off at the point, & shot half in two near the hilt, & his sword knob was also shot off. Besides all this he was struck on the shoulder with a grape shot (which bruised it severely) and was also struck on the breast & leg with fragments of spent shell."[23]

The question remaining at that moment for Federal forces still on the field was could they retake the road and reopen the path south to Malvern Hill? The survival of the Army of the Potomac, and perhaps the future of the Federal Union, would depend upon the answer.

The question remaining for Jenkins and the Confederate high command was could they maintain and expand their grip on the all important Quaker Road, thus virtually sealing a monumental victory with the destruction of the fleeing Federal foe?

One thing was certain, however. With Colonel Jenkins' advance to the Quaker Road, the Southern Confederacy was at that moment very near both victory and independence, nearer indeed, than it had ever been before, or would ever come close to thereafter.

CHAPTER 21

One Blood-Chilling
Cry of Pain

Longstreet's initial assault had finally managed — after repeated assaults and great loss of life — to drive McCall from the center of the Federal position, but those three brigades that had done the damage to the Union line were in turn shattered themselves during the accomplishment of the task. Many of the units had lost half their number and were subsequently enfeebled to the point of wreckage. What they had gained they could not hold without immediate support.

Beyond that, the Federal line still far overlapped the Confederate breakthrough, as neither Kearny to the north nor Hooker to the south had been as yet seriously engaged, thus those Union forces might still easily take the Confederates by the flank at either extreme. Should that occur, the Confederate advance, still bent on enveloping the Federal Army, might well be quickly enveloped and swallowed itself. Thus what had been gained by the Confederates early that evening might still easily be lost if it were not aggressively reinforced. "There was nothing to do but to throw in the remaining brigades in an effort to consolidate and hold the ground already won."[1] This reinforcement would have to be done rapidly and efficiently, however, and that, like most other Confederate operations that day, was not to be.

To begin with, Lawrence Branch's brigade, which had been placed on the far right and rear of Kemper to cover his right flank, made the first and most critical mistake. Branch's brigade, as T.J. Goree previously noted, had not come properly to Kemper's support, thus leaving Kemper far out front and entirely alone to try and stave off the efforts of closing Federal infantry. Kemper's brigade, exhausted and outgunned, could not hold the battery they had stormed, and slowly had to retire before superior numbers.[2] Apparently searching for the right flank of the initial Confederate attack, Branch's brigade then appeared on Jenkins' far right and rear. Jenkins, at first elated by Branch's appearance, and thinking it the reinforcements he desperately needed to hold the Quaker Road, was very soon forced to reconsider his fortunes.

Branch's brigade, in what can only be considered one of the greatest blunders of the war, began firing into their own men from behind. Jenkins, writing in his after battle report, stated, "I had a very strong position and, with my weakened numbers, could have made it good for some time, but here occurred a painful and disastrous event."[3] The painful and disastrous event Jenkins refers to was the appearance of Branch's undisciplined brigade on his right. "The ability of Jenkins' brigade to hold its strategically important position on the Quaker Road depended entirely on the support he was supposed to have received from Lawrence O. Branch's brigade of A.P. Hill's division. Unfortunately, when they came up on Jenkins' right rear, Branch's men started firing through Jenkins' line at the Federals."[4]

Branch's troops, somehow in the confusion of battle, swirling smoke, or perhaps the fading light of early evening, massed on Jenkins' right regiment, throwing it into "confusion" and then firing through it at the Federals opposite.[5] Jenkins was suddenly taking fire from both front and rear, from friend and foe alike, and his brigade was naturally thrown into utter bewilderment. Worse still, Branch then withdrew his brigade as rapidly and in as much confusion as it had appeared, leaving Jenkins to face the gathering Union reinforcements alone. Goree, watching the affair from the rear, argues that Branch's brigade simply panicked when "as soon as they reached the place and saw how far in advance it was & the number of the enemy a half mile farther on, they turned & fled."[6] So there it is. In the blink of an eye the opportunity of a lifetime for Confederate hopes appeared to have evaporated. Facing growing numbers of Federal infantry all across his front, and with no support near at hand or on the horizon, Jenkins was forced to withdraw from the Quaker Road himself, conceding to the Federals — for the time being at least — the one possible artery for their evacuation.

No Federal advance, defense, or action had even so much as altered the field, but rather another inexplicable Confederate miscue had again derailed Rebel aspirations. Had Abraham Lincoln been pulling the strings of a puppet show, he could not have yanked Branch's brigade from the stage with more precision or to better effect for the Federal cause that day.

What would have happened had Branch come to Jenkins' support rather than disrupting his brigade and then pulling off for some unknown reason will never be known. But it is at least reasonable to assume that, had Jenkins been able to hold his position for awhile as he maintained in his report he could have done (the Union center was entirely disorganized at this point, and Jenkins' insistence that he could have held his position seems reasonable), and had Branch's full force been added to Jenkins' blocking deployment defending the Quaker Road, Lee's plan for cutting the Army of the Potomac in half may very well have worked to success that evening.

As the historian Stephen Sears points out, "At that moment the break in McCall's line was very close to achieving General Lee's design for cutting the Army of the Potomac in half. Should the attack now drive on across the Quaker Road, everything north of that point — better than five divisions — would be isolated from the rest of McClellan's army."[7]

Had Branch gone to Jenkins' assistance as he had been ordered, McClellan's army might well have permanently been cut in two. For Longstreet had already detailed two additional brigades — those of Charles Field and Dorsey Pender — to move to Jenkins' support in the center, and had they come up with the Quaker Road still in Confederate hands, there is little doubt that those three (including Branch's) brigades could have held against almost anything the Federals might have thrown at them until nightfall, even allowing for the withdrawal of Jenkins' much depleted command.

It is, of course, impossible to say with any precision what may have happened that night, or what the reaction of officers such as Kearny or Heintzelman might have been to being trapped north of Glendale, but there is little question they would have realized quickly that they were cut off and in very serious trouble. Their potential responses would have been both limited and desperate. Barring some almost miraculous escape, the following morning they would have been virtually encircled. Magruder had his division once again at the Glendale front, and Jackson was finally up and alert, his entire force prepared to pounce upon any fragmented Federal forces between Riddell's Shop and White Oak Swamp. Those Union forces ensnared in such a trap would have found themselves in an almost hopeless situation.

But Branch was nowhere to be seen, thus Jenkins had to withdraw from the vital artery south, and once Pender and Field arrived later that evening the road had been flooded with newly arrived Federal units. No longer would the fight be to hold the Quaker Road, but rather to try and seize it again. And in this the Confederates would ultimately fail.

Not only had Longstreet designated support for the center of his line, but for the left and right of his front as well. On the right, to try and extend Kemper's modest gains and assist Branch (wherever he might next be found), Archer's and Pickett's brigades had been detailed. Field and Pender, as told, were marched straight for the center, while the three additional brigades of Pryor, Featherston, and Gregg were shifted to the far Confederate left to support Wilcox's fading efforts, and hopefully extend the left wing still further.[8] Those three brigades would strike headfirst into Phil Kearny's division, deployed north of Riddell's Shop, between the Long Bridge and Charles City roads. For the Confederates, only the brigade of General R.H. Anderson remained in reserve. The intent thus was clear: If the Army of Northern Virginia was going to break the Federal line at all, it would have to be done here and now, and with virtually every unit left at its disposal. Lee would hold nothing back.

Micah Jenkins may have been forced to withdraw for the time being from the Quaker Road due to Branch's error, but he was by no means finished for the day. Noting Wilcox's ongoing struggle over Randol's battery only some 300 yards north of his position, he quickly reorganized his brigade, then made a hard left turn to assault the battery — which had been butchering his troops for the entire afternoon and early evening — from the south. So effective had the fire from Randol's battery been upon the South Carolinians, many of those who managed to survive the day at Glendale swore they would never forget it. "The sullen 'thug' of the grape shot as they bury themselves into the bodies of the men is an appalling sound — one that can never be forgotten.... Whole companies are decimated," recalled one South Carolina infantryman.[9] Jenkins, it can be presumed, intended to even the score.

Charging due north, Jenkins swept across the Long Bridge Road, stumbled over the bodies of the countless dead and wounded, then swept directly into the battery with what little remained of his command. His small force "then combined with Cadmus Wilcox's brigade in an advance which resulted in the capture of six of the twelve Federal guns on their left. These were the guns from Alanson M. Randol's battery, which had killed and wounded so many of Jenkins's men during their charge against McCall's division earlier that afternoon."[10] Once again the fighting became fierce and hand to hand. General McCall, still desperately trying to fend off the Confederates, years later remembered the scene: "It was here my fortune to witness one of the fiercest bayonet fights that perhaps ever occurred on this continent.... I saw skulls crushed by the butts of muskets, and every effort made by either party in this life-or-death struggle, proving indeed that here Greek had met Greek."[11]

With the taking of Randol's battery, the fighting that day finally ended for Micah Jenkins and his South Carolina brigade. They had driven through Cooper's battery, taken it twice, driven off a third of McCall's division, taken the key strategic point of the entire operation — the Quaker Road — and finally assisted Wilcox in the successful assault of Randol's battery.[12] Had Branch come properly to his support as ordered, Micah Jenkins may well have changed the course of American history. But for Jenkins, who had seen many a good friend die that afternoon and evening, the cumulative effect of the day's combat had taken its toll. Thomas Goree, who was present when Jenkins came off the field, tried to console his friend. "I met him just as he was coming out of the fight and he was weeping like a child at the destruction of his brave, noble men."[13]

As the bodies accumulated in gruesome heaps in and around Randol's battery early that evening, fresh Confederate brigades headed off to the left and right. "Forgetful of the slaughter of Mechanicsville and unmindful of their frightful losses at Gaines's Mill, regiments moved forward at the order of command. The left of the line was threatened anew, but it was held against a vigorous fire. Finding the Federals in strength, the right regiments charged bayonets and soon were at grips with the enemy."[14]

On the far right of the Federal line Phil Kearny was waiting. He had but three brigades in his division. Of those he had placed two across his front while holding Hiram Berry's brigade of Michigan and New York regiments in close reserve. Along the front Kearny had eight pieces of artillery (a far cry from McCall's twenty-six), but they were well positioned, well supported, and would soon do deadly service.

Phil Kearny had made absolutely certain that his infantry was well supplied with enough extra rounds of ammunition to make a stand that day. "Before entering White Oak Swamp, Kearny insisted that every man in his division must be issued all the extra ammunition he 'could carry on his person.' Knapsacks and pockets were crammed with cartridges, and personal belongings such as extra clothing were thrown away. 'A soldier can fight in soiled underwear, but not without bullets,'" Kearny had schooled them, and his martial instincts were soon to be proven prescient.[15] "An officer in his division flatly stated that 'nothing saved the Union army in White Oak Swamp but those extra rounds of ammunition in the Third Division. If it had not been for Phil Kearny our corps would have been destroyed and with it the army."[16]

The ground in front of Kearny's division was dark and low and tree covered in spots, and when Featherston's and Pryor's Confederate brigades first came bounding through the woods with a yell it must have seemed to Kearny as if the gates of hell had suddenly been hurled open and the Rebel hordes let loose. Kearny had fought all over the world as a professional soldier, but he had never seen anything to match what was now approaching. The enemy appeared suddenly on his front, Kearny later recalled, "in such masses as I had never witnessed."[17] As the Rebels poured through the woods Kearny's artillery opened on them, at first with case shot — shells that exploded with thunderous cracks over and among the closing infantry raining grapeshot through the air — and later with canister as the Confederates neared

Kearny's battle line at Glendale. Fighting in the woods north of the Longbridge Road as drawn by Alfred R. Waud (Library of Congress).

the Union lines. Just over a hundred yards out the Rebel attack finally slowed and then came apart in the perfect hail of artillery fire Kearny's batteries were offering. Bloodied but not beaten, the Confederates drifted back into the woods.[18]

The Rebels were hardly finished. Twice they regrouped and came bounding through the woods, twice more straight into the muzzles of the waiting Federal artillery, and twice more they were blasted backward. With each charge the Confederates came closer and closer to Kearny's lines. In desperation the gunners "switched to double charges of canister, fired fast without sponging out the gun barrels between rounds, a highly dangerous expedient that risked a premature explosion while loading."[19] The killing ground in front of the guns became piled with Confederate bodies, the wounded writhing in pain. The screams of the dying men, Kearny later recalled, "blended into one blood-chilling cry of pain."[20]

Still, the Rebels came on. So far the Federal artillery had done a masterful and lethal job holding the Confederate assault at bay, but that could only hold so long as there was ample ordinance for the task, and soon — firing double charges at close range as they were — the batteries began to run low, and the rate of fire slackened. It would take time to bring up more ammunition. The infantry support behind James Thompson's Battery G, immediately grasping the situation, leaped to their feet with a shout, raced out through the guns, and assaulted the approaching Rebels.[21] "In a flash, yelling like incarnate fiends," Colonel Alexander Hays later wrote, "we were upon them."[22]

Just as with the various other clashes that day that had criss-crossed both Cooper's and Randol's batteries, this confrontation also exploded into fierce hand-to-hand combat. Here men were stabbed, slashed, knocked sense-less, and shot at close range in a wild brawl that spun up and down the line. The human tally in dead and wounded was again staggering. "In the smoky dusk individual regiments suffered severe losses. One third of the 63rd Penn-sylvania went down making its charge, and a second regiment defending Thompson's battery, the 1st New York, suffered 230 casualties, the highest in any Federal regiment on June 30."[23]

With his forward brigades now taxed and reeling all along the front, Kearny had little choice but to bring up his only reserve and toss it too into the fray. Just as with the Confederates facing him, the choice for Phil Kearny had become one of all or nothing. The last man standing, it seemed, would prevail that day at Glendale.

On the other side the Confederates threw in Maxey Gregg's brigade of South Carolina infantry, and the fight exploded anew. Darkness was now approaching, especially in the woods, and distinguishing one army from the other in the smoky, drab underbrush became increasingly difficult. Men fired at rifle flashes or at vague forms seeming to move in the distance, rarely sure of what they had hit, or if, in fact, they had hit anything at all. Bullets filled the night air. One Indiana infantryman declared, "We fired so rapidly that our guns were too hot to hold to."[24]

Precisely at this point the Army of Northern Virginia would begin to pay a heavy price for its long catalogue of mistakes, miscues, and ineptitude that June 30. Federal regiments that would have been held in place by means of a vigorous demonstration on the part of Stonewall Jackson at White Oak Swamp, or Benjamin Huger's advance along the Charles City Road, began to curl back into the fight near Glendale on their way south toward the James River. Just to the north of Keanry's now embattled line, for instance, Slocum's three brigades were resting on their arms as Benjamin Huger slowly cut an entirely new road out of the woods to avoid the timbers Heintzelman had ordered cut and laid across the road. With no heavy work on their hands, Slocum offered Kearny his former New Jersey brigade, and the boys, appar-ently grasping the fact that their old commander was in need, leaped to their feet. "Seemingly the whole brigade heard the request, for it went forward at the double-quick without further orders."[25] When they arrived on the field, Kearny, the old warrior, led them into battle himself, just as he had done previously at Williamsburg,[26] and Gregg's attack, for the moment at least, was stymied.

More fresh Federal troops were arriving to stem the Confederate tide, marching down the Long Bridge Road from the direction of White Oak Swamp. Francis Barlow, a young lawyer and capable officer who would one day rise high in the ranks of the Army of the Potomac, was this day commanding a regiment of New York infantry. Returning to Glendale from White Oak Bridge, and instinctively marching to the sound of the guns, he was immediately directed into the battle by David Robinson of Kearny's command.[27] Barlow would long remember the action in the dark and smoke and confusion along Kearny's front, and later wrote that "we could not distinctly see the enemy on the open ground but they heard us coming and broke and ran."[28]

Phil Kearny, fearlessly commanding from up front as usual, was personally plugging units into the fury and directing combat all along his front. With the help of the fresh Yankee regiments arriving from White Oak Swamp, his line, although seriously pressed by repeated and desperate Confederate assaults, was holding. For the time being, at least, the road behind him that wound its way south to the James remained safely in Federal hands. If he could hold his line until darkness enfolded the field, the Army of the Potomac might yet survive the day. Sadly, however, there was little if anything Kearny, or any other officer within earshot, could do to stop the "blood-chilling cry of pain" that was rising in painful volume across the woods and fields just west of Glendale.

CHAPTER 22

I'll See You All in Hell

Like a fire that could not be doused, the fight in and around the abandoned artillery along McCall's shattered front flared, then flamed anew as fresh troops approached the vacated Federal center from opposite poles. Rarely had a contest swayed so often or so consistently across a singular line of objectives, and the battered debris of battle, along with the human wreckage those numerous clashes had wrought, was now tossed about and left behind like the discarded, forgotten wake from some depraved carnival of fiends.

Dead horses, exploded limbers, discarded pistols, swords, rifles, caps, cups, and knapsacks, all the accoutrements of war simply littered the ground. Scattered among this debris, of course, were the pitiful wounded and dead, those still clinging to life begging for mothers, or water, or help, or mercy, or simply someone to come and put an end to their misery. Around and about the guns still boomed and smoke still swirled as darkness quickly descended like a black curtain slowly draped across a grisly stage, the approaching darkness turning what little time remained for battle into a deadly contest of hide and seek. Into this pathetic patchwork of human folly new players were yet arriving, some in gray, some in blue, but in the diminishing light few could discern the difference. Nevertheless, the drama played on.

"The contest for Cooper's and Randol's batteries flared up once more. Yankee troops reached the abandoned pieces first, but lacked the gunners to man them and horses to haul them away and the twelve guns were still fair game when Charles Field's brigade of A.P. Hill's division came on the field."[1] In the closing darkness Field's brigade passed through the wreckage of both Wilcox's and Jenkins' brigades, then moved ahead through Cooper's battery. They did not discharge their weapons, but swept forward instead at charge bayonets, an advancing wall of cold, lethal steel more reminiscent, perhaps, of Alexander's unstoppable Greek phalanx from a time long since gone than any current tactical conception of Civil War combat.[2] They quickly chased the defending Union soldiers out of the battery, over the abandoned breast-work behind, and into the open fields and wood lots just west of the Quaker Road. Here desperate fighting erupted anew, men slashing and firing at shadows, gunned down by invisible attackers, fighting an enemy that could hardly be seen. "One private was confronted by four Federals at the same instant. Although several times stabbed with bayonets, he killed three of his four antagonists. The other was dispatched by his brother."[3]

Due north of this furious contest, a regiment of Field's brigade once more moved toward Randol's battery, the elusive prize that had already been taken and lost and retaken and re-lost by both sides countless times that day. The 47th Virginia chased the Union troops back then struggled to turn the guns and open a deadly fire on the fleeing fugitives. "It so happened that the men of Company K of the 47th had originally enlisted as artillerists, and using that skill they turned one of Randol's Napoleons against the enemy and until dark blazed away with as much ammunition as they found with the gun."[4] From Knieriem's battery south near Joe Hooker's position, north to the Charles City Road, the battle still flashed and boomed and raged, desperate in character.

Along Phil Kearny's front Gregg's assault continued unabated, but through sheer attrition, seemed now to be losing steam. Still, the fight was close and a breakthrough possible, and while Kearny's line had not wavered, he fully grasped the implications of the moment. Sensing the need to patch in more troops to hold off the Confederates, Kearny rode to his left and finally located General McCall, still desperately trying to hold what remained of his battered division together while fending off the Rebels once more near Randol's guns. The two agreed that more had to be done. Assessing the situation in that sector, Kearny suggested, "If you can bring on another line in a few minutes I think we can stop them."[5] With that in mind both officers parted company, and rode off in separate directions in search of available units to cobble together.

In the Union center, regiments were moving up from White Oak Swamp, and these were being sent off by generals Sumner and Heintzelman to try and plug the still gaping chasm that had once been McCall's left wing. Captain Oliver Wendell Holmes, Jr., who had last been seen struggling south en route to Savage Station, was with the 20th Massachusetts Volunteers, and they were one of the regiments sent directly into the gap to contend with the approaching Rebels.

The 20th had spent most of the day in the woods near White Oak Swamp but had now been raced off into the woods and open lots just west of the Quaker Road. Holmes' note to his parents in Boston captures the hectic and desperate nature of his deployment: "Marched all night rested at early dawn—marched and rested in the woods noon—afternoon terribly thirsty (hardly any water to be had) came up double quick on to the field of action (knapsacks on backs) Nelson's Farm."[6]

The 20th Massachusetts deployed rapidly from column into line of battle, superbly as Holmes would later recall it, and started moving forward into the darkness in search of the enemy. "Forward in line (whole battalion front) better than the Regt generally does it on drill—*Whang* goes a shell two men drop in Co. Go. 'Captain! Noonan's hit!' 'No Matter, Forward Guide Right.'"[7]

Opposite Holmes's 20th Massachusetts that evening was Dorsey Pender's North Carolina brigade, five regiments strong, also just recently arrived on the field. Both lines began a withering fire at one another. The twentieth moved forward through the wreckage of an abandoned Federal battery as another Union regiment, the 7th Michigan, came up in support on their left. But the Michigan regiment panicked and ran, displaying the "white feather," the dreaded term for cowardice in the face of the enemy, and leaving the 20th in an exposed and dangerous position. "We go forward passing a deserted battery the dead lying thick round it and then begins the deuce of a time the Mich 7th on our left breaks & runs *disgracefully* (private) they lay it to Col Grosvenor [commander of the 7th Michigan] who they say showed the white feather."[8]

Outgunned and surely outmanned, the 20th fought hard until it appeared the overlapping Confederate lines might encircle them. They then began an orderly retreat, stopping to fire as they withdrew to the rear. "Not a waver in our Regt (Our Co. behaved better than most I may say) till Palfrey ... gave the order to march double quick in retreat. We were flanked & nearly surrounded and that saved us—After that we couldn't avoid confusion and what with straglers of other Regts &c. didn't form a good line."[9] The 20th escaped, but the fighting had been heavy, as Holmes notes. "The guns got so hot & dirty we couldn't load or fire more than ⅔ of 'em."[10]

On the Confederate side, Pender and Fields pressed forward, and in the darkness encountered more and more resistance, but they would push the Federal line back considerably, and eventually remove a substantial number of artillery pieces from the abandoned batteries. "A little later," Porter Alexander recalled, "Field's brigade of Hill's division, in a counter charge, again had bayonet fighting, and drove McCall's line back for a half-mile, and held the ground until the captured guns were carried safely to the rear."[11]

But the Rebels would never again take possession of the Quaker Road and here, once again, it had been previous Confederate miscues that had sabotaged the day. Had Magruder's entire command, for instance, been left to rest the day at Timberlake's Store as originally planned, then brought up in support of Pender and Field, there would have been little doubt as to the outcome. Magruder's command contained three full infantry divisions consisting of 27 regiments, and sixteen batteries of artillery, some 14,000 effective troops.[12] If Magruder had been available to move in support of Pender in the center, the center would have been taken and held by Confederate arms that evening, and the Army of the Potomac would have suffered the consequences.

Indeed, had Branch gone earlier to Jenkins' support as previously discussed, and had Field and Pender then also moved forward as reinforcements for those two brigades, Magruder's entire command might then have been used to attack the Federal retreat. One of Magruder's divisions could have moved north along the Long Bridge Road toward White Oak Swamp, another south down the Quaker Road toward Malvern Hill, with the final division held in reserve. That, essentially, would have represented the sort of envelopment General Lee had been hoping to execute that day. But it was not to be. Branch had failed, Field and Pender as a result had come up too late, and Magruder was all the while off marching in circles.

As the evening wore on, more Federal units continued flowing down the Long Bridge Road from White Oak Swamp. These were fed immediately into the fight, and over time the Union line was slowly restored. "With the fresh infusion of strength the Federals were able to retake Diederich's abandoned battery and to stymie the further advance of Field's and Pender's brigades."[13] But the fighting continued. "The battle raged with almost equal fury along the whole line. Hill, on the Confederate left, pressing forward his brigades in mass, and gained ground at first, capturing two full batteries, which he retained; but he was unable to gain any ground permanently, and at last it became apparent that Hooker and Kearny ... were slowly gaining, while the earlier repulse of McCall's flanks had been retrieved."[14]

Indeed, so aggressive did the Federals become at this point in time that, according to Alexander, Lee's recall of Magruder from the River Road was done to insure stability along his own line, and not for offensive purposes.[15] In order to hold all the ground the Confederates had taken, and to blunt any new Union aggressive aspirations, Longstreet finally committed the last brigade he was holding in reserve, that of J.R. Anderson, of Hill's division.

Hill, apparently aware of the threatening attitude of the Federal units on his front, resorted to a sly ruse to try and defuse the situation. Hill explains:

> About dark the enemy were pressing us hard along our whole line and my last reserve, Gen. J.R. Anderson, with his Ga brigade, was directed to

advance cautiously, and be careful not to fire on our friends. His brigade was formed in line, two regiments on each side of the road [the Long Bridge Road], and obeying my instructions to the letter, received the fire of the enemy at 70 paces before engaging themselves. Heavy reinforcements to the enemy were brought up at this time, and it seemed that a tremendous effort was being made to turn the fortunes of the battle. The volume of fire that, approaching, rolled along the line, was terrific. Seeing some troops of Wilcox's brigade, with the assistance of Lt. Chamberlayne and other members of my staff, they were rapidly formed, and being directed to cheer long and loudly moved again to the fight. This seemed to end the contest, and in less than five minutes all firing ceased and the enemy retired.[16]

With Anderson's advance, and more importantly, the coming of darkness, the fighting around Glendale finally sputtered out. To a great extent, the battle had ended in a tactical draw, the Confederates having pushed ahead and taken some ground and removed numerous pieces of artillery, while the Federals had prevailed in their principle objective, the defense and retention of the Quaker Road. In that sense, both sides had a little something to crow about, and both did a little crowing. Longstreet, for instance, reported, "The enemy was driven back slowly and steadily, contesting the ground inch by inch. He succeeded in getting some of his batteries off the field, and, by holding his last position till dark, in withdrawing his forces under cover of night."[17] But General Sumner's report for the Federals had a different take on the action that day. "After a furious contest, lasting till dark, the enemy was routed at all points, and driven from the field."[18]

The casualty counts at Glendale, when measured against other Civil War clashes, were minor, this because only a small percentage of either army actually met in combat that day, and the contest, while extraordinarily fierce where and when it flashed, lasted but a few hours. Among those units that had taken part in the day's carnage, however, the fight had taken a significant toll. "The Confederates lost 638 dead, 2,814 wounded, and 221 missing, a total of 3,673. The cost to the Federals came to 297 dead, 1,696 wounded, and 1,804 missing, a total of 3,797."[19] Most significantly, Longstreet, whose division had done most of the heavy lifting that day, lost over 25 percent.[20]

But no statistic — not casualty counts, or ground taken, or the number of artillery pieces carried off by the Southerners — could in any way diminish the magnitude of Confederate failure that June 30. Despite all the hard fighting by Longstreet's and Hill's troops — and they had fought ferociously!— those few disjointed brigade assaults were in the end the best the entire Army of Northern Virginia could muster on a day when the annihilation of their enemy, and the prospect of their own independence, had been placed at their fingertips. In that sense, for Confederate arms — indeed, for the entire Southern Confederacy — the day had not only been lost, but botched almost beyond reckoning. All things considered, General Lee attempted to put a good face on a bad day, but his words would ring hollow: "The enemy had been driven with great slaughter from every position save one, which he maintained until he was enabled to withdraw under cover of darkness. At the close of the struggle nearly the entire field remained in our possession."[21]

The one position the Confederates would not drive that day was the position occupied by Phil Kearny, and Kearny later reported fiercely, "Not a single man of my division fell back."[22] As Lee reported, at the end of the day's hostilities the Confederates held the field, but this was an accomplishment utterly devoid of true meaning, for as Douglas Southall Freeman points out, "the field was not the battle, and on the battle the campaign had hung.... The ambitious plan for the convergence of Jackson, Huger, Longstreet, A.P. Hill, Magruder, and Holmes had failed tragically."[23]

As night closed upon Glendale, George McCall and Phil Kearny were off on their separate errands in search of fresh troops to feed the hungry battle. Riding with his staff up to a group of unknown soldiers milling about in the darkness of the woods, McCall reined his horse in, and demanded urgently of the troops, "What command is this?"

The men responded quickly that they belonged to the command of General Field.

McCall shook his head, unfamiliar with any General Field, and started to turn and ride off when one of the soldiers quickly grabbed his horse by the bridle. "Not so fast," he said.[24] George McCall had become a prisoner of war.

In another wood on yet another trail, Phil Kearny like George McCall before him, eased himself into group of soldiers in the gathering darkness. Thinking that Federal troops occupied the woods, Kearny had stopped to study the position, when he suddenly realized he had ridden into a group of Confederate skirmishers. He sat his horse quietly. "Fortunately it was already dark and his cloak concealed his uniform. Apparently mistaking Kearny for his own commander, a Rebel officer strode up and asked, 'My men are all in position, sir. What shall I do now?"

Seizing the moment, Kearny, pulled himself up, then snapped at the mistaken officer. "Do as I have always directed you to do in such a situation, you fool!" Kearny barked. Then he yanked the horse's reins, and galloped off into the darkness before the startled man could respond.

Kearny rode back toward his own lines, then stopped and turned, once out of effective rifle range. "Good-bye, Rebels!" he called out. "I'll see you all in Hell!"[25] Then he yanked the reins again, and rode off into the night.

The battle for the crossroads at Glendale was over.

CHAPTER 23

Cowardice or Treason

On July 1, 1862, the day following the catastrophic Confederate failure at Glendale, and exactly one year prior to the day that General Lee would make the fateful decision to remain on the field and fight at Gettysburg, Lee would choose to remain firmly on the aggressive at Malvern Hill when perhaps discretion might have been the better part of valor. During the morning of the 1st Rebel forces trailed the Union Army down the Quaker Road to the foot of Malvern Hill, there finding the Federals in a firm defensive posture on the summit. In late afternoon the Confederates would attack in what can only be described as one of the most misguided, mishandled, and misbegotten affairs witnessed during the Civil War, one that would put a resounding exclamation mark on a week of Confederate operational incompetence.

In retrospect, the Rebel assault at Malvern Hill seems to have been as much an overreaction to their failure at Glendale the day before as it was any sensible tactical evaluation of the true prospects for victory that day. Lee, exhausted now himself, and feeling somewhat ill,[1] apparently fell victim to the then current hope that the Union Army had scrambled off from the fight at Glendale in a state of near demoralization and that if pushed would simply implode. Daniel Harvey Hill had discussed the formidable defensive features of the Federal position with a local resident, and had told Lee directly that "if General McClellan is there in force, we had better let him alone."[2] But this view would be scoffed at by Longstreet and others who presumed the Federal troops nearly beaten already. "It was this belief in the demoralization of the Federal army," Hill later explained, "that made our leader risk the attack."[3] Whatever the motivation, the attack would prove yet another glaring example of General Lee's insufficient command of his subordinates, and 5,650[4] Confederate officers and men would pay the price during an operation that would spin awkwardly out of control like a string of defective fireworks.

One thing, however, does seem clear. No matter how daunting the Federal position atop Malvern Hill may have appeared to Lee that morning, there was little question that it still represented his last opportunity to destroy McClellan's army and end the war with a total victory. Yet it was also painfully apparent to Lee that what could have been accomplished with relative ease the day before would require a mighty effort to accomplish today, and that any assault, even if successful, against such a dominating, well-fortified position, would require an enormous expenditure in blood. The price of failure on June 30 would be the greatly diminished prospect for success on July 1. Harvey Hill put it succinctly: "Had all our troops been at Frayser's farm, there would have been no Malvern Hill."[5] This Hill could state with certainty, because had all the Confederate columns converged on Glendale as Lee had planned and ordered, there would have been no more Army of the Potomac.

Throughout the long night of June 30 the Union army slipped away from its positions north and west of Glendale, and made the weary, nighttime march to Malvern Hill. Oliver Wendell Holmes, Jr., would not soon forget the exhausting trip: "That night June 30 we marched again (all this time I only eating about 3 pieces of hard bread a day & not wanting more hardly sleeping at all & never washing).... The next morn'g a splendid line of battle (of the whole army) at Malverton."[6]

The successful retreat had nothing at all to do with General McClellan, who had not been in touch with his army for hours. "His lieutenants on the battlefield, having no word and no orders from the general commanding for twelve hours, had once again acted on their own.... Leaving their dead and wounded behind, the Yankees marched for the James."[7] By dawn the entire army, directed independently by corps and division commanders, had made the march and was concentrated on the heights.

General McClellan, returning from his junket aboard the *Galena*, twice stopped by to visit his army, once late on the 30th after the battle at Glendale had subsided, then once again early on the 1st of July, before the battle at Malvern Hill had begun.[8] Despite having no first hand knowledge of the day's events, nor having been even remotely near the fighting at Glendale, McClellan had dispatched a telegram to Washington nonetheless late on the 30th. "My Army has behaved superbly," he gushed, "and have done all that men could do. If none of us escape," he continued, without even the slightest trace of embarrassment, "we shall at least have done honor to the country. I shall do my best to save the Army."[9]

Apparently the absolute best to save his army the Young Napoleon could conceive on the morning of July 1, as his troops readied themselves for another

Confederate assault, was to ride off to Haxall's Landing once more and board the *Galena* for another day on the water. To provide that his men would receive his best he once again left no second in command, thus virtually assuring a disunited effort once the army was attacked. Indeed, the only way General McClellan was going to "not escape" the day's efforts was if the *Galena* were to run aground and sink in the middle of the James.

Meanwhile, the Confederates were having their own unique sort of problems. Out on the Charles City Road that morning, General Huger, having still sent no one forward to reconnoiter the Federal force on his front, remained as a result entirely unfamiliar with the position and strength of his foe. Somewhat mysteriously, he had designed a bit of strategy to turn the Yankee position presumably as he conceived it, and had designated two full brigades to the task. Unbeknownst to Huger, of course, the Yankees had abandoned all their defensive positions around Glendale the night before, and as dawn approached there were no Federals in strength within miles of the crossroads, thus no one out there for Huger's brigades to flank. This fact did not deter him, however. Huger would continue fumbling about on the Charles City Road for hours, his brigades marching through the woods and lots looking for someone to flank, until finally advised by one of Lee's staff members of the actual situation — the Federals were concentrated miles away on Malvern Hill. The befuddled general then required yet another staff officer to guide his division to the front.

Early on the morning of the 1st General Lee met with his lieutenants at his headquarters near Glendale to plot the day's course of action. At long last the entire army was together, and Jackson was up and present, apparently rested after a good night's sleep. Lee was reportedly calm, but worn, and when General Jubal Early expounded on the fact that McClellan might be able to slip away undamaged if not aggressively pursued, Lee exploded with uncharacteristic wrath. "Yes, he will get away," he snapped, "because I cannot have my orders carried out!"[10] Hopes for success that morning were not terribly high, as Douglas Freeman points out: "On the morning of July 1 the depleted army was now united again for the last stage of a pursuit that every one felt was well-nigh hopeless. Lee's disappointment at the outcome of the previous day's failure to concentrate was apparent to all."[11]

Still, there seemed to be opportunity at Malvern Hill, no matter how slim, and after the disappointment at Glendale, slim was at least better than none. After some routine reconnaissance, Longstreet proposed the idea of establishing two grand batteries on the Confederate left and right on suitable ground that had been discovered in order to bring to bear on the Yankee defenses a converging fire that might swamp their artillery, thus opening the way for a full scale infantry assault to carry the hill. In theory Longstreet's idea had merit, but for the Confederates during the Seven Days, theory and execution had proven remarkably incompatible, and this day was to be no different.

Lee accepted Longstreet's idea, but the two grand batteries never came close to reality as the principle road leading to the front remained clogged with infantry, wagons, etc., and the necessary artillery could not even be assembled on the field. A few humble batteries valiantly unlimbered, both left and right, and attempted the convergence of fire originally hoped for, but these were promptly buried under a tornado of answering metal from the numerous Federal guns on the hill. The firing would continue for a few hours with virtually no effect whatsoever on the Yankee guns, while the Confederate batteries were consistently wrecked by the pinpoint accuracy of the Federal gunners. Harvey Hill wrote, "Instead of ordering up 100 or 200 pieces of artillery to play on the Yankees, a single battery, Moorman's was ordered up, and knocked to pieces in a few minutes. One or two others shared the same fate of being beat in detail."[12] It was yet another Confederate operational fiasco, this time mismanagement of the artillery so inept that Daniel Harvey Hill could think of no term save "most farcical"[13] to describe the paucity of results.

Orders, unfortunately, for the infantry assault had already been drafted by General Lee's chief of staff, Colonel Chilton, to read as follows: "Batteries have been established to rake the enemy's line. If it is broken, as is probable, Armistead, who can witness the effect of the fire, has been ordered to charge with a yell. Do the same. By order of Gen. Lee."[14] The entire operation, therefore, was dependent upon a successful artillery bombardment that a single brigade commander, Lewis Armistead, was to interpret, and then, if appropriate, charge "with a yell" which in turn would initiate the general advance. The order was simply a prescription for misinterpretation and mayhem, which is exactly what it inaugurated.

By late afternoon it had become apparent to all that the strategy of grand batteries to dull the Federal defense was a failure, and Lee rode off to the left to try and discern a possible turning movement of the Union defense. While en route, Lee received supposed intelligence from General Whiting that he had in fact observed Yankee troops and wagons moving off the summit of Malvern Hill, and from this Whiting had arrived at the conclusion that McClellan, panicked, was once again in retreat. In truth what Whiting had observed were simply some Yankee redeployments, which he entirely misinterpreted, then reported as fact. Added to this bubbling cauldron of misinformation was the fact that Armistead had advanced some troops to support the artillery in his rear, and this had been overzealously reported to Lee as a "success"[15] when in reality it had been nothing of the kind.

Interpreting these factors as a Yankee retreat in response to a moderate Confederate success, Lee ordered Magruder, newly arrived on the field after yet another all day march due to misunderstood directions, to attack at once. Magruder, of course, still painfully mindful of the fact that Lee seemed to have lost confidence in him, did not hesitate. Magruder's weary, overmarched troops were not yet all on the field, however, thus he had to pull together a patchwork of brigades. This he had accomplished by about 5:30 P.M., but the number of troops — about 5,000 — was far less than requisite to carry the difficult Federal position, and even these were tossed into the assault piecemeal rather than as an entire, coordinated assault. Rather than waiting and explaining the problem to Lee, however, Magruder attacked, unfortunately "with a yell," and upon his attack all other Confederate commands immediately moved to cooperate — exactly as they had been ordered.

Daniel Harvey Hill, watching from the Confederate center, saw Magruder's assault go in. "I never saw anything more grandly heroic than the advance after sunset of the nine brigades under Magruder's orders. Unfortunately, they did not move together, and were beaten in detail. As each brigade emerged from the woods, from fifty to one hundred guns opened upon it, tearing great gaps in its ranks; but the heroes reeled on and were shot down by the reserves at the guns, which a few squads reached. Most of them had an open field half a mile Wide to cross, under the fire of field-

Alfred R. Waud's depiction of Magruder's attack at Malvern Hill viewed from behind the Federal line (Library of Congress).

artillery in front, and the fire of the heavy ordinance of the gun-boats in their rear. It was not war — it was murder."[16]

Murder it would be for hours, as separate Confederate commands sought to cooperate separately and were all wrecked in detail as they too joined the fight. By day's end the slopes of Malvern Hill would be littered with Confederate dead and dying, all to no profit whatsoever. The Federal line remained entirely intact. "Our loss was double that of the Federals at Malvern Hill," recalled Harvey Hill. "Not only did the fourteen brigades which were engaged suffer, but also the inactive troops and those brought up as reserves too late to be of any use met many casualties from the fearful artillery fire which reached all parts of the woods. Hence, more than half the casualties were from field-pieces — an unprecedented thing in warfare."[17]

For Confederate arms the battle of Malvern Hill proved nothing but a very bloody and emphatic repulse, and once again conclusive evidence that its command structure was sorely lacking. Lee, still far on the left when Magruder committed his troops, did not know what had started the battle, and once begun, no idea how to stop it.

But it did not matter! Despite urges on the part of his lieutenants to launch an immediate counterattack, George McClellan, not one to be delayed by a complete thrashing of the enemy, was bound for the James River, and nothing, it seemed, was going to stop him. "Retreat! Never!" a division commander in Porter's corps shouted. "It's madness! We can't retreat! We have them on the run!"[18]

Further orders for a withdrawal to Harrison's Landing were issued, and the despondent Federal Army again began its backward march. When advised of McClellan's decision to retreat still further, a flabbergasted Philip Kearny tossed his cap into the mud at his feet, and raged defiantly, "I, Philip Keanry, an old soldier, protest this order to retreat. We ought, instead of retreating, to follow up the enemy and take Richmond. And in full view of all the responsibility of such a declaration I say to you all, such an order can only be prompted by cowardice or treason."[19]

The Union Army would once again slip away, this time to a safe haven on the James River at Harrison's Landing. The Seven Days battles had come to an end.

In Richmond the sound of battle had for days rattled windows and troubled hearts, and Constance Cary Harrison recalled the bittersweet end of the campaign: "When the tide of battle receded, what wrecked hopes it left to tell the tale of the Battle Summer! Victory was ours, but in how many homes was heard the voice of lamentation to drown the shouts of triumph! Many families, rich and poor alike, were bereaved of their dearest; and for many of the dead there was mourning by all the town.... Losses like these are irreparable in any community; and so with lamentations in nearly every household, while the spirit along the lines continued unabated, it was a chastened 'Thank God' that went up among us when we knew the siege of Richmond was over."[20]

CHAPTER 24

The Lost Day
of the Lost Cause

Almost before the smoke had drifted away from the field at Malvern Hill, the previous day's fighting at Glendale had become, for most participants, a thing of the past. Indeed, such was the nature of the conflict at Glendale that few above the top officers who were directly involved along with their staffs understood immediately the strategic configuration of the contesting forces on the field that day, and thus the remarkable opportunity that had been squandered. Only over time and correspondence would others come to grasp the significance of that day in June '62 and what had been fumbled away. The reality of what occurred at Glendale, however, subverts a number of ideas that over time have come to be accepted as truths of the Civil War, and thus of American history, and these misconceptions will be dealt with in this chapter.

For Robert E. Lee, however, the reality of Glendale would never quite disappear, for as Freeman states clearly, "It was the bitterest disappointment Lee ever sustained, and one that he could not conceal. Victories in the field were to be registered, but two years of open campaign were not to produce another situation where envelopment seemed possible."[1] For Lee (and thus for the entire Confederacy) the failure at Glendale had been monumental, and while McClellan had been driven — at least in a sense — from the gates of Richmond, any honest evaluation of the operations of the Army of Northern Virginia during the entire Seven Days, and particularly during its sputtering, inept performance at Glendale, would of necessity require a complete reevaluation of those numerous failures, and the officers who contributed to them, from top to bottom.

That evaluation began promptly. Lee's plans during the Seven Days had backfired with such consistency, and often so spectacularly, that to remedy the situation he could have done one of two things — or possibly both. He could have changed his theory of command, that is his concept of how he, as general commanding, contributed to the fight once battle had begun, from that of an inactive player, whose job it had been to bring the disparate elements of battle together at the right time and the right place only, to that of an active, involved participant. Or he could simply have changed the personnel at the top of his chain of command, removing those who had failed him, and substituting more capable officers who would understand and act on his orders. Or he could have done both. Lee, as Freeman has noted, would not change his concept of command until the confrontation with Grant in the Wilderness in 1864, thus maintaining his seemingly odd detachment once combat began. Lee's obvious choice, then, after the Seven Days was to change his personnel, yet this would create for General Lee almost as many problems as it solved.

To begin with, over a series of newspaper articles a serious spat erupted almost immediately between Longstreet and A.P. Hill. Heated correspondence flew back and forth which led ultimately to Hill's arrest by Longstreet. "No adjustment could be reached. Friends were called in. All the indications pointed to a duel, though arrangements were made with such secrecy that even Sorrel [Longstreet's aide] did not know what was afoot."[2] Douglas Southall Freeman elaborates on the complexities of the situation that confronted Lee.

> Could the perplexities of the reorganization of the Army of Northern Virginia after the Seven Days have been illustrated more dramatically than by the threat of this duel? Huger had proved "too slow"; Magruder was to leave Virginia with the assurance that, when opportunity offered, he would deal with his critics; Jackson, in the eyes of many, had not fulfilled expectations; Whiting's conduct had raised a question; D.H. Hill was overcritical, though competent, and had been sent a challenge by Toombs [for another duel]. Of the division commanders only Ewell, A.P. Hill and Longstreet had come through the campaign with a record for meeting creditably, and without quarrel or cavil, all the opportunities that had come to them; and now two of these three might seek to kill each other![3]

Lee temporarily solved not only his problem, but the rather delicate issue between Hill and Longstreet as well, with a simple but basic reorganization. Hill was sent off to serve under Jackson temporarily in the Valley, while Longstreet maintained his leading role as Lee's chief lieutenant (Hill, by the way, would have just as many problems with Jackson as he'd had with Longstreet, as would many other officers). The army was then divided fundamentally into two corps (this was a de facto reorganization, as Confederate law at the time did not allow for any military configuration beyond the division), the largest under Longstreet, the smaller under Jackson. Through these two officers from that point forward Lee's orders would flow, and through these officers Robert E. Lee would achieve his finest military results.

In that sense Lee's decision over the coming months would prove brilliant, and a penetrating assessment of both these officers' martial skills. This was no small achievement. For a great deal would be required of Jackson and Longstreet as corps commanders. To begin with, both would have to grasp Lee's conceptual designs, an achievement many officers were incapable of, and secondly — and perhaps more importantly — turn those designs into practical applications despite the constantly changing, harried conditions of 19th century combat. During the Seven Days fighting, for instance, Lee's grasp of the strategic had often been complete, his tactical conceptions brilliant, but conception alone serves only the philosopher, rarely if ever the battlefield commander. The battlefield requires above all else *execution* of the tactical plan, and it was in execution that the Army of Northern Virginia, and Lee by association, had failed miserably. Refusing to change his methods, Lee could only alter his subordinates, and this he accomplished with rare insight.

Once the dust had settled from the Seven Days, two erroneous conclusions would be drawn from the campaign's final results, both understandable, both demonstrability incorrect. The first was that Lee had conducted a brilliant campaign to drive McClellan to the brink, when in fact, while the conception had been brilliant, the actual campaign — that is the *execution* of the campaign — had been bungled from start to finish. What Lee *had* accomplished was to conduct an aggressive campaign, indeed so aggressive that that aggression alone had spooked McClellan into a fearful, irrational retreat that no success, logic, or argument could inhibit. Thus in a matter of days only, what had once appeared to be doom had been turned into a Southern dawn. To the residents in Richmond, and for citizens all across the South, it is entirely understandable that the results at the time seemed to speak for themselves, but McClellan's irrational behavior ought not be confused with Confederate operational excellence, no matter how seemingly apparent the connection.

The positive effect of the Seven Days success for General Lee was to anoint both him and his command with a new aura of capability, no matter how undeserved, but which would soon — with the staff reorganization in place — be turned into firm reality. With Jackson and Longstreet in corps command, Lee would mold the Army of Northern Virginia for a time into one of the most mobile, aggressive, and fearless fighting forces in modern military history. Their success at Second Bull Run, Antietam, Fredericksburg, and Chancellorsville, always against difficult odds, would prove a run of remarkable skill, resilience, and spirit. Not until Jackson was lost would Lee be revisited by command failures (most notably at Gettysburg) that would again point directly to the underlying problem — without the proper lieutenants in place, Lee's tactical conceptions had a tendency to misfire. It remains a matter of speculation what might have been had Lee decided prior to the Wilderness to take firmer control of his army. His fight on the defensive against Grant's overwhelming numbers in the war's latter years serves as testimony to his genius, and quite possibly the success he might have crafted had he adopted that attitude at an earlier date.

The second misconception drawn from the Seven Days campaign's results — and one even more irrational and therefore in stark conflict with the facts — was that George McClellan had conducted a brilliant disengagement and retreat in the face of a hostile foe. The simple fact that the Army of the Potomac had survived to fight again is hardly proof that McClellan, the general, had much if anything at all to do with that survival. Indeed, even a cursory review of the record demonstrates that McClellan's hand and direction was generally nowhere to be found. Yet often, and to this day, George McClellan has been credited with something he had little part in creating, as stated here in a 21st century military critique of the campaign: "Certain historians have questioned the wisdom of McClellan's decision, yet few can question its execution. In fact, while in many cases Civil War tactics appear archaic by today's standards, McClellan's withdrawal has stood the test of time. An Analysis of McClellan's execution based on current military doctrine for retrograde operations indicates that McClellan's withdrawal was nearly flawless."[4] Nearly flawless? McClellan's "change of base" was nearly flawless except for the demonstrable fact that on every day of the retreat — except, perhaps, the first — his long column had been entirely vulnerable to assault, envelopment, and rout. Nearly flawless, except for the fact that on June 30 at Glendale, the Federal retreat faced almost certain doom from four converging Confederate columns that should have, by any reasonable reckoning, devoured it.

The facts are that McClellan had little if anything to do with the movements or decisions of his troops. These, from the rearguard actions at Savage Station on the 29th forward, were handled by corps and even division commanders on their own, often without even the slightest help or guidance from General McClellan. Heintzelman vacated Savage Station on his own prerogative, leaving Bull Sumner to fight alone and independently. Franklin then made the decision to vacate White Oak Swamp, while Heintzelman and Sumner followed suit at Glendale. And these were but a few of the independent decisions and movements made by McClellan's subordinates. Where was General McClellan? Absent.

On the two most critical days of the retreat, the 30th of June at Glendale, and the 1st of July at Malvern Hill, McClellan had fled the field for the safety of the gunboat *Galena*, purposely leaving no second in command and his army to fight for its life without him. Colonel Francis Barlow, who had fought with Kearny at Glendale, summed up the feelings of most officers and men in the Army of the Potomac when he later stated, "I think the whole army feel that it was left to take care of itself and was saved only by its own brave fighting."[5]

At Glendale the Potomac army took up a position far too long for the troops allocated, placed McCall's battered unit in the center of the line (where another, fresh division should have been utilized), and deployed with large gaps between the numerous units. There was no sensible reserve, no true understanding of the enemy, and no guiding operational structure for the day. That the army survived was a testament to many fine officers and men who fought desperately in a desperate situation, but none of that can be attributed to George McClellan. How could it? General McClellan was long gone and out of touch.

Moreover, the Potomac army survived fundamentally not due to its own hard fighting, but rather to Confederate miscues, mistakes, and command failures so numerous, widespread, and bewildering in scope that it is truly hard to imagine a collective failure more debilitating short of the actual physical paralysis of the entire Confederate high command. The one true opportunity the Confederacy had during the course of the entire war to gain its independence was the one day in which the Army of Northern Virginia simply failed to function as a military organization, and *that* breakdown was what saved the Army of the Potomac at Glendale.

The thrust of this book has been that the Southern Confederacy not only could have won the American Civil War at Glendale, but that it could have done so easily, and indeed, even despite all the command failures that took place, still came remarkably close to doing so. Yet directly associated with this idea is the question of McClellan's masterful retreat, for the two ideas are in fact mutually exclusive; that is, they cannot both be simultaneously true. If McClellan conducted a masterful retrograde operation, for instance, then by definition his army could not have been placed in a posture where it might have been easily destroyed. Likewise, if it can be factually demonstrated that the Army of the Potomac could have been easily routed from the field at Glendale, then by definition McClellan could not have conducted a masterful retreat.

Starting with what actually occurred at Glendale — and then progressing to some of the more likely potentials — as has been well documented, Jenkins' South Carolina brigade actually took the Quaker Road, thus cutting the Army of the Potomac in half that afternoon. That brigade, according to Jenkins' own report, could have held their position for at least a period of time, even if not supported. Had Branch's brigade come to Jenkins' support, as was its mission, rather than firing into the South Carolinians from the rear, then fleeing the scene, the Civil War may well have resolved in a Confederate victory that evening, as two more full Confederate brigades had already been dispatched to their support. But either way, the fact that the Federal Army was in fact cut in half, and that the potential was imminent for that break to be made permanent, rests today as proof positive that the Army of Northern Virginia came at least very close to destroying McClellan's army on the 30th of June 1862. It was, at that point, the thinnest slice of good fortune that ultimately sustained the Army of the Potomac, not its hard fighting, and certainly not George McClellan.

Had Stonewall Jackson simply cooperated with the rest of Lee's army and conducted a strong demonstration at White Oak Swamp, the Union rear guard would have been held in place, and the flood of units returning to the Federal center would never have taken place. *Those* units wrested the field from the Confederates, and were ultimately responsible for the aggressive outlook that forced Longstreet to commit his final reserve. Without them the fight would have been lost and the Federal Army cut in two. Had Jackson, on the other hand, been even half-awake and conducted the requisite reconnaissance required of his position, he would have discovered the situation at Brackett's Ford, only a mile from White Oak Bridge, connected by good roads, and launched the assault (previously explained) that would have swept the Federal line into oblivion. And Brackett's Ford was just one of many potential crossing points that could have been utilized that day to turn and possibly force the Federal rear guard from its blocking position at the swamp. Whether utilized or not, the mere fact that they were discovered and available is yet further evidence that not just one but multiple opportunities existed for Confederate victory that day. That these opportunities were all mishandled by the Confederates hardly infers skill on the part of the Federal defenders, nor does it confer any sort of martial competence, better yet mastery, upon George McClellan.

Add to this, then, the other obvious potentials that day for a sweeping Confederate victory — had Huger brought up his infantry on the Charles City Road; had Holmes moved aggressively and taken Malvern Hill in the early morning; had Longstreet launched his attack in coordinated fashion rather than piecemeal, not to mention the various *combinations* inherent in those opportunities, and the list of possibilities grows exponentially. When considered fairly, the facts demonstrate clearly that the potential for Southern victory at Glendale was abundant almost beyond measure, and that the failure to capture that victory rests most principally with Confederate leadership, from top to bottom, and as well to a small band of Federal officers and men who, with their backs to the wall, fought as noble and desperate a fight as ever has been witnessed on the North American continent.

George McClellan did not conduct a masterful retrograde action, although his claim to have done so — and the simple fact that his army did indeed survive — appears to have been the germ from which this myth took flight. McClellan, for instance, safe finally at Harrison's Landing on the James, trotted out this rather remarkable explanation of events: "Attacked by vastly superior forces, and without hope of reinforcements, you have succeeded in changing your base of operations by a flank movement, always regarded as the most hazardous of military expedients."[6] The assertion, current to this day, that McClellan's retreat was nearly flawless in terms of its execution, remains one of the more baffling misconceptions of American history. The facts, when viewed in the clear light of day, demonstrate that George McClellan was almost nowhere to be found during the course of his army's retreat, that he left the retreat to the often confused discretion of his subordinates, that his army could have been interdicted and destroyed at any number of points, and that by fleeing his army for the safety of the river he was at a minimum guilty of dereliction of duty. These, unfortunately for George McClellan, are all facts, and "facts," as John Adams once observed, "are stubborn things."

What would have happened had Lee's army succeeded that day at Glendale? To begin with, unlike other Confederate victories like those at Fredericksburg, or Chancellorsville, where the victories were over a prepared, consolidated adversary, a victory at Glendale would have been over an adversary that was strung out over miles of narrow roads, its long train of wagons, supplies, and artillery immediately exposed, its various divisions dispersed over a wide section of countryside and subsequently ill-prepared to defend themselves. Those factors are what would have made a victory at Glendale so complete. As it was, after the Seven Days the Army of Northern Virginia virtually reequipped itself from the long trail of equipment McClellan's army had left behind. Should the Confederates have won at Glendale, *all* the stores, supplies, ammunition, reserve artillery, etc., of the Army of the Potomac would have fallen into Rebel hands, not merely enough to reequip itself, but to reinvent itself. Overnight, the Army of Northern Virginia would become the strongest fighting force on the North American continent, one of the strongest in the world, and there would have been no serious Federal force, or combination of forces, that could have challenged it anytime soon — and this includes John Pope's newly raised Federal Army of Virginia.

Moreover, the majority of Federal officers and men in the Potomac army would probably have been forced to surrender, cut off as they were, thus providing the Confederacy with an enormous bargaining chip for a negotiated peace. Whether Abraham Lincoln would have been open to such a bargain, considering his aggressive stance, would have been highly questionable, but whether in a fighting mood or not, there would have been no place for him to turn in the short run. Lincoln's principal army would have been removed from the table, and the likelihood of raising another to replace it not only a question of national policy but also of time. Thus, whether Abraham Lincoln liked it or not, after a Confederate victory at Glendale, his hands would have been tied, at least for the immediate future, and the Confederacy thus a de facto reality. Additionally, with the Federal government suddenly impotent as to its wartime goals, who knows what might have transpired in terms of international relations. Such a lopsided victory as Glendale would have provided the South may have been just enough to bring to the Confederacy the foreign recognition it so desperately sought but could never achieve.

Then finally, what sort of future might that Confederacy have actually experienced should it have achieved its independence at Glendale, de facto or other? Could that Southern Confederacy have actually survived, founded upon the principle of slavery as it was, based fundamentally on agrarian myth, configured in a governmental format already proven powerless and unworkable almost a hundred years prior? This is a question rarely asked, but it was both asked and answered by Edward Porter Alexander, years later and after much thought and contemplation. Alexander's answer remains one of the most remarkable and insightful statements of its period, most certainly by an ex–Confederate officer of stature, and his conclusions still resonate today: "Had our cause succeeded, divergent interests must soon have further separated the States into groups, and this continent would have been given over to divided nationalities, each weak and unable to command foreign credit. Since the days of Greece, Confederacies have only held together against foreign enemies, and in times of peace have soon disintegrated. It is surely not necessary to contrast what would have been our prospects as citizens of such States with our condition now as citizens of the strongest, richest, and — strange for us to say who once called ourselves 'conquered' and our cause 'lost'— the freest nation on earth."[7]

Out of the carnage of Civil War the freest nation on earth slowly and painfully emerged, a nation that would gradually become in fact what earlier it had been in theory only. John Gordon, another ex–Confederate general and friend of Alexander's, would confirm Porter Alexander's assertion as the re–United States entered the early years of the 20th century, and here Gordon puts the final, finishing touch on the story: "So the Republic, rising from its baptism of blood with a national life more robust, a national union more complete, and a national influence ever widening, shall go forever forward in its benign mission to humanity."[8]

Once, however, and only *once*, during the long course of the American Civil War would the future course of that "benign mission to humanity" come dangerously close to wreckage, and the Confederacy very near a de facto reality. This did not occur at Gettysburg, Second Bull Run, Chancellorsville, or Fredericksburg, or any of the other great battles now commonly well known. Rather it was at a small, unknown crossroads town in southeastern Virginia where the national light flickered precariously one Monday afternoon when the Army of Northern Virginia came within a hair of victory so compelling that it would have catapulted the Confederacy to its independence, and as a result destroyed, perhaps forever, the Federal Union of states. The date was June 30, 1862. The place was Glendale.

Epilogue

Those in Gray

Benjamin Huger was born in Charleston, South Carolina, in 1805, and graduated from West Point with the class of 1825. Huger served in the pre–Civil War army with some distinction. He saw action in the Mexican War where he rose to the rank of colonel and was appointed chief of ordnance by General Winfield Scott. With the outbreak of the Civil War Huger resigned his commission, was appointed brigadier general in the Confederate Army, and later rose to the rank of major general. His actions at Norfolk, Seven Pines, and during the Seven Days battles were severely criticized, however, and later led to an investigation by the Confederate Congress. Removed from command shortly after the Battle of Malvern Hill, Huger was reassigned to inspector of artillery and ordnance and transferred to the Trans-Mississippi Department. He remained there until the end of hostilities. After the war Huger lived out his remaining days on a farm in Fauquier County, Virginia. He died in 1877 at the age of 82. He is buried in Baltimore, Maryland.

Thomas Stonewall Jackson was born in Clarksburg, Virginia (now West Virginia), in 1824, and graduated from West Point with the class of 1846. Jackson served in the Mexican War and was promoted to the brevet rank of major. He resigned his officer's commission in 1852 at which time he became an instructor at the Virginia Military Institute. With the outbreak of the Civil War Jackson was appointed colonel of Virginia militia and later promoted to brigadier general. Jackson served with particular distinction at First Manassas where General Barnard E. Bee by chance dubbed him "Stonewall" for his stand on Henry House Hill. From there Jackson rose to become one of the most famous generals in American military history. In 1862 he waged a brilliant campaign in Virginia's Shenandoah Valley against three separate Federal armies, which is today considered nothing less than a classic.

Jackson also served brilliantly at Second Manassas, Antietam, and Fredericksburg. His behavior during the Seven Days battles, however, was lackluster at best, and many suggestions have been offered — from exhaustion, to indifference, to religious conviction — to account for his poor performance. By all accounts Jackson slept through the Battle of Glendale when even a half-hearted advance by his division might well have tipped the scales of battle in favor of the Confederacy. Most of the Federal brigades that reestablished the shattered Yankee line that day were in fact recovered from in front of Jackson because of his inactivity, a redeployment that would have been impossible had Jackson been more aggressive. Stonewall Jackson would recover from his lethargy, however, and rise to prominence in subsequent actions. Jackson was accidentally shot by his own troops on May 2, 1863, while performing an advanced reconnaissance at night during the Battle of Chancellorsville, arguably his finest victory. He would die eight days later of his wounds. Stonewall Jackson is buried in Lexington, Virginia.

Wade Hampton was born in Charleston, South Carolina, in 1818 to a family of considerable wealth and resources. He graduated from the South Carolina College in 1836. By the time of the Civil War Hampton was reputed to be the largest land owner in all the South. He served in both houses of the South Carolina legislature, where his views on slavery ran counter to almost all of his colleagues. It was Hampton's view that slavery was an inefficient means of labor, and that the institution actually hindered rather than helped Southern business and finance. He argued fervently against secession, but once war came Hampton organized the Hampton Legion at his own expense. Wounded at First Manassas, Hampton commanded a brigade of infantry under Stonewall Jackson during McClellan's Peninsular Campaign. After Glendale Hampton assumed command of a brigade of cavalry under J.E.B. Stuart and served in that capacity until 1864. Severely wounded at Gettysburg, Hampton was promoted to major general and assumed command of the cavalry corps after Stuart's death. Hampton performed brilliantly in that role until the end of the war, and was ultimately promoted to the rank of lieutenant general. After the war Wade Hampton was elected governor of South Carolina, and later served as the commissioner of the Pacific Railways. He died in 1902 at the age of 84. Hampton is buried in Columbia, South Carolina.

Theophilus Hunter Holmes was born in 1804 in North Carolina and graduated from West Point with the class of 1829. Holmes saw service in the Mexican War, and rose to the rank of major in the pre-war army. Holmes was appointed brigadier general in 1861, then major general, and finally promoted to lieutenant general in 1862. But Holmes was clearly not up to the task of performing as a lieutenant general, and after his failures at Glendale (and the following day at Malvern Hill) he was reassigned to the Trans-Mississippi Department, where he was ultimately relieved of duty by Kirby Smith. After the war Holmes worked a small farm in North Carolina and died in 1880 at the age of 75. Theophilus Holmes is buried in Fayetteville, North Carolina.

James Longstreet was born in Edgefield, South Carolina, in 1821, and graduated from West Point with the class of 1842. Prior to the Civil War Longstreet served in numerous Indian campaigns and with distinction in the Mexican War. Longstreet was appointed brigadier general in 1861 and major general later that year. He saw service at First Manassas and later during McClellan's Peninsula Campaign. Longstreet was promoted to the rank of lieutenant general later in the war and served under Lee in numerous campaigns including Second Manassas, Antietam, Fredricksburg, and Gettysburg. He was severely wounded in May 1864 during the Battle of the Wilderness but returned to active duty and served with Lee up through the Confederate surrender at Appomattox. After the war Longstreet moved to New Orleans and switched his political affiliation to the Republican Party. A personal friend of U.S. Grant, Longstreet was appointed minister to Turkey in 1880 and later returned to serve as commissioner of the pacific railroads under presidents McKinley and Roosevelt. Longstreet died in Gainesville, Georgia, in 1904 at the age of 82.

Robert E. Lee was born in 1807 in Westmoreland County, Virginia, and graduated from West Point with the class of 1829. Lee was born the fifth child of Revolutionary War hero "Light-Horse Harry" Lee, but his father's financial mismanagement virtually bankrupted the Lee family, and Robert was raised in a small home in Alexandria under meager conditions by his struggling mother, Ann Hill Lee. After graduation from West Point, Lee served in numerous roles with distinction including commandant of the military academy. He was married to Mary Ann Randolph Custis in 1831, and together they raised seven children. In 1859 Lee was at home in Virginia on extended leave at the time of John Brown's raid on Harper's Ferry, and he was placed in command of the forces sent to quell the revolt. By marriage Lee had come to acquire an estate — Arlington on the Potomac River, which by the end of the Civil War would be forever transfigured into Arlington National Cemetery — along with numerous slaves, but Lee manumitted those whom he had come to own prior to the outbreak of hostilities. On April 18, 1861, Lee refused command of all Union forces, and on April 20, when it became apparent that he would be called upon to march against Virginia in the name of the United States, he promptly resigned his commission. Lee then offered his services to the Confederate government and served in a number of staff and minor field positions, until his appointment to commander of the Army of Northern Virginia in June 1862. Lee's actions quickly catapulted him to virtually legendary status. During the Seven Days battles he drove the Federal Army under George McClellan from the gates of Richmond, and during the remaining years of Civil War led the Army of Northern Virginia to numerous victories. Fighting against enormous odds, Lee held the Confederacy together until the cause of Southern independence became entirely hopeless. In April 1865 he surrendered to the forces of U.S. Grant at Appomattox Court House, and returned to Richmond as a paroled prisoner. He later accepted the presidency of Washington College (now Washington and Lee University). Robert E. Lee, perhaps the most venerated figure in American military history, died in 1870 at the age of 63. He is buried in Lexington, Virginia.

Micah Jenkins was born on Edisto Island, South Carolina, in December 1835, and graduated first in his class from The Citadel in 1854 at the age of only 19. Jenkins then moved to Yorkville, South Carolina, where he was cofounder of the Kings Mountain Military School. Jenkins served in that capacity until the coming of war. In 1855 he married Caroline Jamison, daughter of the future secretary of war of South Carolina. With the coming of secession Jenkins was appointed colonel of the 5th South Carolina Regiment. Jenkins then served with distinction at First Manassas and later drove his command with such ferocity at Seven Pines that Longstreet's aide, T.J. Goree exclaimed: "Genl. Anderson's S.C. brigade under Col. Jenkins *immortalized* itself." Confederate general D.H. Hill would call that same advance a "march to victory, which has had but few parallels in history." For his conduct at Glendale Jenkins was promoted to brigadier general in July 1862. He was then severely wounded at Second Manassas but recovered in time to accompany the 1st Corps west where he commanded Hood's division at the battle of Chickamauga. Jenkins returned with Longstreet's corps to Virginia in the spring of 1864 where on the 2nd day of the Battle of the Wilderness he was accidentally shot in the head by his own troops while riding forward on reconnaissance with Longstreet, not far from where Stonewall Jackson had been struck down in a similar manner only a year prior. Micah Jenkins, once referred to by Longstreet as the finest officer in the Army of Northern Virginia, died within hours on May 6, 1864, at the age of 28. He is buried in Charleston, South Carolina.

Edward Porter Alexander was born in Washington, Georgia, on May 26, 1835, and graduated third in the class of 1857 from West Point. Alexander then served on an expedition to Utah to quell a Mormon revolt, and later returned to West Point as assistant professor of engineering. When war came he resigned from the Federal Army and was appointed captain of engineers in the Confederate Army. He served under General Beauregard at First Manassas after which he was promoted to chief of ordnance for the Army of Northern Virginia with the rank of lieutenant colonel. Alexander also handled duties involving the signal corps and military intelligence. He was one of the Confederacy's first aeronauts, gathering invaluable intelligence during the Seven Days fighting, but he was grounded a few days after the battle at Malvern Hill. After the *Gazelle*'s descent that day, the *Teaser* ran aground and was captured by a Federal gunboat. Alexander served in virtually all the major eastern campaigns, was later appointed chief of artillery for Longstreet's corps and was principally in charge of the cannonade on the third day at Gettysburg that preceded Pickett's Charge. He was promoted to brigadier general in February 1864. Alexander was seriously wounded at Petersburg but returned and was with the army on its final march to Appomattox. After the war he served as a railroad president, professor of engineering, and planter. He also handled a number of government posts with distinction. In his later years Alexander finally found time to sit down and pen his memoirs, along with a critical examination of the war. That critique, *Military Memoirs of a Confederate: A Critical Narrative*, was an immediate success and is still regarded as a classic by students of the war. His more personal memoirs were not discovered and published until 1989. Titled *Fighting for the Confederacy—The Personal Recollections of General Edward Porter Alexander*, his memoirs offer one of the most intelligent, candid and compelling accounts of the Civil War ever published. Alexander died in Savannah, Georgia, on April, 28, 1910, at the age of 74. He is buried in Augusta, Georgia.

Those in Blue

George Brinton McClellan was born in Philadelphia and graduated second in the West Point class of 1846. McClellan served with distinction in the Mexican War, and was promoted to the brevet rank of captain. He later served as an instructor at West Point and also traveled to Europe to study the Crimean War. In 1857 he resigned from the army, and at the outbreak of Civil War was president of the Ohio & Mississippi Railroad. McClellan quickly rose through the ranks, and after the debacle of First Manassas, was promoted to command the Army of the Potomac, and in November of 1861— in conjunction with the retirement of General Winfield Scott — general in chief of the armies of the United States. While unquestionably bringing a sense of energy and organization to the army, McClellan's subsequent military career would be seriously compromised by inertia, and an almost delusional overestimation of his opponents resources. After McClellan fought Lee to a draw at Antietam in September 1862 but once again refused to budge further, Lincoln removed him from command once and for all. McClellan then ran as the Democratic nominee for president against Lincoln in 1864, but carried only three states. He served briefly as governor of New Jersey, and died in Orange, New Jersey, in 1885 at the age of 58. George McClellan is buried in Trenton, New Jersey.

Samuel Peter Heintzelman was born in Manheim, Pennsylvania, in 1805 and graduated from West Point with the class of 1826. Prior to the Civil War, Heintzelman served in the Mexican War and with some distinction while on garrison duty in the western territories. He achieved the rank of lieutenant colonel in 1851 and with the outbreak of war was commissioned colonel of infantry. He fought gallantly at First Manassas where he was wounded, and was promoted to major general in May 1862. At Second Manassas Heintzelman fought under John Pope where his attack on Stonewall Jackson was repulsed. He spent the remainder of the war in command of sections of the Washington defenses and on court-martial duty. He retired from the army in 1869. He died in Washington in May 1880 at the age of 74. Samuel Heintzelman is buried in Buffalo, New York.

George Archibald McCall was born in Philadelphia in 1802, and graduated from West Point with the class of 1822. He fought in the Seminole Wars in Florida, and later in the War with Mexico where he was brevetted for bravery. McCall achieved the rank of colonel and retired from the service in 1853 but returned to active duty with the coming of the Civil War. He was appointed brigadier general by Abraham Lincoln and fought with distinction at Mechanicsville, Gaines's Mill, and Glendale. Late on the evening of June 30, McCall was taken prisoner at Glendale after riding too far forward while attempting to rally his troops. He was confined to Libby Prison in Richmond until exchanged in August 1862. He then remained on sick leave until his resignation from the service in March 1863. He retired to his estate near West Chester, Pennsylvania, where he died in 1868 at the age of 65. George McCall is buried in Philadelphia, Pennsylvania.

Oliver Wendell Holmes, Jr., was born in Boston in 1841 into one of the city's most prominent families and graduated from Harvard College in 1861. He was then promptly commissioned a lieutenant with the 20th Massachusetts Volunteers, where he served with distinction on line for three years. Wounded at Ball's Bluff, Antietam, and Chancellorsville, in 1864 Holmes would be assigned to the headquarters staff of General Horatio

Wright. Holmes would see the war through to the summer of 1864, after which he was mustered out of the service along with the other survivors of the 20th Massachusetts. Holmes then returned to Boston where he took up the study of law. He was to become editor of the *American Law Review*, later a professor at Harvard, and in 1902 was appointed to the United States Supreme Court. Known as the "Great Dissenter" Holmes has been called "the most illustrious figure in the history of American law" and would serve on the court until 1932. He died on March 6, 1935, in Washington, D.C., at the age of 93. Buried in Arlington National Cemetery, on the very top of his headstone Holmes insisted what he considered his greatest accomplishment in life be listed first — "Captain and Brevet Colonel, 20th Mass. Volunteer Infantry."

Philip Kearny was born in New York City on June 2, 1815, to the wealthy, aristocratic family of Philip and Susan Kearny. His father was one of the founders of the New York Stock Exchange, but young Philip exhibited no great interest in business. Rather, he modeled himself after his uncle, Major General Stephen Watts Kearny, who would later earn fame in the Mexican War. Phil graduated from Columbia University with honors in 1833 and worked briefly as a law clerk until his grandfather's death in 1836 at which time he inherited a substantial fortune. He promptly quit the practice of law, determined to pursue his lifelong ambition as a soldier. In 1837 he was commissioned a lieutenant of dragoons at Fort Leavenworth, where he immediately displayed enormous skill and potential. Kearny was soon selected by the secretary of war to attend the distinguished French Cavalry School at Saumar. There he learned to fight in the style of the *1st Chasseurs d'Afrique,* sword in one hand, pistol in the other, and reins in his teeth. For his utter fearlessness in battle the French dubbed him *"Kearny le Magnifique."* He then returned to the United States where he served as aide-de-camp to General Winfield Scott. In the Mexican War Kearny served with particular distinction, charging the gates at Churubusco in an effort to capture General Santa Anna. His arm would be shattered by grape in the effort and require amputation. Kearny was brevetted major for his courage and daring, but after the war Kearny went through a difficult divorce when his first wife left him, and later he grew bored and impatient in the peacetime army. In 1851 he resigned his commission and traveled the globe. In France Kearny met his second wife, Agnes, and the two returned to New Jersey where Kearny began construction of a fabulous estate known as Bellegrove in what is present day Kearny, New Jersey. Philip and Agnes also traveled widely, and with the outbreak of the Italian Wars Phil promptly enlisted in the French army. There he took part in every cavalry charge at Solferino and Magenta and

was awarded the Cross of the Legion of Honor. At the outbreak of the Civil
War Kearny hurried home and offered his services to the state of New York.
Because of his divorce and subsequent remarriage, however (which appeared
unseemly in the Victorian 19th century), Kearny's appointment was denied,
so he turned to nearby New Jersey where he was finally appointed brigadier
of volunteers. Perhaps the most qualified, respected, and commanding officer
in the Federal service, Kearny's rise through the ranks proved meteoric. At
Williamsburg he brought his division up to save the day, and at Seven Pines
he drove two brigades into the flank of the freewheeling Rebel attack and
brought it to a virtual halt. Then he held the line firmly at the battle of Oak
Grove. Four days after his extraordinary performance at Glendale Kearny
was promoted to major general. Phil Kearny's division was then transferred
to the Army of Virginia where he fought with Pope at Second Manassas.
There he was once again called upon to take part in a severe rearguard action
that saved the army by allowing it to slip across Bull Run at night. The following day, September 1— and while reportedly furious over the incompetent
leadership of both McClellan and Pope — Kearny again covered the army's
line of retreat. During a horrendous thunderstorm that evening his division
faced elements of Stonewall Jackson's command advancing toward Washington along the Little River Turnpike, not far from an estate named Chantilly. A brief but sharp fight ensued, and the Rebels were repulsed. Kearny,
in what one infantryman called simply "an ungovernable rage," once again
spurred his horse far out ahead of his front lines and into a group of waiting
Confederates. Cursing them all furiously, Kearny attempted to flee but was
brought down by a single bullet. As rumors of his replacing McClellan swirled
around Washington, Phil Kearny was killed instantly on the field at Chantilly,
perhaps only weeks or even days away from high command. Upon hearing
the news of Kearny's death a stunned Stonewall Jackson issued orders that
"his body, sword, and all his personal belongings be brought to his [Jackson's]
Headquarters at Chantilly." The following morning, and accompanied by a
host of officers from both Lee and Jackson's headquarters, Kearny's body was
delivered across the lines under a flag of truce. The mood was somber. Lee's
chief of staff, Walter Taylor recalled, "There was no place for exultation at
the death of so gallant a man." News of his death stunned the nation, and
Secretary of War Edwin Stanton called Kearny's loss nothing less than "a
national calamity." Phil Kearny, the officer Winfield Scott once called "the
bravest and most perfect soldier" he had ever known, was dead at the age of
47. He is buried in Arlington National Cemetery.

Chapter Notes

Preface

1. Edward Porter Alexander, *Fighting for the Confederacy* (Chapel Hill: University of North Carolina Press), as quoted, 109.
2. Douglas Southall Freeman, *R.E. Lee* (New York: Touchstone Books), 214.
3. Alexander, *Fighting for the Confederacy*, 108.
4. Freeman, *R.E. Lee*, 214.

Prologue

1. Ivan Musicant, *Divided Waters* (New York: Castle Books), 135.
2. *Ibid.*, 136.
3. *Ibid.*, 150.
4. *Ibid.*, as quoted, 156.
5. *Ibid.*, 156.
6. *Ibid.*, 158.
7. *Ibid.*, 161.
8. Irving Werstein, *Kearny the Magnificent* (New York: The John Day Co.), 182.
9. *Ibid.*, 182.
10. *Ibid.*, as quoted, 186.
11. Stephen Sears, *To the Gates of Richmond* (New York: Houghton Mifflin), as quoted, 19.
12. *Ibid.*, 23.

Chapter 1

1. Stephen Sears, *To the Gates of Richmond* (New York: Houghton Mifflin, 1992), 36–37.
2. Oliver Wendell Holmes, Jr., *Touched with Fire* (New York: Fordham University Press, 2000), 38–39.
3. Irving Werstein, *Kearny the Magnificent* (New York: The John Day Co., 1962.), 211.
4. Stephen Sears, *To the Gates of Richmond*, 24.
5. *Ibid.*, 98–99.

6. Edward Porter Alexander, *Military Memoirs of a Confederate* (New York: DaCapo Press, 1993), 55.
7. *Ibid.*, xix–xxvi.
8. *Ibid.*
9. *Ibid.*, 55.
10. Sears, *To the Gates of Richmond*, 98.
11. Alexander, *Military Memoirs of a Confederate*, 63.
12. *Ibid.*
13. Sears, *To the Gates of Richmond*, 103.
14. Alexander, *Military Memoirs of a Confederate*, 74.
15. *Ibid.*, 72–73.
16. Sears, *To the Gates of Richmond*, 87.
17. Douglas Southall Freeman, *Lee's Lieutenants*, Vol. 1 (New York: Charles Scribner's Sons, 1942), as quoted, 363.
18. Alexander, *Military Memoirs of a Confederate*, 73–74.
19. Wyman S. White, *The Civil War Diary of Wyman S. White* (Baltimore: Butternut and Blue, 1993), 68–69.
20. Sears, *To the Gates of Richmond*, as quoted, 111.
21. Freeman, *Lee's Lieutenants*, Vol. 1, 244.
22. John B. Gordon, *Reminiscences of the Civil War* (Baton Rouge: Louisiana State University Press, 1993), 57.
23. *Ibid.*, 58.
24. Holmes, *Touched with Fire*, 50–51.
25. Edward Porter Alexander, *Fighting for the Confederacy* (Chapel Hill: University of North Carolina Press, 1989), 88.
26. Freeman, *Lee's Lieutenants*, Vol. 1, 262–263.
27. Douglas Southall Freeman, *R.E. Lee* (New York: Touchstone Books, 1961), 19.
28. Alexander, *Fighting for the Confederacy*, 91.
29. Freeman, *Lee's Lieutenants*, Vol. 1, 266.
30. Alexander, *Military Memoirs of a Confederate*, 111.

31. Sears, *To the Gates of Richmond,* as quoted, 154.

32. Alexander, *Military Memoirs of a Confederate,* 112.

33. Irving Werstein, *Kearny the Magnificent* (New York: The John Day Co., 1962), as quoted, 220–221.

34. Alexander, *Military Memoirs of a Confederate,* 118.

35. Sears, *To the Gates of Richmond,* 209.

36. *Ibid.,* 251.

37. Holmes, *Touched with Fire,* 56.

38. Alexander, *Military Memoirs of a Confederate,* 139.

39. Sears, *To the Gates of Richmond,* 280.

40. Holmes, *Touched with Fire,* 58.

Chapter 2

1. Douglas Southall Freeman, *R.E. Lee* (New York: Touchstone Books, 1961), 207.

2. Edward Porter Alexander, *Fighting for the Confederacy* (Chapel Hill: University of North Carolina Press, 1989), 104.

3. Stephen Sears, *To the Gates of Richmond* (New York: Houghton Mifflin, 1992), 255–256.

4. Alexander, *Fighting for the Confederacy,* 115.

5. *Ibid.,* 116.

6. *Ibid.,* 553.

7. *Ibid.,* 117.

8. *Ibid.,* 116.

9. *Ibid.,* 117.

10. Sears, *To the Gates of Richmond,* 257–258.

11. Freeman, *R.E. Lee,* 207–208.

12. *Ibid.,* 208.

13. *Ibid.,* 207.

14. Edward Porter Alexander, *Military Memoirs of a Confederate* (New York: Da Capo Press, 1993), 134.

15. *Ibid.,* 117.

16. *Ibid.,* 116–117.

17. Douglas Southall Freeman, *Lee's Lieutenants,* Vol. 1 (New York: Charles Scribner's Sons, 1942), 485.

18. Henry Kyd Douglas, *I Rode with Stonewall* (Chapel Hill: University of North Carolina Press, 1940), 40.

Chapter 3

1. Douglas Southall Freeman, *Lee's Lieutenants,* Vol. 1 (New York: Charles Scribner's Sons, 1942), 550.

2. *Ibid.,* 551.

3. *Ibid.*

4. *Ibid.,* 620.

5. Edward Porter Alexander, *Military Memoirs of a Confederate* (New York: Da Capo Press, 1993), as quoted, 138.

6. John B. Gordon, *Reminiscences of the Civil War* (Baton Rouge: Louisiana State University Press, 1993), 70–71.

7. Edward Porter Alexander, *Fighting for the Confederacy* (Chapel Hill: University of North Carolina Press, 1989), 105–106.

8. Henry Kyd Douglas, *I Rode With Stonewall* (Chapel Hill: University of North Carolina Press, 1940), 106.

9. Freeman, *Lee's Lieutenants,* Vol. 1, 564.

10. Alexander, *Fighting for the Confederacy,* 106.

11. Alexander, *Military Memoirs of a Confederate,* 139.

12. Stephen Sears, *To the Gates of Richmond* (New York: Houghton Mifflin, 1992), 274.

13. Freeman, *Lee's Lieutenants,* 555.

14. *Ibid.*

15. *Ibid.*

16. Irving Werstein, *Kearny the Magnificent* (New York: The John Day Co., 1962), as quoted, 203.

17. *Ibid.*

18. *Ibid.,* as quoted, 204.

19. *Ibid.,* as quoted.

20. *Ibid.,* as quoted.

21. *Ibid.,* 79.

22. *Ibid.,* as quoted, 88.

23. *Ibid.,* as quoted, 211.

24. *Ibid.,* as quoted, 223.

25. *Ibid.,* as quoted, 225.

Chapter 4

1. Douglas Southall Freeman, *Lee's Lieutenants,* Vol. 1 (New York: Charles Scribner's Sons, 1942), 568.

2. Bryan Conrad, *The William & Mary Quarterly* 14, 2nd ser., 220.

3. *Ibid.,* 217.

4. Douglas Southall Freeman, *R.E. Lee* (New York: Touchstone Books, 1961), 209.

5. Stephen Sears, *To the Gates of Richmond* (New York: Houghton Mifflin, 1992), 281.

6. *Ibid.,* 281–282.

Chapter 5

1. Edward Porter Alexander, *Military Memoirs of a Confederate* (New York: Da Capo Press, 1993), 134.

2. Douglas Southall Freeman, *Lee's Lieutenants,* Vol. 1 (New York: Charles Scribner's Sons, 1942), as quoted, 569.

3. *Ibid.*, as quoted.

4. Alexander, *Military Memoirs of a Confederate*, 138.

5. *Ibid.*, 139.

6. *Ibid.*, 138.

7. Freeman, *Lee's Lieutenants*, Vol. 1, 568.

8. Henry Kyd Douglas, *I Rode with Stonewall* (Chapel Hill: University of North Carolina Press, 1940), 101.

9. Freeman, *Lee's Lieutenants*, Vol. 1, 570.

10. *Ibid.*

11. *Ibid.*, as quoted.

12. Stephen Sears, *To the Gates of Richmond* (New York: Houghton Mifflin, 1992), 284.

13. Thomas J. Goree, *Longstreet's Aide: The Civil War Letters of Major Thomas J. Goree* (Charlottesville: University Press of Virginia, 1995), 94.

14. Freeman, *Lee's Lieutenants*, Vol. 1, 565.

Chapter 6

1. Stephen Sears, *To the Gates of Richmond* (New York: Houghton Mifflin, 1992), 123

2. Douglas Southall Freeman, *Lee's Lieutenants*, Vol. 1 (New York: Charles Scribner's Sons, 1942), 558.

3. Irving Werstein, *Kearny the Magnificent* (New York: The John Day Co., 1962), 102.

4. *Ibid.*, 14.

5. *Ibid.*, as quoted, 208.

6. Freeman, *Lee's Lieutenants*, Vol. 1, 577.

7. *Ibid.*, 567.

8. Edward Porter Alexander, *Military Memoirs of a Confederate* (New York: Da Capo Press, 1993), as quoted, 143.

Chapter 7

1. Stephen Sears, *To the Gates of Richmond* (New York: Houghton Mifflin, 1992), as quoted, 274.

2. Irving Werstein, *Kearny the Magnificent* (New York: The John Day Co., 1962), 24.

3. *Ibid.*, 42–43.

4. *Ibid.*, 130.

5. *Ibid.*, 45.

6. *Ibid.*, 131.

7. *Ibid.*, 151–153.

8. *Ibid.*, as quoted, 153.

9. *Ibid.*, as quoted, 151.

10. *Ibid.*, as quoted, 151–152.

11. *Ibid.*, as quoted, 152.

12. Wyman S. White, *The Civil War Diary of Wyman S. White* (Baltimore: Butternut and Blue, 1993), 6.

13. Oliver Wendell Holmes, Jr., *Touched with Fire* (New York: Fordham University Press, 2000), xii.

14. Werstein, *Kearny the Magnificent*, 44.

15. Sears, *To the Gates of Richmond*, 54.

16. *Ibid.*, 303.

17. Werstein, *Kearny the Magnificent*, 167.

18. *Ibid.*, 99.

19. *Ibid.*, 111.

Chapter 8

1. Douglas Southall Freeman, *Lee's Lieutenants*, Vol. 1 (New York: Charles Scribner's Sons, 1942), 570.

2. *Ibid.*, as quoted, 570.

3. Daniel Harvey Hill, "McClellan's Change of Base and Malvern Hill." In *Battles and Leaders of the Civil War*. Vol. 2. *North to Antietam*. Robert Underwood Johnson, ed. (Secaucus, NJ: Castle Books, 1956), as quoted, 385.

4. Edward Porter Alexander, *Military Memoirs of a Confederate* (New York: Da Capo Press, 1993), 149–150.

5. Freeman, *Lee's Lieutenants*, Vol. 1, as quoted, 570–571.

6. Alexander, *Military Memoirs of a Confederate*, 144.

7. *Ibid.*

8. *Ibid.*, 145.

9. Edward Porter Alexander, *Fighting for the Confederacy* (Chapel Hill: University of North Carolina Press, 1989), 96.

10. *Ibid.*, 97.

11. Freeman, *Lee's Lieutenants*, Vol. 1, 571.

12. *Ibid.*, 572.

13. Alexander, *Fighting for the Confederacy*, 108.

14. Stephen Sears, *To the Gates of Richmond* (New York: Houghton Mifflin, 1992), 287.

15. Hill, "McClellan's Change of Base and Malvern Hill," 388.

16. Alexander, *Military Memoirs of a Confederate*, as quoted, 148–149.

17. Alexander, *Fighting for the Confederacy*, as quoted, 97.

Chapter 9

1. Stephen Sears, *To the Gates of Richmond* (New York: Houghton Mifflin, 1992), 289.

2. Edward Porter Alexander, *Military Memoirs of a Confederate* (New York: Da Capo Press, 1993), 139.

3. *Ibid.*, 140.

4. Library of Congress, *Civil War Desk Ref-*

erence (New York: Simon & Schuster, 2000), 178.

5. Constance Cary Harrison, "Richmond Scenes In '62." In *Battles and Leaders of the Civil War*. Vol. 2. *North to Antietam*. Robert Underwood Johnson, ed. (Secaucus, NJ: Castle Books, 1956), 446–447.

6. Sears, *To the Gates of Richmond*, 289.

7. *Ibid.*, 290.

8. Alexander, *Military Memoirs of a Confederate*, 140.

9. *Ibid.*

10. Douglas Southall Freeman, *R.E. Lee* (New York: Touchstone Books, 1961), 502.

11. *Ibid.*

12. *Ibid.*

13. Thomas J. Goree, *Longstreet's Aide: The Civil War Letters of Major Thomas J. Goree* (Charlottesville: University Press of Virginia, 1995), 95.

14. James J. Baldwin III, *The Struck Eagle* (Shippensburg, PA: Burd Street Press, 1996), 132.

Chapter 10

1. Stephen Sears, *To the Gates of Richmond* (New York: Houghton Mifflin, 1992), 290.

2. *Ibid.*, 294.

3. *Ibid.*, as quoted, 290.

4. *Ibid.*, 295.

5. James J. Baldwin III, *The Struck Eagle* (Shippensburg, PA: Burd Street Press, 1996), 132.

6. *Ibid.*, 132.

7. Thomas J. Goree, *Longstreet's Aide: The Civil War Letters of Major Thomas J. Goree* (Charlottesville: University Press of Virginia, 1995), 94.

8. Douglas Southall Freeman, *Lee's Lieutenants*, Vol. 1 (New York: Charles Scribner's Sons, 1942), 249.

9. Goree, *Longstreet's Aide*, 87.

10. Baldwin, *The Struck Eagle*, 3.

11. James Lee Conrad, *The Young Lions: Confederate Cadets at War* (Mechanicsburg, PA: Stackpole Books, 1997), as quoted, 15.

12. *Ibid.*, 13.

13. *Ibid.*, vii.

14. *Ibid.*, as quoted, 38.

15. Freeman, *Lee's Lieutenants*, Vol. 1, 710.

16. Conrad, *The Young Lions*, 152.

17. Baldwin, *The Struck Eagle*, 10.

18. Goree, *Longstreet's Aide*, 87.

19. *Ibid.*, 95.

20. James Longstreet, "The Seven Days, Including Frayser's Farm." In *Battles and Leaders of the Civil War*. Vol. 2. *North to Antietam*. Rob-

ert Underwood Johnson, ed. (Secaucus, NJ: Castle Books, 1956), 400–401.

21. Sears, *To the Gates of Richmond*, 290.

22. Alexander, *Military Memoirs of a Confederate*, 142.

Chapter 11

1. Constance Cary Harrison, "Richmond Scenes In '62." In *Battles and Leaders of the Civil War*. Vol. 2. *North to Antietam*. Robert Underwood Johnson, ed. (Secaucus, NJ: Castle Books, 1956), 443.

2. *Ibid.*, 446.

3. *Ibid.*, 445–446.

4. Stephen Sears, *To the Gates of Richmond* (New York: Houghton Mifflin, 1992), 284.

5. Douglas Southall Freeman, *Lee's Lieutenants*, Vol. 1 (New York: Charles Scribner's Sons, 1942), 557.

6. *Ibid.*

7. Edward Porter Alexander, *Military Memoirs of a Confederate* (New York: Da Capo Press, 1993), 143.

8. *Ibid.*, as quoted.

9. *Ibid.*, as quoted.

Chapter 12

1. Edward Porter Alexander, *Military Memoirs of a Confederate* (New York: Da Capo Press, 1993), 148.

2. *Ibid.*, as quoted, 149.

3. Douglas Southall Freeman, *Lee's Lieutenants*, Vol. 1 (New York: Charles Scribner's Sons, 1942), 576.

4. Daniel Harvey Hill, "McClellan's Change of Base and Malvern Hill." In *Battles and Leaders of the Civil War*. Vol. 2. *North to Antietam*. Robert Underwood Johnson, ed. (Secaucus, NJ: Castle Books, 1956), 388.

5. Freeman, *Lee's Lieutenant's*, Vol. 1, 577.

6. Alexander, *Military Memoirs of a Confederate*, as quoted, 151.

7. *Ibid.*, 142.

8. *Ibid.*

9. Edward Porter Alexander, *Fighting for the Confederacy* (Chapel Hill: University of North Carolina Press, 1989), 109.

10. *Ibid.*

11. Alexander, *Military Memoirs of a Confederate*, 148.

12. Freeman, *Lee's Lieutenants*, Vol. 1, 576.

13. Alexander, *Military Memoirs of a Confederate*, 144.

14. *Ibid.*, 142.

15. Hill, "McClellan's Change of Base and Malvern Hill," 389.
16. *Ibid.*, 388.

Chapter 13

1. Douglas Southall Freeman, *Lee's Lieutenants*, Vol. 1 (New York: Charles Scribner's Sons, 1942), 565.
2. Daniel Harvey Hill, "McClellan's Change of Base and Malvern Hill." In *Battles and Leaders of the Civil War*. Vol. 2. *North to Antietam*. Robert Underwood Johnson, ed. (Secaucus, NJ: Castle Books, 1956), 385.
3. Edward Porter Alexander, *Fighting for the Confederacy* (Chapel Hill: University of North Carolina Press, 1989), 106.
4. Stephen Sears, *To the Gates of Richmond* (New York: Houghton Mifflin, 1998), 278.
5. Freeman, *Lee's Lieutenants*, Vol. 1, 585.
6. *Ibid.*, 581.
7. Edward Porter Alexander, *Military Memoirs of a Confederate* (New York: Da Capo Press, 1993), 139.
8. Freeman, *Lee's Lieutenants*, Vol. 1, 581.
9. *Ibid.*
10. *Ibid.*, 582.
11. Alexander, *Military Memoirs of a Confederate*, 140.
12. Freeman, *Lee's Lieutenants*, Vol. 1, as quoted, 582.
13. *Ibid.*, as quoted, 583.
14. Hill, "McClellan's Change of Base and Malvern Hill," 390.
15. Freeman, *Lee's Lieutenants*, Vol. 1, 584.
16. *Ibid.*, as quoted.
17. Sears, *To the Gates of Richmond*, 292.

Chapter 14

1. Douglas Southall Freeman, *Lee's Lieutenants*, Vol. 1 (New York: Charles Scribner's Sons, 1942), 585.
2. *Ibid.*
3. *Ibid.*
4. *Ibid.*, 586.
5. *Ibid.*, 585–586.
6. *Ibid.*, 586.
7. *Ibid.*, 15.
8. Stephen Sears, *To the Gates of Richmond* (New York: Houghton Mifflin, 1992), 24.
9. Freeman, *Lee's Lieutenants*, Vol. 1, 16.
10. Sears, *To the Gates of Richmond*, 26.
11. Freeman, *Lee's Lieutenants*, Vol. 1, 18.
12. *Ibid.*, as quoted, 19.
13. Sears, *To the Gates of Richmond*, 293.

14. Freeman, *Lee's Lieutenants*, Vol. 1, 586.
15. *Ibid.*
16. *Ibid.*
17. *Ibid.*, 586–587.

Chapter 15

1. Stephen Oates, *With Malice Toward None* (New York: Harper Perennial, 1977), 304.
2. James McPherson, *Tried by War* (New York: Penguin Press, 2008), as quoted, 99.
3. *Ibid.*, 89.
4. Stephen Sears, *To the Gates of Richmond* (New York: Houghton Mifflin, 1992), 281.
5. McPherson, *Tried by War*, as quoted, 97.
6. Paul M. Angle, and Earl Schenck Miers, *The Living Lincoln* (New York: Barnes & Noble Books, 1955), as quoted, 471–472.
7. Sears, *To the Gates of Richmond*, as quoted, 65.
8. Oates, *With Malice Toward None*, 303.
9. McPherson, *Tried by War*, as quoted, 99.
10. *Ibid.*, as quoted, 100.
11. Angle and Miers, *The Living Lincoln*, as quoted, 483.
12. *Ibid.*, as quoted, 484.
13. *Ibid.*, as quoted.
14. *Ibid.*, as quoted, 485.
15. *Ibid.*, as quoted, 484–485.
16. Constance Cary Harrison, "Richmond Scenes In '62." In *Battles and Leaders of the Civil War*. Vol. 2. *North to Antietam*. Robert Underwood Johnson, ed. (Secaucus, NJ: Castle Books, 1956), 448.

Chapter 16

1. Douglas Southall Freeman, *R.E. Lee* (New York: Touchstone Books, 1961), 210.
2. *Ibid.*, 210.
3. James J. Baldwin, III, *The Struck Eagle* (Shippensburg, PA: Burd Street Press, 1996), as quoted, 133–134.
4. Edward Porter Alexander, *Military Memoirs of a Confederate* (New York: Da Capo Press, 1993), 153.
5. *Ibid.*
6. Thomas J. Goree, *Longstreet's Aide: The Civil War Letters of Major Thomas J. Goree* (Charlottesville: University Press of Virginia, 1995), 94.
7. Baldwin, *The Struck Eagle*, 134.
8. *Ibid.*, 138.
9. *Ibid.*, 126–127.
10. Alexander, *Military Memoirs of a Confederate*, 82.
11. Stephen Sears, *To the Gates of Richmond*

(New York: Houghton Mifflin, 1992), 293–294.

12. Baldwin, *The Struck Eagle*, 134.

13. Edward Porter Alexander, *Fighting for the Confederacy* (Chapel Hill: University Of North Carolina Press, 1989), 118.

14. Baldwin, *The Struck Eagle*, as quoted, 129–130.

15. Goree, *Longstreet's Aide*, 94.

Chapter 17

1. Edward Porter Alexander, *Military Memoirs of a Confederate* (New York: Da Capo Press, 1993), 147–148.

2. *Ibid.*, 148.

3. *Ibid.*, 152.

4. Daniel Harvey Hill, "McClellan's Change of Base and Malvern Hill." In *Battles and Leaders of the Civil War.* Vol. 2. *North to Antietam.* Robert Underwood Johnson, ed. (Secaucus, NJ: Castle Books, 1956), 389.

5. Alexander, *Military Memoirs of a Confederate*, 153.

6. *Ibid.*, as quoted, 150.

7. *Ibid.*, as quoted.

8. *Ibid.*, as quoted.

9. Edward G. Longacre, *Gentleman and Soldier* (Nashville: Rutledge Hill Press, 2003), xiv.

10. *Ibid.*, xv.

11. *Ibid.*, 16.

12. *Ibid.*, 3.

13. *Ibid.*, 53.

14. Edward Porter Alexander, *Fighting for the Confederacy* (Chapel Hill: University of North Carolina Press, 1989), 108.

Chapter 18

1. Kevin Dougherty, and J. Michael Moore, *The Peninsula Campaign Of 1862* (Jackson: University Press of Mississippi, 2005), 132.

2. Stephen Sears, *To the Gates of Richmond* (New York: Houghton Mifflin, 1992), 293.

3. Douglas Southall Freeman, *R.E. Lee* (New York: Touchstone Books, 1961), 211.

4. Sears, *To the Gates of Richmond*, 293.

5. Freeman, *R.E. Lee*, 211.

6. Sears, *To the Gates of Richmond*, 298.

7. *Harper's Pictorial History of the Civil War* (New York: Random House, 1987), 372.

8. Freeman, *R.E. Lee*, 211.

9. *Ibid.*

10. *Ibid.*

11. Sears, *To the Gates of Richmond*, 298.

12. *Ibid.*

13. Freeman, *R.E. Lee*, 211.

14. Sears, *To the Gates of Richmond*, 298.

15. *Harper's Pictorial History of the Civil War*, as quoted, 372.

16. *Ibid.*

17. Edward Porter Alexander, *Military Memoirs of a Confederate* (New York: Da Capo Press, 1993), 154.

18. *Ibid.*

19. *Harper's Pictorial History of the Civil War*, 373.

20. Sears, *To the Gates of Richmond*, 299.

Chapter 19

1. Edward G. Longacre, *Gentleman and Soldier* (Nashville: Rutledge Hill Press, 2003), 78.

2. Edward Porter Alexander, *Military Memoirs of a Confederate* (New York: Da Capo Press, 1993), as quoted, 150–151.

3. *Ibid.*, as quoted, 146–147.

4. Stephen Sears, *To the Gates of Richmond* (New York: Houghton Mifflin, 1992), 288.

5. Douglas Southall Freeman, *R.E. Lee* (New York: Touchstone Books, 1961), 214.

6. Henry Kyd Douglas, *I Rode with Stonewall* (Chapel Hill: University of North Carolina Press, 1940), 107.

7. Alexander, *Military Memoirs of a Confederate*, 147.

8. *Ibid.*

9. Edward Porter Alexander, *Fighting for the Confederacy* (Chapel Hill: University of North Carolina Press, 1989), 96.

10. *Ibid.*

Chapter 20

1. James J. Baldwin, III, *The Struck Eagle* (Shippensburg, PA: Burd Street Press, 1996), 134.

2. Stephen Sears, *To the Gates of Richmond* (New York: Houghton Mifflin, 1992), as quoted, 295.

3. Baldwin, *The Struck Eagle*, 134.

4. Sears, *To the Gates of Richmond*, as quoted, 296.

5. Thomas J. Goree, *Longstreet's Aide* (Charlottesville: University of Virginia Press), 95.

6. James J. Baldwin, III, *The Struck Eagle*, 134.

7. *Ibid.*, 134.

8. Thomas J. Goree, *Longstreet's Aide: The Civil War Letters of Major Thomas J. Goree*

(Charlottesville: University Press of Virginia, 1995), 95.

9. Baldwin, *The Struck Eagle*, 135.
10. *Ibid.*
11. *Ibid.*
12. Sears, *To the Gates of Richmond*, 299.
13. *Ibid.*
14. *Ibid.*, 299–300.
15. Goree, *Longstreet's Aide*, 94.
16. *Ibid.*
17. Baldwin, *The Struck Eagle*, as quoted, 135.
18. Goree, *Longstreet's Aide*, 95.
19. Baldwin, *The Struck Eagle*, 138–139.
20. *Ibid.*, 139.
21. *Ibid.*, 138.
22. *Ibid.*, 138.
23. Goree, *Longstreet's Aide*, 95.

Chapter 21

1. Douglas Southall Freeman, *R.E. Lee* (New York: Touchstone Books, 1961), 211.
2. Thomas J. Goree, *Longstreet's Aide: The Civil War Letters of Major Thomas J. Goree* (Charlottesville: University Press of Virginia, 1995), 94.
3. James J. Baldwin, III, *The Struck Eagle* (Shippensburg, PA: Burd Street Press, 1996), as quoted, 135.
4. *Ibid.*
5. *Ibid.*, 136.
6. Goree, *Longstreet's Aide*, 94.
7. Stephen Sears, *To the Gates of Richmond* (New York: Houghton Mifflin, 1992), 300–301.
8. *Ibid.*, 300.
9. Baldwin, *The Struck Eagle*, as quoted, 135.
10. *Ibid.*, 136.
11. *Ibid.*, as quoted.
12. *Ibid.*
13. Goree, *Longstreet's Aide*, 95.
14. Freeman, *R.E. Lee*, 212.
15. Irving Werstein, *Kearny the Magnificent* (New York: The John Day Co., 1962), as quoted, 226.
16. *Ibid.*, as quoted.
17. Sears, *To the Gates of Richmond*, as quoted, 302.
18. *Ibid.*
19. *Ibid.*
20. Werstein, *Kearny the Magnificent*, as quoted, 226.
21. Sears, *To the Gates of Richmond*, 302.
22. *Ibid.*, as quoted.
23. *Ibid.*, 302–303.
24. *Ibid.*, as quoted, 303.
25. *Ibid.*

26. Werstein, *Kearny the Magnificent*, 226.
27. Sears, *To the Gates of Richmond*, 303–304.
28. *Ibid.*, as quoted, 304.

Chapter 22

1. Stephen Sears, *To the Gates of Richmond* (New York: Houghton Mifflin, 1992), 304.
2. *Ibid.*
3. Douglas Southall Freeman, *R.E. Lee* (New York: Touchstone Books, 1961), 212.
4. Sears, *To the Gates of Richmond*, 304–305.
5. *Ibid.*, as quoted, 306.
6. Oliver Wendell Holmes, Jr., *Touched with Fire* (New York: Fordham University Press, 2000), 58–59.
7. *Ibid.*, 59.
8. *Ibid.*
9. *Ibid.*
10. *Ibid.*
11. Edward Porter Alexander, *Military Memoirs of a Confederate* (New York: Da Capo Press, 1993), 154.
12. Sears, *To the Gates of Richmond*, 389.
13. *Ibid.*, 306.
14. *Harper's Pictorial History of the Civil War* (New York: Random House, 1987), 373.
15. Alexander, *Military Memoirs of a Confederate*, 154.
16. *Ibid.*, as quoted, 155.
17. *Harper's Pictorial History of the Civil War*, as quoted, 373.
18. *Ibid.*, as quoted.
19. Sears, *To the Gates of Richmond*, 307.
20. *Ibid.*
21. *Harper's Pictorial History of the Civil War*, as quoted, 373.
22. Sears, *To the Gates of Richmond*, as quoted, 304.
23. Freeman, *R.E. Lee*, 212.
24. Sears, *To the Gates of Richmond*, 306.
25. Irving Werstein, *Kearny the Magnificent* (New York: The John Day Co., 1962), as quoted, 226–227.

Chapter 23

1. Stephen Sears, *To the Gates of Richmond* (New York: Houghton Mifflin, 1992), 313.
2. Daniel Harvey Hill, "McClellan's Change of Base and Malvern Hill." In *Battles and Leaders of the Civil War*. Vol. 2. *North to Antietam*. Robert Underwood Johnson, ed. (Secaucus, NJ: Castle Books, 1956), 392.
3. *Ibid.*

4. Sears, *To the Gates of Richmond*, 335.
5. Hill, "McClellan's Change of Base and Malvern Hill," 389.
6. Oliver Wendell Holmes, Jr., *Touched with Fire* (New York: Fordham University Press, 2000), 59.
7. Sears, *To the Gates of Richmond*, 308–309.
8. *Ibid.*, 308.
9. *Ibid.*, as quoted.
10. Douglas Southall Freeman, *R.E. Lee* (New York: Touchstone Books, 1961), as quoted, 215.
11. *Ibid.*, 214.
12. Edward Porter Alexander, *Military Memoirs of a Confederate* (New York: Da Capo Press, 1993), 159.
13. *Ibid.*, as quoted.
14. *Ibid.*, as quoted, 157.
15. Sears, *To the Gates of Richmond*, 322.
16. Hill, "McClellan's Change of Base and Malvern Hill," 394.
17. *Ibid.*
18. Irving Werstein, *Kearny the Magnificent* (New York: The John Day Co., 1962), as quoted, 230.
19. *Ibid.*, as quoted, 231.
20. Constance Cary Harrison, "Richmond Scenes In '62." In *Battles and Leaders of the Civil War*. Vol. 2. *North to Antietam*. Robert Underwood Johnson, ed. (Secaucus, NJ: Castle Books, 1956), 448.

Chapter 24

1. Douglas Southall Freeman, *R.E. Lee* (New York: Touchstone Books, 1961), 214.
2. Douglas Southall Freeman, *Lee's Lieutenants*, Vol. 1 (New York: Charles Scribner's Sons, 1942), 667.
3. *Ibid.*
4. Kevin Dougherty and Michael J. Moore, *The Peninsula Campaign of 1862* (Jackson: University Press of Mississippi, 2005), 155.
5. Stephen Sears, *To the Gates of Richmond* (New York: Houghton Mifflin, 1992), as quoted, 331.
6. *Ibid.*, as quoted, 345.
7. Edward Porter Alexander, *Military Memoirs of a Confederate* (New York: Da Capo Press, 1993), viii.
8. John B. Gordon, *Reminiscences of the Civil War* (Baton Rouge: Louisiana State University Press, 1993), 465.

Bibliography

Books

Alexander, Edward Porter. *Fighting for the Confederacy.* Chapel Hill: University of North Carolina Press, 1989.

_____. *Military Memoirs of a Confederate.* New York: Da Capo Press, 1993.

Angle, Paul M., and Earl Miers Schenck. *The Living Lincoln.* New York: Barnes & Noble, 1955.

Baldwin, James J., III. *The Struck Eagle.* Shippensburg, PA: Burd Street Press, 1996.

Chaffin, Tom. *Sea of Gray.* New York: Hill and Wang, 2006.

Coblentz, Stanton A. *From Arrow to Atomic Bomb.* New York: Perpetua, 1953.

Conrad, James Lee. *The Young Lions: Confederate Cadets at War.* Mechanicsburg, PA: Stackpole Books, 1997.

Cowley, Robert, ed. *With My Face to the Enemy.* New York: G.P. Putnam's Sons, 2001.

Dougherty, Kevin, and Michael J. Moore. *The Peninsula Campaign of 1862.* Jackson: University Press of Mississippi, 2005.

Douglas, Henry Kyd. *I Rode with Stonewall.* Chapel Hill: University of North Carolina Press, 1940.

Dupuy, Trevor N. *The Evolution of Weapons and Warfare.* New York: Da Capo Press, 1984.

Freeman, Douglas Southall. *Lee's Lieutenants.* Vol. 1. New York: Charles Scribner's Sons, 1942.

_____. *R.E. Lee.* New York: Touchstone Books, 1961.

Gordon, John B. *Reminiscences of the Civil War.* Baton Rouge: Louisiana State University Press, 1993.

Goree, Thomas J. *Longstreet's Aide: The Civil War Letters of Major Thomas J. Goree.* Charlottesville: University Press of Virginia, 1995.

Guernsey, Alfred H., and Henry M. Alden. *Harper's Pictorial History of the Civil War.* New York: Random House, 1866.

Holmes, Oliver Wendell, Jr. *Touched with Fire.* New York: Fordham University Press, 2000.

Keegan, John. *The American Civil War.* New York: Knopf, 2009.

Library of Congress. *Civil War Desk Reference.* New York: Simon & Schuster, 2002.

Longacre, Edward G. *Gentleman and Soldier.* Nashville: Rutledge Hill Press, 2003.

McPherson, James M. *Tried by War.* New York: Penguin Press, 2008.

Meacham, Jon. *American Lion.* New York: Random House, 2008.

Musicant, Ivan. *Divided Waters.* New York: Castle Books, 2000.

Oates, Stephen B. *With Malice Toward None.* New York: Harper Perennial, 1977.

O'Connell, Robert L. *Of Arms and Men.* New York: Oxford University Press, 1989.

Page, Dave. *Ships Versus Shore.* Nashville: Rutledge Hill Press, 1994.

Palmer, Michael A. *Lee Moves North.* New York: John Wiley & Sons, 1998.

Sears, Stephen. *Chancellorsville.* New York: Houghton Mifflin, 1996.

_____. *Controversies & Commanders.* New York: Houghton Mifflin, 1999.

_____. *Gettysburg.* New York: Houghton Mifflin, 2003.

_____. *To the Gates of Richmond.* New York: Houghton Mifflin, 1992.

Sun-tzu. *The Art of War.* New York: Viking Press, 2002.

Taylor, Walter H. *Four Years with General Lee.* New York: Bonanza Books, 1962.

Werstein, Irving. *Kearny the Magnificent.* New York: The John Day Co., 1962.

Wertz, Jay, and Edwin C. Bearss. *Smithsonian's Great Battles and Great Battlefields of the Civil War.* New York: Morrow, 1993.

White, Wyman. *The Civil War Diary of Wyman S. White.* Baltimore: Butternut & Blue, 1993.

Wills, Garry. *Lincoln at Gettysburg.* New York: Touchstone Books, 1992.

Articles

Conrad, Bryan. "The Seven Days Campaign, 1862. *The William & Mary Quarterly*, 14, 1934.

Harrison, Constance Cary. "Richmond Scenes in '62." In *Battles and Leaders of the Civil War*. Vol. 2. *North to Antietam*. Robert Underwood Johnson, ed. Secaucus, NJ: Castle Books, 1956.

Hill, Daniel Harvey. "McClellan's Change of Base and Malvern Hill." In *Battles and Leaders of the Civil War*. Vol. 2. *North to Antietam*. Robert Underwood Johnson, ed. Secaucus, NJ: Castle Books, 1956.

Longstreet, James. "The Seven Days, Including Frayser's Farm." In *Battles and Leaders of the Civil War*. Vol. 2. *North to Antietam*. Robert Underwood Johnson, ed. Secaucus, NJ: Castle Books, 1956.

Index

Alexander, Edward P. 14, 17, 22, 23, 27, 31, 32, 40, 79, 80, 86, 87, 103–108, 112–114, 135, 137, 140, 141, 144, 145, 157, 175, 193, 194, 198–199
Armistead, Lewis 182
Army of Northern Virginia 28, 32, 44, 53, 69, 85, 87, 89, 96, 123, 126, 135, 171, 177, 186, 188, 191, 192
Army of the Potomac 13, 14, 44, 56, 75, 84, 110, 132, 155, 164, 172, 176, 180, 189–192

Barlow, Francis 172, 190
Berry, Hiram 70, 169
Birney, David 70
Brackett's Ford 50, 107, 108, 109, 111, 191
Branch, Lawrence 86, 145, 146, 165, 166, 167, 176, 191
Brent, Joseph 59, 118

Charles City Road 33, 36, 54, 64, 100, 112, 168, 174, 181
Chickahominy River 18, 23, 30, 31, 37, 49, 50
Chilton, R.H. 122, 125, 182
The Citadel 94, 95, 96, 136
Confederate Pursuit 34
U.S.S. Congress 5
Cooper's battery 93, 134, 137, 138, 139, 145–151, 158, 162, 173
Crutchfield, Stapleton 80, 81, 83, 156
U.S.S. Cumberland 6

Dabney, Robert 60, 62, 78, 112
Darbytown Road 33, 36, 84, 120, 124
Davis, Jefferson 20, 85, 92, 144
Douglas, Henry K. 36, 40, 61, 79, 155

Ericsson, John 7

Federal Blocking Positions 54
Field, Charles 167, 173–178
Fortress Monroe 7, 10, 13, 132
Franklin, William 10, 43, 55, 83, 107, 108, 110, 111, 139, 141, 144, 153, 154, 155, 189

Freeman, Douglas S. 53, 94, 112, 113, 133, 178, 181, 186, 187

Gaines's Mill 26, 29, 31, 35, 136
U.S.S. Galena 180, 181, 190
Gazelle 30, 32, 114
Glendale 12, 22, 28, 36, 41, 49, 53, 54, 83, 107, 145, 153, 167, 172, 180, 186, 194
Gordon, John 19, 20, 39, 194
Goree, Thomas J. 93, 94, 135, 145, 159–166, 169
Grapevine Bridge 60, 78

Hampton, Wade 40, 78, 81, 139–144, 145, 153, 154, 196
Harrison, Constance 85, 99, 100, 132, 184
Heintzelman, Samuel P. 43, 44, 55, 162, 167, 171, 189, 200
Hill, Ambrose P. 24, 35, 40, 41, 63, 84, 86, 120, 145, 155, 173, 176–178, 187
Hill, Daniel H. 44, 79, 81, 82, 83, 106, 112, 113, 139, 140, 154, 179, 180–184
Holmes, Oliver W. 20, 26, 27, 73, 84, 174–176, 180, 200–201
Holmes, Theophilus 41, 63, 113–119, 120, 121–126, 178, 191, 196–197
Hooker, Joseph 42, 43–45, 57, 110, 122, 149, 174, 176
Huger, Benjamin 33, 36, 40, 41, 63–69, 84, 86, 100–104, 111, 112, 120, 133, 146, 171, 178, 181, 191, 195

Jackson, Andrew 95
Jackson, Thomas J. 17, 18, 23, 24, 33–35, 40, 49, 60–63, 77–83, 105–112, 120, 133, 139–144, 146, 153–157, 171, 178, 181, 187–191, 195–196
Jackson's Attack at Brackett's Ford 109
James River 13, 24, 25, 30, 33, 49, 51, 154
Jenkins, Micah 86, 91, 92, 133–138, 139, 145–146, 158–164, 165–169, 176, 191, 198
Johnston, Joseph 8, 11, 16, 17, 18, 88

213

Kearny, Philip 10, 23, 42–48, 57, 64, 66–
    69, 70–76, 110, 133, 142, 143, 147, 153,
    162, 167, 168–172, 174, 176, 178, 184, 201–
    202
Kemper, James 86, 146, 147–150, 161, 165,
    167

Lee, Robert E. 17, 20–25, 29–36, 37–42,
    59–63, 84–91, 98, 113–119, 120–126, 132,
    133, 134, 143, 145–146, 154, 155, 157, 167,
    168, 176, 178, 179, 180, 181–185, 186–189,
    197–198
Lincoln, Abraham 7, 9, 10, 73, 75, 127–132,
    166, 193
Long Bridge Road 84, 86, 92, 133, 134, 147,
    149, 168, 172
Longstreet, James 33, 36, 40, 41, 63, 84–91,
    120–126, 133–135, 145–146, 156, 161, 165,
    167, 176, 177–182, 187, 188, 191, 197
Longstreet's Attack 148

Magruder, John B. 33, 37–39, 59, 60, 118,
    120–126, 176, 183
Mahone, William 65–69, 101–104
Mallory, Stephen 6
Malvern Hill 31, 41, 51, 84, 97, 113–119, 120–
    126, 139, 146, 164, 179–185
McCall, George 55, 110, 133, 137, 149, 150,
    158, 161, 165, 168, 173, 174, 178, 200
McClellan, George B. 5–12, 13–28, 29–36,
    47, 48, 77, 84, 87, 113, 123, 127–132, 157,
    167, 179, 180, 181, 184, 186–192, 199–200
McDowell, Irvin 17, 18
Meade, George G. 42, 56, 137, 147, 149–151,
    153, 155, 161
U.S.S. Merrimack 6
U.S.S. Minnesota 6
U.S.S. Monitor 7
Munford, Thomas 78, 81–83, 106, 111, 139,
    140, 156

Nelson's Farm 91, 93, 136, 159, 162, 175
New Market, Virginia 113–119

Palmetto Sharpshooters 93, 136, 163
Pender, Dorsey 167, 175, 176

Quaker Road 51, 54, 84, 149, 158, 159, 162,
    164–168, 174, 175, 177, 179, 191

Randol's battery 137, 147, 149, 150, 151, 168,
    173, 174
Riddell's Shop 36, 41, 53, 55, 64, 133, 167, 168
River Road 33, 113–119
Robinson, John 70, 172
Rosser, Thomas 97, 122

Savage Station 39, 42, 59, 61, 77, 120, 174,
    189
Sears, Stephan 114, 124, 149, 154, 167
Seven Pines, Battle of 19, 22, 65, 136
Seymour, Truman 137, 159, 161
Simmons, Seneca 158, 159, 161
Slocum, Henry 55, 110, 153, 171
Stanton, Edwin 7, 127, 129, 130
Stuart, J.E.B. 23

Theater of Operations 21
Thompson, James 171

Urbana, Virginia 9, 11

C.S.S. Virginia 5
Virginia Military Institute 95, 96, 101

Waud, Alfred 47, 82, 170, 183
Welles, Gideon 7, 8
West Point 14, 20, 31, 44, 56, 71, 85, 94, 95,
    123
White Oak Bridge 105, 107, 139, 191
White Oak Swamp 17, 37, 40, 42, 49, 50, 51,
    54, 78, 81, 83, 107, 111, 120, 139, 153, 167,
    169
Wilcox, Cadmus 146, 147–151, 153, 155, 159,
    161, 167
Williamsburg, Battle of 44, 45, 47
Wright, Rans 67, 68, 106, 108, 156